Studying the Old Testament

A Companion

More praise for Rhonda Burnette-Bletsch's Studying the Old Testament:

"Rhonda Burnette-Bletsch's book prepares students to read the Bible and prompts them to reflect upon and discuss what they have read. The CD-ROM is not only a databank for maps and charts but also a valuable resource of pedagogical instruments and ideas. Burnette-Bletsch is ultimately concerned about the education of students. We are fortunate that she shares the fruits of her experience with us in this textbook."

—James H. Pace, Professor of Religious Studies, Elon University

"Professor Burnette-Bletsch has written a very clear and readable introduction to the Hebrew Scriptures/Old Testament. The scholarship in this book is quite up-to-date but takes into account the older ideas that still are generally agreed upon. The book can be used with confidence by instructors even if one does not always agree with the conclusions presented. Pedagogically speaking, this is a useful tool for introductory classes in this field for undergraduates, seminarians, and laity."

—James M. Efird, Professor Emeritus of Biblical Interpretation,
  Duke Divinity School

Studying the Old Testament

A Companion

Rhonda Burnette-Bletsch

Abingdon Press
Nashville

STUDYING THE OLD TESTAMENT
A COMPANION

Copyright © 2007 by Abingdon Press

Library of Congress Cataloging-in-Publication Data

Burnette-Bletsch, Rhonda, 1970-
  Studying the Old Testament : a companion / Rhonda Burnette-Bletsch.
    p. cm.
  Includes index.
  ISBN 978-0-687-64623-4 (binding: adhesive pbk. with cd insert : alk. paper)
  1. Bible. O.T.--Textbooks. 2. Bible. O.T.--Criticism, interpretation, etc. I. Title.

BS1194.B74 2007
221'.61--dc22

2007009707

07 08 09 10 11 12 13 14 15 16—10 9 8 7 6 5 4 3 2 1
MANUFACTURED IN THE UNITED STATES OF AMERICA

CONTENTS

ACKNOWLEDGMENTS

This project would not have been possible without the support of colleagues, friends, and family. Thanks are owed to my former teachers at Duke University—especially James Crenshaw, Carol Meyers, and Orval Wintermute—for initiating me into the study of these fascinating texts. I have also been blessed with a supportive colleague in Barnes Tatum, who has served as a valued conversation partner on this project. I am indebted as well to the last decade of Greensboro College students who have indirectly shaped this book by teaching me what does and does not work in the classroom. In addition, Greensboro College has generously supported my research with grants from the Royce and Jane Reynolds Endowment Fund for Faculty Development and the Kathleen and Joseph M. Bryan Family Foundation Summer Fellowship Program. My tireless research assistant, Carol Lewis, read multiple versions of each chapter and offered many helpful comments. Mickey Efird, James Pace, Michael Penn, and Philip Rolnick also read portions of this manuscript and made invaluable contributions. Thanks to the fine editorial staff at Abingdon Press—especially John Kutsko, Tim West, and J. Campbell—for gently shepherding me through the final stages of preparing the manuscript and making the CD-ROM a functioning reality. Above all, I am indebted to my parents for their unfailing support and to my husband, John, for his constant encouragement. Finally, this book is lovingly dedicated to my children, Jonah, Ethan, and Daniel, without whom I would probably write faster but would most certainly laugh less.

A JOURNEY WORTH MAKING

The importance of the Bible can hardly be overestimated. Not only is it foundational to three of the world's great religions—Judaism, Christianity, and Islam—it is undoubtedly the most influential book in the history of Western civilization. Even Westerners who do not consider themselves particularly religious are consciously or unconsciously affected by the Bible on an almost daily basis. This ancient text has inspired some of the world's greatest art, music, and literature. Popular culture likewise abounds with biblical images and allusions. Appeals to biblical texts and precepts are commonplace on both sides of current debates about appropriate gender roles, reproductive rights, gay and lesbian rights, criminal justice, ecological issues, and public education. The relative merits of such arguments cannot be evaluated without firsthand knowledge of the Bible and its contents. Anyone who aspires to be an educated person or a responsible global citizen must grapple with the biblical text.

However, many people are understandably intimidated by the prospect of navigating this massive tome. After all, despite its continuing importance in the modern world, the Bible was originally written in languages that most of us do not understand and for audiences who lived long ago in cultures very different from our own. Reading biblical texts requires a willingness to venture into unfamiliar territory. This textbook is intended to serve as a traveling companion and guide for readers who are bold enough to undertake such a journey.

But before we set out on this journey, we must plot the course that we intend to travel. The Bible is actually an anthology of religious texts, whose contents and order vary for different religious communities. The particular collection of books that is regarded as sacred and authoritative by a given community is called its **canon**, a word that literally means "rule" or "measure." Thus, what is meant by *the Bible* actually depends on your frame of reference.

The Jewish Bible, for example, contains twenty-four books that were originally composed in **Hebrew** and, in the case of a few late passages, **Aramaic**. This canon divides easily into three main sections represented by the consonants of the acronym **Tanakh**: the **T**orah ("Instruction"), the **N**evi'im ("Prophets"), and the **K**etuvim ("Writings"). The Torah is dominated by a long narrative that extends from the creation story at the beginning of Genesis to the death of Moses at the end of Deuteronomy. The middle section of the Jewish canon may be divided into books that provide a historical narrative about ancient Israel (called the Former Prophets) and books that are associated with individual prophets (called the Latter Prophets). The final part of the Jewish canon is a varied collection of writings that reflect the emergence of early Judaism in the late biblical period.

Because Christianity originated as a branch of Judaism, Christian Bibles include these same twenty-four books but order them differently and repartition them into thirty-nine volumes (for example, Samuel becomes 1 and 2 Samuel). These books are usually labeled the Old Testament to distinguish them from the twenty-seven books that form the second part of the Christian canon, which is called the New Testament. Some Christians prefer to call the earlier section of their canon the First Testament, avoiding the false implication that those books have been rendered obsolete by the New or Second Testament.

In addition, Catholic and Orthodox Christians grant secondary or **deuterocanonical** status to several other books and supplements like Tobit, Judith, and the additions to Esther. These texts, which are sometimes called the **Apocrypha**, had been included in the **Septuagint**, the early Greek translation of Jewish scripture that was used by Greek-speaking Jews and the early church. This material is scattered throughout the Old Testament in Catholic and Orthodox Bibles and sometimes appears in a separate section in modern study Bibles. But because this deuterocanonical literature was rejected by sixteenth-century reformers like Martin Luther, it generally does not appear in Protestant Bibles.

Jewish Bible	Protestant Old Testament	Catholic and Orthodox Old Testament
Torah/Instruction	Pentateuch	Pentateuch
Genesis	Genesis	Genesis
Exodus	Exodus	Exodus
Leviticus	Leviticus	Leviticus
Numbers	Numbers	Numbers
Deuteronomy	Deuteronomy	Deuteronomy
Nevi'im/Prophets	Historical Books	Historical Books
(Former Prophets)	Joshua	Joshua
Joshua	Judges	Judges
Judges	Ruth	Ruth
Samuel	1 Samuel	1 Kings (1 Samuel)
Kings	2 Samuel	2 Kings (2 Samuel)
	1 Kings	3 Kings (1 Kings)
(Latter Prophets)	2 Kings	4 Kings (2 Kings)
Isaiah	1 Chronicles	1 Chronicles
Jeremiah	2 Chronicles	2 Chronicles
Ezekiel	Ezra	1 Esdras (Ezra)
Book of the Twelve	Nehemiah	2 Esdras (Nehemiah)
(which includes	Esther	Tobit
Hosea, Amos,		Judith
Micah, Joel,	Poetic and Wisdom	Esther with
Obadiah, Jonah,	Books	additions
Nahum,	Job	1 Maccabees
Habakkuk,	Psalms	2 Maccabees
Zephaniah,	Proverbs	
Haggai,	Ecclesiastes	Poetic and Wisdom
Zechariah, and	Song of Songs	Books
Malachi)		Job
		Psalms

Jewish Bible	Protestant Old Testament	Catholic and Orthodox Old Testament
Ketuvim/Writings	**Prophetic Books**	Proverbs
Psalms	Isaiah	Ecclesiastes
Job	Jeremiah	Song of Songs
Proverbs	Lamentations	Wisdom of Solomon
Ruth	Ezekiel	Ecclesiasticus
Song of Songs	Daniel	
Ecclesiastes	Hosea	**Prophetic Books**
Lamentations	Joel	Isaiah
Esther	Amos	Jeremiah
Daniel	Obadiah	Lamentations
Ezra-Nehemiah	Jonah	Baruch
Chronicles	Micah	Ezekiel
	Nahum	Daniel with
	Habakkuk	additions
	Zephaniah	Hosea
	Haggai	Joel
	Zechariah	Amos
	Malachi	Obadiah
		Jonah
		Micah
		Nahum
		Habakkuk
		Zephaniah
		Haggai
		Zechariah
		Malachi

A thorough exploration of the Apocrypha and New Testament is left to other textbooks, although we will occasionally consider the interpretive trajectories that are taken in this literature. But, as its title suggests, *Studying the Old Testament: A Companion* focuses primarily on the earlier books that appear in both the Jewish Bible and Christian Old Testament. Because this collection of books is canonical for two different religious traditions, we will refer to it by the neutral title **Hebrew Bible** or Hebrew scripture.

There are already many textbooks devoted to Hebrew scripture. Why another one? Simply put, most other introductions either summarize the Bible itself or distill the current consensus of biblical scholarship. Either of these approaches encourages rote memorization rather than active engagement with primary sources. Instead, this book deliberately focuses on the process of critically reading and seriously thinking about biblical texts. This book should not be mistaken as a substitute for the Bible itself and for that reason provides only minimal summary of the biblical storyline. Its primary goal is to help people become better readers of the Bible through guided firsthand experience. To that end, suggested biblical readings and at least one preliminary exercise should ideally be completed before your assigned textbook reading. Readers of this text are usually offered a choice between two possible preliminary exercises for each unit: one traditional worksheet and one creative activity.

Main chapters follow the sequence of the Jewish canon: the Torah (chapter 2), the Former Prophets (chapter 3), the Latter Prophets (chapter 4), and the Writings (chapter 5). Each chapter gives readers the chance to experience interpretive issues in real texts before introducing classic theories. These theories are not treated as foregone conclusions but are continually evaluated against firsthand observations. Thus, readers are encouraged to become active participants in biblical scholarship rather than mere spectators.

Most other introductions spend an inordinate number of pages evaluating the historical value of biblical accounts as a source for reconstructing "what really happened." In contrast, this book approaches the Bible as religious literature that was composed mainly for purposes other than preserving history. While it is certainly necessary to read biblical texts against their proper historical and cultural contexts, it is equally imperative to focus on genre-appropriate questions, literary origins, and theological significance. Accordingly, our journey through scripture will not be directed by an attempt to recover what really happened but by this guiding question: "Why did ancient Israel create and preserve these particular traditions?"

The CD-ROM accompanying this text contains preliminary exercises, charts, maps, timelines, and a variety of study aids. Bibliographies, lists of key terms, study guides, and discussion questions accompany each chapter. Key terms from each chapter are linked to a glossary. In addition, Special Topics on the CD-ROM discuss tangential but frequently asked questions (for example, what is the origin of Satan?) and explore points of contact between the Bible and contemporary culture (for example, biblical themes in music and film). These resources are mentioned parenthetically within the text of this book and listed at the end of major units in each chapter.

CHAPTER ONE

PREPARING FOR THE JOURNEY

A ny seasoned traveler knows the importance of preparing for a
journey, especially when visiting a faraway place for the first time.
This chapter offers three short but crucial orientations to the biblical
world, the biblical text, and biblical studies as a prelude to our own journey through Hebrew scripture. The first orientation provides an
overview of the environment and historical contexts in which this literature was produced. The second section of this chapter explores the
literary history of the biblical text itself and how this collection of writings was eventually transmitted to us as scripture. The final orientation
introduces the major interpretive goals and methods that characterize
the academic discipline of biblical studies.

THE BIBLICAL WORLD

We cannot begin to understand biblical literature without first
gaining a basic familiarity with the geographical setting and historical
circumstances in which it originated. The Hebrew Bible did not emerge
in a vacuum but was a product of ancient **Israel** and the larger environment of the ancient **Near East**. Most readers have some familiarity with
this part of the world, which comprises the modern-day countries of
Turkey, Syria, Lebanon, Israel, the Palestinian Authority, Jordan, Saudi
Arabia, Egypt, Iraq, and Iran. However, we should take care not to
confuse ancient Israel with the modern state of Israel, which was

founded in 1948. We should also distinguish between the **Israelites**, who inhabited the biblical world, and modern-day citizens of Israel, who are called Israelis.

Israel's Ancient Near Eastern Environment

Our orientation to the biblical world begins with a closer look at ancient Israel's geographical setting (CD Special Topic IA.1). Compared to other powers in the ancient Near East, Israel was a small and fairly insignificant political entity (CD Map IA.1). Although its boundaries and political status changed many times during more than one thousand years of biblical history, ancient Israel was even at its greatest extent no bigger than the state of Vermont (CD Map IA.2). Despite the small size of this territory, which was sandwiched for the most part between the Mediterranean Sea and the Jordan River, it nonetheless served as an important land bridge between larger and more powerful nations. Its location meant that Israel was frequently traversed by merchants during times of peace and by armies during times of war. Because of its strategic significance, powerful empires frequently struggled for control of this region in their efforts to extend and protect their borders.

Throughout its history, the land of Israel was called by many names, which are used interchangeably within the biblical text. Before and even after the emergence of an Israelite state this land was often called **Canaan**. Less than a century after the formation of an Israelite monarchy, the name Israel was restricted to the northern part of this region while the southern part became known as Judah. Later in the biblical period, invading empires had their own names for this territory. The Assyrians transformed the northern kingdom of Israel into the province of **Samaria**. Later Persian rulers referred to Judah as the province of **Yehud** (or Judea), while Greek conquerors called the entire region **Palestine** (a name derived from an Aegean group called the **Philistines,** who had settled on the southern coast of Canaan centuries earlier).

STUDYING THE OLD TESTAMENT

In the pages of Hebrew scripture, we will encounter several peoples who interacted with Israel, ranging from small tribal groups to great empires. Important civilizations arose early along the larger rivers that meander through the ancient Near East. Sumerian, Akkadian, and Amorite cultures thrived between the Tigris and Euphrates rivers long before the emergence of Israel. In later years, this geographical region called **Mesopotamia** (literally "between the rivers") was the seat of many empires that would politically dominate Israel and her smaller neighbors.

Many of the people who occupied Mesopotamia shared similar languages and a common cultural heritage with Israel. Biblical traditions tracing Israel's origins to this region reflect the connections among these Semitic groups. Archaeologists have unearthed libraries of ancient texts from Mesopotamian cultures that contribute to our understanding of Israel's ancient Near Eastern environment. Some of these texts have important affinities to biblical literature. For example, the *Gilgamesh Epic* contains a universal flood account that is much older than the one preserved in Genesis. The Code of Hammurabi includes significant parallels to much later biblical laws.

If Mesopotamian civilizations may be considered one of Israel's cultural parents, then the other parent was most assuredly ancient **Egypt,** which sat astride the Nile River in northeast Africa. That this great civilization looms large in Israel's historical memory is clearly attested by the exodus account and innumerable other biblical references. During periods of political strength, Egypt exercised considerable influence over neighboring regions. This may account for certain affinities between Israelite and Egyptian culture, such as the practice of circumcision.

Egypt and Mesopotamia cast looming shadows over the ancient Near East, often eclipsing the smaller states that lay between them. Israel's nearest neighbors included the Canaanites, Arameans, Ammonites, Moabites, and Edomites. These peoples were likewise Semitic in origin and the ethnic boundaries that separate them from the Israelites are sometimes unclear. This is reflected in biblical traditions that connect these peoples genealogically with Israel's own ancestors. Nevertheless, these rival groups at times competed viciously with one another for survival and dominance.

Map IA.1: The Ancient Near East
Map IA.2: The Land of Israel
Special Topic IA.1: The Topography of Ancient Israel

An Overview of Israelite History

An orientation to the biblical world also requires an overview of ancient Israel's history. However, we must distinguish between Israelite history and the stories about Israel that are found in the biblical text. The Bible's central storyline obviously has some basis in historical fact (scholars debate exactly how much), but the people who produced and preserved this literature were not primarily historians. They were more interested in shaping the faith and identity of their own communities than in preserving historical data for its own sake. Although the narrative found in Genesis through Kings appears to tell the story of Israel in a linear fashion, almost all of these traditions were written long after the events that they claim to describe and were shaped by the concerns of later communities. We are better readers when we appreciate this feature of biblical literature instead of stubbornly insisting upon reading the Bible as a series of eyewitness accounts.

This chapter provides essential background information for our upcoming journey through Hebrew scripture. The following outline covers the broad sweep of historical events, while later chapters will fill in details as they become relevant to the discussion of particular texts. Throughout this text we will adopt the more neutral convention of using B.C.E. (Before the Common Era) and C.E. (Common Era) in place of the Christian notations B.C. (Before Christ) and A.D. (*anno domini*, "Year of Our Lord"). For convenience Israelite history may be divided into seven eras:

STUDYING THE OLD TESTAMENT

1. Pre-Israelite Period (before 1020 B.C.E.) Although biblical traditions trace Israel's origins from Abraham and Sarah through the conquest of Canaan, it is impossible to verify any details of Israel's history prior to the monarchic period. Our only record is found in the biblical text itself and archaeological data pertaining to this era lends itself to a variety of interpretations. However, we do know that before the emergence of an Israelite monarchy, Egypt controlled Canaan for the better part of a millennium and in later centuries periodically attempted to reassert its dominance over this region (1 Kgs. 14:25; 2 Kgs. 23:29-35). Around 1200 B.C.E., the Egyptians repelled Aegean invaders who then settled in southwestern Canaan, where they became known as the Philistines. Several smaller states emerged in Canaan as Egyptian control receded toward the end of the eleventh century.

2. United Monarchy (1020–922 B.C.E.) Israel's emergence as a political entity was a defensive response to hostile incursions by the Philistines. Israelite tribes first banded together under the successive rules of Saul, David, and Solomon. The biblical text credits David with finally suppressing the Philistine threat and temporarily subjugating several small neighboring states, and it credits his son Solomon with extensive building projects. However, some scholars view these accounts as a much later glorification of the Davidic dynasty. During this period **Jerusalem** became Israel's administrative center and the site of a **temple** for Israel's patron deity **Yahweh**.

3. Divided Monarchy (922–722 B.C.E.) and Assyrian Period (745–612 B.C.E.) After Solomon's death what had been a united monarchy split into two separate states, the northern kingdom of Israel and the southern kingdom of Judah. Israel eventually established its capital in Samaria under a series of dynasties, while Davidic kings continued to rule Judah from Jerusalem. Beginning in the latter half of the eighth century, both kingdoms were forced to pay tribute to the

Assyrian Empire, which was the first in a series of eastern powers to dominate the biblical world. Ill-fated attempts to regain their independence resulted in the destruction of Israel in 722 B.C.E. and the near destruction of Judah in 701 B.C.E. As Assyria weakened toward the end of the seventh century, Judah enjoyed a short-lived resurgence under a reforming king named Josiah.

4. Babylonian Period (612–539 B.C.E.) The Assyrian capital fell in 612 B.C.E. to a coalition of Babylonians and Medes. Seven years later, the **Babylonian Empire** established its supremacy over the ancient Near East by defeating Egyptian and Assyrian armies at the Battle of Carchemish. In 597 B.C.E. Babylonian forces captured Jerusalem and deported many of Judah's most influential citizens. A foolhardy rebellion by Judah led to more deportations and the destruction of Jerusalem and its temple in 587 B.C.E. This devastating crisis was a watershed moment in biblical history. Attempts to reinterpret older religious traditions in light of the **Babylonian exile** left a deep imprint on biblical literature. Changes that begin during this period mark the transition from Israelite religion (sometimes called **Yahwism**) to early Judaism.

5. Persian Period (539–330 B.C.E.) The Babylonian Empire was short-lived, and in 539 B.C.E. Babylon fell without a fight to Persian forces. The **Persian Empire** won the support of Babylon's former subjects through benign policies such as allowing deportees to return to their native lands and financing the restoration of local temples. After spending half a century in exile, only some of the deported Judeans chose to return to their ancestral homeland, while many others continued to live abroad in the **Diaspora** (meaning "scattering"). The returned community completed the construction of another temple in Jerusalem in 515 B.C.E., marking the beginning of what is called the **Second Temple Period** (515 B.C.E.–70 C.E.).

6. Greek Period (330–164 B.C.E.) The biblical world was again transformed in the late fourth century by the conquests of Alexander the Great, who established a vast empire from Greece to western India. Following Alexander's premature death in 323 B.C.E., this empire was divided among his generals. Ptolemy and Seleucus vied for control of Palestine, but eventually the **Seleucid Dynasty** prevailed. During this period some Jews voluntarily adopted aspects of Greek (or Hellenic) culture while others resisted **Hellenization**. In the mid-second century, a Seleucid ruler named Antiochus IV Epiphanes attempted to impose Hellenic culture on all of his subjects and forcibly prohibited the practice of Judaism.

7. Maccabean Period (164–63 B.C.E.) Under the leadership of a Torah-observant group called the **Maccabees**, Jewish rebels managed to drive out the Seleucids and establish a semi-autonomous state by 142 B.C.E. This brief period of relative independence ended in 63 B.C.E. when Roman troops occupied Palestine.

THE BIBLICAL TEXT

Another important way to prepare for our journey through scripture is by familiarizing ourselves with the long and colorful history of the biblical text itself. Many people vaguely assume that the Bible simply fell from heaven bound between leather covers and printed in King James English. But the formation, transmission, canonization, and translation of this literature were long and complicated processes. A more developed understanding of the Hebrew Bible's literary history can make us better readers of biblical texts.

In addition, readers who are unaccustomed to the Bible may also need a crash course in interpreting biblical citations (CD Charts IIA.1 and IIA.2). Just as world travelers must learn to read maps and signposts, those who peruse the pages of scripture must be able to find particular passages with ease. Conventionally, passages within a given book are cited by a system of chapter and verse numbers. These divisions were not added to the biblical text until the thirteenth and fifteenth centuries C.E. and, as we shall see, do not always appear at natural transition points in the text.

Formation and Transmission

The Hebrew Bible is a diverse collection of traditions that were written gradually over a long period of time by many different people. Much of this material was transmitted orally for generations before attaining a written form. In a real sense, biblical texts have no single author but grew out of the life of Israelite communities that continually shaped these traditions with each retelling. Written texts proved almost as fluid as oral traditions. Many of the **scribes** who handled these texts added explanatory material and updated biblical books in light of Israel's ever-changing circumstances. Unintentional errors also crept into texts as scrolls were copied and recopied over the centuries. Scribal transmission soon produced many different versions of each text, ranging from fairly minor variant readings to more significant variations in content. Some early manuscripts of Jeremiah, for example, are much shorter than what was eventually accepted as the standard version of this book.

Unfortunately, neither the original manuscript (called the **autograph**) nor early copies of any biblical book have survived. Instead we are dependent on copies that in many cases are centuries removed from the initial composition of each text. Scholars must carefully compare all surviving Hebrew manuscripts and analyze their differences to reconstruct the most probable original wording of each biblical book—a painstaking task called **text criticism**. Also useful to text critics are ancient translations of the Hebrew Bible into other languages, especially the Septuagint, since this Greek translation is earlier than any surviving Hebrew manuscripts. All modern language translations are dependent on the efforts of text critics to produce a standard edition of the Hebrew Bible in its original languages from the available manuscript evidence.

Prior to the 1940s, the oldest known Hebrew manuscripts of biblical texts dated from the ninth and tenth centuries C.E. Because these manuscripts were the work of Jewish scholars called Masoretes, who devoted themselves to the correct transmission of biblical texts, they are collectively referred to as the **Masoretic text** (abbreviated MT). The Masoretes not only continued the work of earlier scribes by preserving biblical texts, they also attempted to safeguard them from further corruption. Biblical Hebrew was traditionally written from right to left as a long and unbroken string of consonants without vowels, punctuation, or spaces between words. This situation sometimes allowed different ways of reading a passage depending on which vowels were supplied or how words and sentences were separated by the reader. The Masoretes attempted to standardize the biblical text by adding marks around the consonants to indicate vowels, accent marks, and punctuation.

Text critics continue to rely heavily on these medieval manuscripts, but a series of dramatic discoveries beginning in 1947 brought to light Hebrew texts that are more than a thousand years older than the MT. A large collection of ancient scrolls and scroll fragments dating from the second century B.C.E. to the first century C.E. were found in caves northwest of the Dead Sea near the ancient site of Qumran. This collection, called the **Dead Sea Scrolls**, includes at least partial manuscripts of every biblical book (with the exception of Esther), some of which differ significantly from the MT. Slightly later scrolls that were subsequently discovered to the south of Qumran agree much more closely with medieval manuscripts. This may suggest that a more standard edition of the Hebrew Bible began to develop in at least some circles by the end of the first century C.E.

Canonization

The absence of Esther among the Dead Sea Scrolls may indicate that the Qumran community did not regard this book as authoritative, but many other books are included in the Qumran library that ultimately did not become part of the official Hebrew canon. Likewise, the contents of the Septuagint (which included books like Sirach and Tobit) suggest that Greek-speaking Diaspora Jews recognized a wider collection of texts. Clearly, the formation of the Hebrew canon was a long process that did not occur at a single time or place. No official body ever voted on which books to include in the canon, but rather Jewish communities gradually moved toward consensus on which books should be regarded as normative.

The three-part structure of the Jewish canon (Torah, Prophets, Writings) reflects at least three distinct stages within this canonization process. The Torah gained canonical status by the end of the fifth century B.C.E., when the reforms of Ezra made it the religious constitution of the postexilic community (Neh. 8–9). The Prophets were next accepted as authoritative by at least some influential Jews around the end of the third century B.C.E. New Testament writers presuppose the authority of these two collections whenever they mention "the law and the prophets" (for example, Matt. 22:40; Acts 13:15; Rom. 3:21). The first hint of a third collection occurs in the preface to Sirach (ca. 132 B.C.E.), which refers rather vaguely to "the law, the prophets, and the other books." Similarly, around 85 C.E. the New Testament Gospel of Luke refer to the emerging three-part canon as "the law of Moses, the prophets, and the psalms" (Luke 24:44). As the last part of the Tanakh to be canonized, the Writings likely remained undefined well into the first century C.E., whereas the authority of certain books in this collection continued to be questioned even centuries later (especially Esther, Ecclesiastes, and the Song of Songs).

Translation

Even as the Jewish canon was still developing, translators were already making biblical books available to a wider audience. In the centuries following the destruction of the Jerusalem temple in 597 B.C.E., many Jews lived outside of their ancestral homeland and did not speak Hebrew on a daily basis. Alexander's conquest in the late fourth century made Greek the dominant language of the biblical world and created the need for a Greek translation of Hebrew scripture. This first major translation of the Bible was undertaken in the third century in Alexandria, Egypt. Its name—the Septuagint (abbreviated LXX, "seventy")—derives from a legend that 72 scholars miraculously produced identical Greek translations after working individually for 72 days. The Septuagint was widely used for centuries within Diaspora Judaism and within the early Christian movement. It includes those books that came to be considered deuterocanonical by Catholic and Orthodox churches.

New translations of the Christian Bible began to appear as Latin became the dominant tongue for the western half of the Roman Empire in the early centuries C.E. Acting under a commission from the Roman bishop, a biblical scholar named Jerome produced a complete Latin translation of the Hebrew Bible and New Testament from Hebrew and Greek manuscripts between 385 and 405 C.E. Jerome's translation—called the **Vulgate** because it made the Bible accessible in the common (or "vulgar") language of the day—became the official Bible of the Roman Catholic Church.

Although the Vulgate originated as an attempt to make the Bible accessible to the general population, it ironically remained in use by the Catholic Church long after most Europeans stopped speaking and reading Latin. Preferring to leave biblical interpretation in the hands of an educated clergy, the church began to discourage translation of the Bible into the vernacular. Parts of the Latin Vulgate were first translated into English in the early eighth century by the Venerable Bede, a

Benedictine monk. The first complete translation of Jerome's Vulgate into English was produced by a fourteenth-century priest named John Wycliffe. Church authorities banned Wycliffe's Bible and prohibited further translation.

Nonetheless, the continued translation of the Bible into modern languages was assured by two important events: the invention of the printing press in 1455 and the Protestant Reformation, which began in 1517. Printing presses made books more affordable by eliminating the slow and labor-intensive task of copying them by hand. Protestant Reformers such as Martin Luther insisted that scripture (rather than the church) should serve as the primary authority for the Christian faith and encouraged new translations of the Christian Bible into many European languages. Because of anti-Catholic sentiment among the Reformers, most of these translators rejected the deuterocanonical books and worked directly from Hebrew and Greek manuscripts rather than the Latin Vulgate.

William Tyndale was the first person to translate the New Testament from Greek into English in 1525. He also began a translation of the Hebrew Bible from original-language manuscripts, but before completing it he was arrested by church authorities, tried for heresy, and burned at the stake. Soon after Tyndale's death, Henry VIII decided to encourage English translation of the Bible as a part of his challenge to papal authority. In 1535, he permitted the free distribution of the Coverdale Bible—the first complete printed English Bible, which relied heavily on Tyndale's earlier work. As Protestant and Catholic rulers struggled over control of England throughout the sixteenth and seventeenth centuries, both sides sponsored new translations that were intentionally crafted to bolster their own theological claims (CD Special Topic IIC.1).

These translations culminated in the King James Version (KJV) in 1611. Also known as the Authorized Version, the KJV is a magisterial literary masterpiece whose influence on the English language cannot be overestimated. Although an excellent scholarly achievement for its day, the KJV is not the best translation currently available for several reasons. First, the forty-seven scholars commissioned by James I to work on the KJV had access only to relatively late manuscripts of the Hebrew scripture, whereas better and earlier manuscripts have been made available to Bible translators since 1611. Second, our knowledge of Hebrew grammar and syntax has increased greatly since the seventeenth century. Third, the English language itself has evolved since the production of the KJV, making some of its expressions almost unintelligible to modern readers. Despite the sentimental attachment that many readers still have to the King James Version, its usefulness has been superseded by many more recent English translations.

Modern readers might be justifiably bewildered by the multitude of English Bibles now available on bookstore shelves (CD Special Topic IIC.2). How can there be so many different translations of the same text? What are the differences among these translations? Are some more reliable or useful than others? We have already discussed the necessity of text criticism as a prerequisite for translating biblical texts. Translators sometimes disagree over how best to reconstruct the original wording of the biblical text from available manuscript evidence. Good translations discuss these text-critical choices in footnotes.

Some English Bibles are designed with a specific audience in mind. The books to be included in the translation and the order of those books will vary depending on whether a Jewish, Protestant, Catholic, or Orthodox audience is intended. Bibles that are intended for an **ecumenical** (mixed) or academic audience usually include three separate sections: Hebrew scripture, the deuterocanonical literature (or Apocrypha), and the New Testament.

Translations that are sponsored by a single religious organization are likely to reflect its interpretive biases and assumptions. For example, the New International Version was produced by conservative leaders of the evangelical Christian community who required translators to affirm a particular view of biblical authority. In contrast, the Revised Standard Version was produced by a more diverse group of translators. Readers should be aware that the guiding principles used in a translation are usually specified in the preface of that Bible.

Aside from text-critical, canonical, and ideological issues, translators of biblical texts also have to deal with all of the problems inherent in transferring meaning from one language into another. There are often many different ways to render a given Hebrew expression in English. Because there is no simple semantic and grammatical correspondence between any two languages, a translation is always an approximate interpretation of the original text. Literary features such as rhyme and wordplay may also be difficult to preserve in translation. These problems are compounded by chronological distance and cultural differences. An idiom (for example, *to have someone in stitches*) or a euphemism (for example, *to pass away*) whose meaning is clear in one culture often makes little or no sense in another.

Faced with these issues, translators tend to take one of two approaches in rendering a **source text** (in this case the Hebrew Bible) in the **target language** (in this case English). Some renderings aim for a **literal translation** that preserves the wording and sentence structure of the source text insofar as possible. This approach sometimes results in an awkward-sounding translation that may present difficulties for modern readers. Other renderings aim for a more **dynamic translation** that sounds more natural in the target language but may compromise the meaning of the source text. Most modern translations of the Bible fall on a continuum between completely literal and completely dynamic approaches. A third category of English Bibles is not translations of original language manuscripts at all but **paraphrases** of established English translations (for example, the Living Bible).

Because all translations have strengths and weaknesses, the choice of a particular Bible should be guided by the interpretive goals of the reader. For the purposes of our upcoming journey through scripture, readers should select a translation that is as literal as possible while still being readily comprehensible. It is often helpful to compare literal and dynamic renderings of difficult passages, while paraphrases should almost always be avoided. Up-to-date translations executed by an ecumenical committee are preferable to ones produced by an individual or single denomination, which may promote their own theological agenda.

 Special Topic IIC.1: The Early History of the English Bible
Special Topic IIC.2: Modern English Bibles

BIBLICAL STUDIES

Before we venture into the biblical text, we should carefully consider our reasons for embarking on the journey that lies before us. People read the Bible in a variety of settings for many different purposes. Faith communities (Jewish, Orthodox, Catholic, and Protestant) read scripture passages corporately as part of their worship services. Many individuals read the Bible devotionally to enrich their personal faith or aid in spiritual formation. People sometimes read the Bible as a classic example of world literature that has exerted an enormous influence on Western civilization. Others approach the biblical text as a window into the history and culture of the ancient Near East or as the basis of the world's great monotheistic religions.

Readers of *Studying the Old Testament: A Companion* will be asked to adopt an academic approach to Hebrew scripture. Therefore, our final orientation in this chapter introduces the discipline of biblical studies, which will be presupposed in the chapters that follow. We will first consider how reading the Bible in an academic setting might differ from reading it devotionally in churches and synagogues before introducing some of the major interpretive methods of biblical studies.

The Classroom versus Faith Communities

Reading the Bible in the context of a faith community necessarily differs from the practice of biblical studies as an academic discipline. Jews and Christians who read the Bible for devotional purposes typically focus on the contemporary relevance of a biblical text rather than its original historical context. In religious settings the Bible is primarily a source of ethical teaching used to encourage certain behaviors and discourage others. Members of faith communities usually accept the Bible's religious authority without question although they might understand that authority in many different ways. Very conservative Christians insist that the Bible is factually accurate in every way, while moderate to liberal Christians and Jews tend to view the Bible as inspired but not inerrant.

In contrast, the academic discipline of biblical studies approaches the Bible like any other ancient text while making no assertion (either positive or negative) about its religious authority. Although biblical scholars may or may not belong to a community of faith, they attempt to read the Bible as rationally and objectively as possible. Rather than search for present-day applications, biblical scholars emphasize the need to understand texts in their original settings. For that reason they raise questions concerning the date, author, implied audience, apparent ideology, genre, social setting, and historical context of a given document. To answer these questions, biblical scholars draw upon archaeology, history, literary studies, linguistics, sociology, and a variety of other academic fields.

Despite these undeniable differences, academic and devotional approaches to the biblical text are not necessarily incompatible. In fact, the contributions of biblical studies can be an invaluable resource for Jews and Christians. People who read the Bible in the context of faith communities can easily forget the vast historical and cultural distance between the modern and biblical worlds. Such comfortable familiarity with biblical texts can lull readers into forgetting that this ancient literature does not directly address most modern concerns. The discipline of biblical studies reminds us that the Bible is a collection of texts from the distant past that are often alien to us. Rather than assuming that we already know what the Bible says, we must read it on its own terms. When we place this literature within its originating contexts, we understand it more accurately and are then better prepared to consider its contemporary relevance.

Although many Jews and Christians are receptive to the insights of biblical studies, fundamentalist Christians object to the idea of studying the Bible like any other text. Fundamentalism as a religious movement first began in the late nineteenth century among conservative Protestants in North America reacting against scientific discoveries that seemed to undermine biblical claims. These very conservative Christians believe that the biblical writers were inspired in a way that transcended the limitations of their own time and culture to produce a text that was both infallible and inerrant. Fundamentalists prefer a literal interpretation of scripture and tend to equate factual accuracy with religious truth. According to this all-or-nothing approach, the Bible cannot be regarded as trustworthy unless all of it is factually true. Biblical scholars and most people of faith reject dogmatic claims such as these, which set religious faith in opposition to intellect.

Methods of Biblical Analysis

Reading a text is much like engaging in a conversation. Both activities entail a complex process of interpretation involving three important factors: the speaker/author, spoken or written words, and the listener/reader. Meaning resides neither in the words themselves nor in the mind of either conversation partner but in the creative interplay of all of these elements. For that reason, a productive encounter with a text (much like a good conversation) requires an investment of time and effort.

Communication is obviously enhanced when we get better acquainted with our conversation partner. Similarly in biblical interpretation, we ask questions about the contexts from which this literature emerged.

How, when, and where was a given text written and for what purpose? Who was its original or intended audience? What were the principle concerns of the author or the communities that shaped that text? How was the world that they experienced different from our own? Such information, to the extent that it can be reconstructed, gives us insight into the intended meaning of the author or originating community.

Just as spoken words are the medium of a conversation, the biblical text is the vehicle through which ancient writers expressed themselves to their audiences (and unintentionally to us centuries later). A good translation is essential for readers who are unfamiliar with the Bible's original languages. We can better understand a biblical text by investigating its literary origins. Was it written by a single author at one time and place or did it develop gradually at the hands of multiple editors? We also understand a text more accurately when we are aware of its literary genre. A riddle or a proverb, for example, should not be interpreted in the same way as a legal text. Finally, we should also pay attention to stylistic features such as key words, repetition, plot, and characterization that provide additional clues to direct the interpretation of a text.

The listener or reader also plays a crucial part in the process of interpretation. We are not passive recipients of meaning but necessarily filter the words that we hear or read through our own experiences. For that reason, the perceived meaning of a text is never completely identical to the author's intended meaning. How a reader understands a text is to a great extent dependent on his or her specific **social location**. Gender, ethnicity, race, class, religion, and a host of other identity markers consciously and unconsciously shape the way that we view the world around us. We are better readers of biblical texts when we try to be conscious of the ways in which our own social location affects our worldview. Because every reader views the Bible in light of his or her own experiences, there are many different possible interpretations of any biblical text. But this fact does not mean that they are all equally

STUDYING THE OLD TESTAMENT

valid. The best test of an interpretation is whether it makes sense to other readers.

As biblical studies has developed as an academic field, new methodologies have continued to emerge that aid in the process of interpretation. Some of these methods help us explore the origin and background of a text, whereas others focus either on the final form of text or on the reader. Biblical scholars have traditionally referred to the careful analysis of scripture as biblical **criticism**, a rather unfortunate term that is often misunderstood by people outside the field. When we read the Bible critically, we are not trying to find fault with the text or undermine it in any way. Rather the critical study of a subject means that it is examined as carefully, analytically, and objectively as possible. Just as art critics are people who value artistic expression and are trained to assess the relative merits of a given work, biblical critics appreciate the Bible and attempt to make well-founded judgments about it.

As we explore Hebrew scripture in the next several chapters, readers will have the opportunity to participate firsthand in biblical scholarship. A short introduction to some of the major methods or criticisms used in biblical studies will help us prepare for that experience. Text criticism is a necessary prerequisite for biblical studies. Historical and social science methods attempt to illuminate the world from which the text emerged. Form, source, redaction, and literary criticism focus on the text itself. Canonical, reader-response, and feminist criticism emphasize the role that readers play in interpreting texts. This chapter provides only brief descriptions of these methods, but we will learn more about them in later chapters.

1. Text Criticism involves the careful comparison of Hebrew manuscripts and early biblical translations to determine the most probable wording of the original text, or autograph. Text critics determine which manuscripts are the most reliable, detect common scribal errors, and identify intentional changes in the text. For example, Hebrew manuscripts of

Leviticus 20:10 contain an example of dittography, a copying error in which the same phrase is accidentally recorded twice.

2. Historical Criticism might take one of two directions. Some historical critics evaluate the accuracy of texts that purport to record historical events (the history *in* the text). By comparing biblical accounts of an event with non-biblical evidence, they try to determine what actually happened. Other historical critics investigate the historical situation in which a given text was itself composed (the history *of* the text). These critics assume that the circumstances of the author and his or her intended audience are vital to interpreting a text. We will draw upon this method frequently in the following chapters, but it will be especially emphasized in relation to the Latter Prophets.

3. Social-Science Criticism attempts to understand the social world from which biblical traditions emerged using models borrowed from social-science disciplines. Such models might be used to illuminate social institutions such as Israelite prophecy, as we shall see in chapter 4.

4. Form Criticism focuses on the oral or pre-literary stage of development behind the present text. Form critics analyze small, self-contained units of text that seem to represent distinctive forms or genres like folktales, genealogies, proverbs, hymns, and creeds. Such genres probably circulated in oral form long before they were incorporated into a written text. Because particular forms of communication arise in particular social contexts, words generally spoken at a religious ceremony may be inappropriate for the marketplace. Recognizing this inevitable relationship between form and function, form critics try to determine the real-life settings that most likely gave birth to a given genre. This method will come in handy as we explore the Latter Prophets, Psalms, and Proverbs.

5. Source Criticism is used to identify and describe earlier sources that were combined by editors to produce the present form of biblical texts.

STUDYING THE OLD TESTAMENT

These sources are not always explicitly cited, requiring source critics to rely on clues within the text such as sudden changes in vocabulary, literary style, and theological perspective. Inconsistencies and unnecessary repetition may also indicate the combination of multiple sources. The author of Chronicles, for example, almost certainly used the books of Samuel and Kings as sources for compiling a new history of Israel. Source criticism has also played an important role in the study of the Torah, as we shall see in the next chapter.

6. Redaction Criticism examines how oral and written sources have been artistically shaped and arranged by the final editor of a text. Redaction critics recognize that biblical texts are more than a random amalgam of sources. Instead of attempting to recover earlier stages in the production of a text, they focus on its final shape in order to determine the intention and perspective of its compiler. This method has played an important role in the study of the Torah, the Former Prophets, and Chronicles.

7. Literary Criticism is the analysis of a text as literature, with attention to matters such as plot, character, setting, and point of view. Literary critics are not concerned with the historical development or background of a text but deal with the final form of the text as we now have it. This method highlights literary strategies such as important themes, symbolism, irony, metaphor and simile, and other rhetorical devices. We will rely heavily on this method as we explore the Bible's narrative and poetic texts.

8. Canonical Criticism focuses on the collections of texts that are considered authoritative by Jewish and Christian communities. Rather than reading a given text in isolation, this method insists that it be interpreted in conversation with the larger canon. Canonical critics explore the theological significance of biblical texts for the communities of faith that accept them as sacred and normative. We will take a closer look at this method in relation to the Writings.

9. Reader-Response Criticism emphasizes the reader's role in creating the meaning of a text. This approach discounts the intention of the author as totally inaccessible and denies that the text itself has any inherent meaning. Reader-response critics instead view meaning as whatever readers find in texts. There is no single "correct" reading of a text, although interpretations can be validated by groups (for example, the academic community or a particular community of faith).

10. Feminist Criticism intentionally claims the concerns of modern feminism as its starting point. This approach recognizes that women historically have been denied access to authority, including the production and interpretation of religious texts. Some feminist critics offer reinterpretations of texts that are supportive of women, while others focus on exposing what they see as the inherent sexism of biblical literature. This method informs several special topic discussions in this text as well as our discussions of Ruth and Esther.

Now that we have been introduced to the biblical world, to the biblical text, and to the academic discipline of biblical studies, we are prepared to venture into the pages of the Hebrew Bible. Readers may find it helpful to refer to this chapter periodically as our journey through scripture progresses. The orientations in this chapter aim to paint a "big picture" to which details will be added in later chapters.

CHAPTER TWO

TORAH: THE JOURNEY BEGINS

The first five books of Hebrew scripture tell the story of several significant beginnings. Genesis opens with a majestic story of cosmic origins, whereas the chapters that follow depict the emergence of human communities and world civilization. In the twelfth chapter of Genesis, focus narrows from universal foundations to the formation of a particular people. God selects a single couple, Abram and Sarai, who embark upon a journey that will be continued by their descendants through the next four biblical books. Over the course of this journey, they are transformed from a dysfunctional extended family into an enslaved people and finally into a chosen nation. As Deuteronomy concludes, the fledgling nation of Israel stands at the brink of another journey as they prepare to cross the Jordan River into the promised land.

Beginnings are important because they give us a sense of identity. Just as we might research our ancestors and their life stories to gain self-understanding, the Israelites preserved accounts of their origins to better appreciate their ongoing journey as a people. Therefore, we must remember that these are stories told with a purpose in mind. Biblical authors sought not so much to inform their readers as to inspire them. At critical junctures of Israel's history, storytellers continued to recall and reshape the nation's foundational narratives in ways that met their audiences' changing needs. Stories about their past gave Israel insight into their present situation and a vision to shape their future.

On the opening leg of our journey through Hebrew scripture, we will explore Israel's stories about cosmic, ancestral, and national origins. The books that contain these stories are often referred to collectively as the **Torah**, a common designation for the first of three major divisions within the Jewish canon. Another frequent title for the Bible's first five books is the **Pentateuch**, a term derived from the Greek words *penta* (five) and *teuchos* (scroll), which reflects the ancient tradition of copying each of these books onto a separate scroll made either from papyrus or prepared animal skins. This term was in use by the second century C.E., suggesting that these five books were viewed as a cohesive unit at least by that time.

Yet the terms Torah and Pentateuch are both problematic for different reasons. The first is notoriously difficult to translate and often causes misunderstanding. Although typically translated "law," the word *Torah* actually has a much broader meaning that would be more accurately conveyed by "instruction" or "teaching." In fact, the Torah contains a wide variety of literary forms, including narratives, genealogy, legends, poems, and sermons. Legal materials comprise only a small percentage of the total text within these five books. Moreover, Christians have frequently made unfavorable comparisons between the Old and New Testaments based on the mistaken notion that the former is narrowly legalistic whereas the latter conveys a message of grace. Such misperceptions not only impede interreligious dialogue but also impoverish Christianity's appreciation of its own scriptural heritage. In fact, Judaism regards the Torah as a gift from God and a source of great joy. As it is interpreted and explained by other writings, the Torah provides a comprehensive way of life that transforms everyday actions into constant reminders of one's faith. Collectively, these binding rules and customs are called *halakhah*, which literally means "the path that one walks."

The second designation, Pentateuch, is also problematic. Many biblical scholars argue that the first coherent section of Hebrew scripture is either shorter or longer than the traditional five books. Some scholars point out that Deuteronomy is only loosely connected to the first four books of the Torah. They correctly recognize that it is in some ways more closely related to the books that follow it than to those that precede it. These scholars usually label Genesis through Numbers a **Tetrateuch** ("four scrolls"). Other scholars contend that Deuteronomy does not provide a satisfactory ending to the Torah's story. Not until the end of Joshua, when Israel is settled in the land, are most of God's promises to Abraham fulfilled. Including Joshua would produce a six-volume work, or a **Hexateuch** ("six scrolls").

However, any proposal either to contract or expand the Pentateuch discounts the long-standing tradition of reading the first five books of the Bible as a self-contained unit. Although modern readers might long for a happy ending or a neat resolution to the Bible's first story, this is not what the Pentateuch provides. The Torah is a story of origins rather than conclusions. Faced with this reality, modern readers should ask themselves why Israelite storytellers might have chosen to end their foundational narrative with a cliffhanger.

COSMIC ORIGINS: THE PRIMEVAL HISTORY

As we begin our journey through the Torah, we might notice that both the English title "Genesis" and the Hebrew title *bereshit* ("in the beginning") suggest that the first book is concerned with origins. Genesis 1–11 is the Bible's version of **primeval history**, a description of events that allegedly precede recorded history. Thus, the stories contained in these chapters were written down long after the events that they describe. Many past cultures preserved more than one account of primeval history, and Israel was no less curious and creative in expressing her own vision of cosmic origins. Tales set at the dawn of time provided a powerful vehicle for ancient people to articulate their understanding of abstract concepts such as the nature of the world, human nature, the supernatural, and the divine-human relationship.

Consequently, a primeval story tells us more about the worldview of the community that produced it than it does about cosmic origins as such.

Much of Israel's primeval history consists of etiologies. An **etiology** is a story intended to explain a natural phenomenon such as the appearance of rainbows, a cultural practice such as a dietary restriction, or a religious practice such as observance of the Sabbath day. Etiologies that also describe the origin of the world or a significant portion of it might be labeled a **cosmogony**, or a creation story. Almost all ancient cultures possessed at least one cosmogony and frequently had several. Conflicting cosmogonies either represented the religious worldviews of different groups within the society or complementary ways for a single group to express its beliefs.

Creation (Gen. 1–2; CD Preliminary Exercises IA.1 and IA.2)

We find what appear to be two separate cosmogonies at the beginning of Genesis (CD Primary Texts IA.1-2). The Bible begins with the spirit of God (Hebrew *elohim* ["god/s"]) hovering majestically over the face of a formless, watery chaos. By simply speaking the words "let there be . . ." Elohim brings into being light, a firmament (sky), dry land, vegetation, and heavenly bodies. Similarly, by the power of speech the deity separates and organizes elements of the emerging creation to produce day and night, waters above (rain) and waters below (seas, rivers, and so on), and all self-perpetuating species of plants (CD Chart IA.1). The theme of classification continues as various types of animals are produced, each reproducing according to their kinds. The repetition of key words and phrases such as *morning and evening* reinforces the overall sense of organization in this chapter as the days of creation are counted out. The habitats established on days one through three are populated with living creatures in the same order on days four through six (CD Chart IA.2). As the crowning act of creation, Elohim simultaneously makes both male and female humans in the divine image, grants them dominion over the animals, and blesses them with fertility. Pleased with this good creation, the deity rests on the seventh day, making it holy.

Genesis 2:4 begins with what reads suspiciously like an ending for the first story: "These are the generations of the heavens and the earth when they were created." After this note of finality, the next sentence appears jarring in more ways than one. Not only does it continue to discuss creation, it recalls *the day* (one day?) in which the LORD God (Hebrew *Yahweh 'Elohim*) made the earth and the heavens (note the reversal of terms). It also rambles on in a manner that would make teachers of English cringe. As opposed to the short, repetitive sentences that characterized Genesis up to this point, the rest of chapter 2 demonstrates a much different literary style and vocabulary. Furthermore, aspects of creation that were completed in the previous chapter are now redone in a different order. Instead of beginning with a formless deep, the cosmos now consists in its pre-creation state as an unwatered and uncultivated desert. The creation of human beings becomes a two-stage process interrupted by the creation of plants and animals.

In Genesis 2:7, Yahweh Elohim forms the first human (Hebrew *ha'adam*) from the earth (Hebrew *ha'adamah*) and breathes life into its nostrils. These two Hebrew words are obviously related, but the intended pun is lost on readers of English unless *'adam* is translated "earthling." This earth-creature is given the task of tilling the garden and commanded not to eat from a particular tree, a restriction that contrasts with the unlimited dominion granted humans in chapter 1. Yahweh Elohim also differs significantly from Elohim. Not only do these two cosmogonies consistently use different names for the deity, they also describe their creative activities in distinctive ways. Whereas Elohim merely hovered and spoke, Yahweh Elohim waters, plants, forms, and breathes in a manner suggestive of a physical presence. In other words, the first story showcases a **transcendent,** or more distant, deity, whereas the second story depicts the deity in an **anthropomorphic,** or human-like, manner. Furthermore, the deliberate and organized creation of chapter 1 is replaced in chapter 2 by a more spontaneous trial-and-error approach. Only after creating the earthling does Yahweh Elohim appear to realize the need for a garden and a mate. The production of a suitable mate itself requires multiple attempts before the deity finds a working solution.

Although it is not uncommon for ancient cultures to have several conflicting cosmogonies, the presence of two creation stories juxtaposed at the beginning of Genesis might puzzle modern readers. Many Christians and Jews have even been taught to overlook or harmonize the inconsistencies between these accounts and read them as a coherent narrative. Clearly the biblical editors were sophisticated enough to recognize the tensions between these accounts, but they chose to include both stories anyway. Some possible reasons have already been suggested. The stories may have been preserved by different groups in ancient Israel to convey their respective views of the world, human nature, and God. Alternatively, a single group might have found both stories useful to communicate different aspects of the divine nature or human existence. As we continue to examine more stories in the Pentateuch, other answers might present themselves as well.

Preliminary Exercise IA.1: Comparing the Genesis Creation Stories
Preliminary Exercise IA.2: What Is a Creation Story?
Primary Text IA.1: The Bible's First Cosmogony (Gen. 1:1–2:4a)
Primary Text IA.2: The Bible's Second Cosmogony (Gen. 2:4b-25)
Primary Text IA.3: *Enuma Elish*
Chart IA.1: The Cosmology of Genesis 1:1–2:4a
Chart IA.2: The Structure of Genesis 1:1–2:4a
Special Topic IA.1: Other Cosmogonies of the Hebrew Bible
Special Topic IA.2: Creationism and Evolution

In the Garden (Gen. 2–3; CD Preliminary Exercises IB.1 and IB.2)

The second creation account continues into Genesis 3 and tells the story of the first human couple, eventually named **Adam** and **Eve.**

Although this story is rarely mentioned again in Hebrew scripture, it has assumed great theological and cultural import for later audiences who read it as an illustration of human nature and appropriate relations between the sexes. These traditional interpretations exert a powerful influence over how this story is translated from Hebrew into English. In turn, such translations tend to reinforce traditional interpretations.

For instance, most English translations portray the creation of Eve as an afterthought for Adam's benefit. Readers will recall that in Genesis 2 the earthling (*ha'adam*) is created from the earth and assigned agricultural duties in the garden. Most English translations obscure this pun by rendering *ha'adam* as "man" or "Adam" even though the Hebrew term is neither a proper name nor male-specific. As in English, Hebrew proper names never appear with a definite article (*ha*/the). Moreover, even though *ha'adam* is grammatically a masculine word (as all Hebrew words are either masculine or feminine), it often refers to human beings in general—both men and women.

A male-specific term does not appear in this story until after the operation in verse 23, when the deity removes part of the earthling to create a woman (*'ishshah*). Only after this bit of surgery does the leftover portion become a "man" (*'ish*). This raises very interesting questions about the nature of the first human and the type of surgery that Yahweh Elohim may have been performing in the garden. The vocabulary suggests that this surgery constitutes not the creation of woman from man, but the creation of gender from genderless humanity.

Readers also commonly assume that Eve is subordinate to her mate because many English translations describe her as a "helper" or "helpmate" (Hebrew *'ezer*). Yet this same Hebrew term often describes the relief that God provides for Israel (2 Kgs. 14:26; Job 29:12; Pss. 30:10; 54:4; 72:12; 107:12). Clearly, this word does not inherently suggest the subordination of the helper to the helped! Instead, the Genesis story insists that the earthling needs a "helper as its partner" (Hebrew *'ezer kᵉnegdo*), not a "helper as its servant."

Readers may also be inclined to argue that Eve is subordinate to Adam because she is the one who first eats from the forbidden tree. She is also the one who converses with the serpent, which is described not as **Satan** but as one of the creatures made by Yahweh Elohim (CD Special Topic IB.2). That the serpent speaks is not unusual since primeval stories from many ancient cultures feature speaking animals. In Genesis 3, this crafty serpent engages the woman in an intelligent conversation concerning the tree and convinces her that instead of death its fruit offers godlike, universal knowledge. Many readers manage to ignore the fact that Adam is described as having been present, if silent, throughout this conversation (CD Special Topic IB.3). Readers must also find ways to explain why eating from the tree results in the serpent's prediction of increased knowledge rather than the deity's earlier decree of an immediate death sentence.

Rather than kill the disobedient humans, Yahweh Elohim delivers three etiological proclamations. The deity's first speech, which is addressed to the serpent, explains why snakes lack legs and bite fearful humans. The third speech, which is addressed to the man, accounts for the difficult toil characterizing a farmer's life and possibly also human mortality (cf. Gen. 3:22). The middle speech to the woman is traditionally understood as explaining painful childbirth, sexual desire, and gender dominance.

Clearly, all of these speeches depict the negative consequences of disobedience rather than the deity's original intention for creation. Moreover, the speeches addressed to the humans explain cultural arrangements that were well known to members of ancient Israelite society. Because they are cultural etiologies, these verses cannot always be generalized to other times and places. Nevertheless, the speech addressed to the woman is often used in contemporary societies to justify gender dominance. Ironically, few modern readers would insist that men must be tillers of the soil based on verses 17-18!

In postbiblical Christian interpretation, the garden story is often titled "The **Fall** of Man" and associated with the idea that all human

STUDYING THE OLD TESTAMENT

beings inherit a sinful nature due to the "**original sin**" of Adam and Eve (CD Special Topic IB.4). However, the Bible never describes Eden as a lost paradise nor do words like *fall* and *sin* appear in this story. The term curse is applied only to the serpent and to the earth, whose original fertility is temporarily impaired until after the flood account (Gen. 8:21). These facts suggest that the interpretation of Genesis 2–3 as a fall story is an example of **eisegesis** rather than **exegesis**. In other words, this interpretation rests upon details that are imposed upon the story rather than observations drawn from it. Yet the overall structure of Genesis 1–11 does suggest that, for good or ill, the consequences of disobedience extend beyond the garden into life east of Eden.

Preliminary Exercise IB.1: Exegesis and Eisegesis of Genesis 2–3
Preliminary Exercise IB.2: Artists' Renderings of Eden
Primary Text IB.1: *The Life of Adam and Eve*
Special Topic IB.1: Adam's First Wife—Lilith
Special Topic IB.2: Who or What Is Satan?
Special Topic IB.3: How Eve Became "the Temptress"
Special Topic IB.4: The "Fall of Man" and "Original Sin"
Special Topic IB.5: Genesis 2:4b–3:24 and Modern Cinema

Life East of Eden (Genesis 4–11; CD Preliminary Exercises IC.1 and IC.2)

Cain, depicted as the elder son of Adam and Eve, introduces the first murder into human society after the deity's unexplained preference for the sacrifices of his brother **Abel.** Later interpreters have tried to understand this story as a paradigm for conflict between agricultural and herding societies. Other interpreters have imposed on the story qualitative distinctions concerning the brothers' offerings or personal characters. God's preference would be understandable if Cain's offering was somehow inferior or if Cain was an evil person. The story, however, allows for divine mystery by not answering all of our questions.

Nor does the story answer such practical concerns as who could threaten Cain's life or marry him when he and his parents are presumably alone in the world following Abel's death. Such problems lead many scholars to conclude that the Cain and Abel story originated independently of Adam and Eve's saga. Biblical editors, also called **redactors**, may have later connected the two accounts by making them a family. Before these stories were knit together, the Cain and Abel tale would have presupposed a larger population.

The editorial arrangement of the Torah depicts human society as rapidly deteriorating in the hands of Cain's descendants (CD Special Topic IC.1). Redactors reinforce this impression by including a fragmentary legend about sexual relations between human women and divine beings that result in a race of giants (Gen. 6:1-4). In many ways, this story seems more at home on Mount Olympus than in the biblical text (CD Special Topic IC.2)! However, it does demonstrate that the boundaries so carefully established in the first creation story have been violated to the extent that the human and divine worlds are now mixed together.

Again the deity intervenes to punish humanity and establish a new beginning with a single family. The flood story in Genesis is a puzzling account to an observant reader who encounters several inconsistencies and repetitions (CD Chart IC.1). Twice the reader is informed of the deity's decision to destroy the earth, and twice the deity commands **Noah** to build an ark and stock it with animals. However, on one of these occasions, Elohim (God) gives detailed instructions for building the ark and for preserving two of every kind of animal, male and female according to their kinds. This language is very reminiscent of the first creation story. On the other occasion, Yahweh (the LORD) tells Noah to preserve seven pairs of all clean animals and birds but only one pair of all unclean animals. Throughout the story, the name of the deity continues to alternate as does the description of the flood, either as a cosmic upheaval that undoes creation or as a natural phenomenon resulting from excessive rainfall. At times the story describes the waters of the flood as rising for 150 days and receding in 220 days. Elsewhere it claims the rains lasted only 40 days and nights and receded in 7 days. Ironing out these difficulties leads many readers to conclude that the present flood story is a combination of two independent accounts (CD Primary Texts IC.1, IC.2, and IC.3). When separated from one another the two accounts are internally consistent, and in many ways each is similar to one of the two cosmogonies that began Genesis (CD Chart IC.2).

Both versions of the flood narrative include a **covenant**, or agreement, formed between the deity and Noah following the deluge. This is the first of four such relationships formalized in this way throughout Hebrew scriptures. In addition to the **Noahide covenant** formed here, the deity later establishes similar agreements with Abraham, Israel (as mediated through Moses), and David (CD Special Topic IC.3). One version of the flood account preserves a **conditional covenant** that obligates both Noah and Elohim. In this case Noah's descendants are commanded to avoid shedding human blood as well as eating meat that contains blood. In return Elohim promises never again to destroy the earth by flood and offers a blessing very similar to the one given humans in the first cosmogony. The rainbow is established as a sign of these promises. In the parallel flood account, Yahweh forms an **unconditional covenant** with Noah that removes the curse placed on the earth in the second cosmogony and ensures the uninterrupted flow of agricultural seasons for the future.

Other ancient flood stories, very similar to the biblical account, existed in cultures that neighbor and predate Israel. These myths, which are preserved in several different languages and in varying degrees of completeness, include the *Atrahasis Epic* and the **Gilgamesh Epic** (CD Primary Text IC.4). These stories also contain the motifs of one person being chosen to survive a universal flood with his family, building an ark, preserving animals, sending out birds, and offering a sacrifice after the flood. Significant differences also occur, especially in the depiction of the deity or deities and the reasons given for causing the flood. However, the parallels at least indicate that biblical writers were aware of the earlier flood myths and may even have consciously adapted them to fit their own religious worldviews.

Following the flood account, the primeval history introduces Noah's genealogy with a short, puzzling narrative in which Noah the vineyard keeper becomes intoxicated. This story criticizes Noah's son **Ham** for the mysterious sin of seeing his father's nakedness. As punishment, Noah curses Ham's son **Canaan** to a future of servitude (CD Special Topic IC.4). This narrative, along with the following **genealogy,** expresses Israel's understanding of its political and ethnic context. Canaan is also a name for Israel's nearest neighbors and occasional enemies. Thus, Ham's son is the **eponymous**, or name-bearing, ancestor of the Canaanites. Ham's line also includes a son named Egypt (where the Israelites were enslaved) and a descendant named Nimrod, who builds Nineveh (capital of the Assyrian Empire, another enemy of Israel). There should be little surprise that Israelites would describe Ham as Noah's least-favored child. Noah's son Japheth is depicted as the ancestor of various coastal peoples including the Philistines, another eventual Israelite enemy. Shem, who appears to be Noah's favorite child, naturally becomes the ancestor of Semitic tribes including the Israelites (Gen. 11:10-32). Thus, genealogy and narrative are used by biblical writers to justify Israel's privileged relationship with the deity as originating in primeval history.

In the final primeval episode, the boundaries between the human and divine worlds are again threatened. Humans aspire to breach the heavens with the construction of a tall tower. Ironically, the deity must descend from on high to view the results of human labor. The description of this tower is reminiscent of temples called **ziggurats,** built in ancient Babylon as holy places connecting heaven and earth. Likewise, the name **Babel** may also hint toward Babylon as the inspiration for this story. As punishment for their arrogance, humans are scattered across the earth and made to speak different languages to prevent future collaboration. The ethnic divisions suggested by the vineyard story and genealogy become a functional reality. Unlike all of the previous stories of punishment in Genesis, the deity this time does not offer mercy or protection even to a few humans. Rather, the primeval history ends with readers wondering whether the creation has become corrupted beyond its creator's desire or ability to repair.

Preliminary Exercise IC.1: Making Sense of the Biblical Flood Story
Preliminary Exercise IC.2: "I Wonder Why?"—Writing an Etiology
Primary Text IC.1: The "Yahweh Version" of the Biblical Flood Story
Primary Text IC.2: The "Elohim Version" of the Biblical Flood Story
Primary Text IC.3: The Combined Version of the Biblical Flood Story
Primary Text IC.4: A Flood Story within the *Gilgamesh Epic*
Chart IC.1: A Comparison of the Two Biblical Flood Stories
Chart IC.2: Parallels between the Flood and Creation Accounts
Special Topic IC.1: Biblical Genealogies and Advanced Old Age
Special Topic IC.2: The Sons of God and the Daughters of Humans
Special Topic IC.3: Covenant
Special Topic IC.4: Racism and the "Curse of Ham"

INTERLUDE:
THE LITERARY ORIGINS
OF THE TORAH

Problems in the Text
(CD Preliminary Exercise IIA.1)

By this point in our journey through Genesis you have seen
enough to begin forming a preliminary understanding of the
Pentateuch's nature. Perhaps you have also been wondering how
this material came to exist in its present form with so many odd-
ities. As your reading has demonstrated, the Torah's story does
not flow seamlessly from beginning to end. Rather it contains a
variety of literary genres such as narrative, poetry, and genealogy.
Each genre itself exhibits many different literary styles and sets
of vocabulary, as evidenced by the two narrative cosmogonies in
Genesis. The highly structured first creation story has a distinctive vocabulary and tends to use short, repetitive sentences. The
second cosmogony is characterized by a completely different
vocabulary, a much looser structure, and very little repetition
within rambling sentences. Further into the Torah, style and
vocabulary continue to vary.

In addition, the Pentateuch appears to contain different views of the divine, of human nature, and of the created world. For instance, the first chapter of Genesis portrays a transcendent deity called Elohim, who brought order from watery chaos by speaking. If producing a play based on Genesis 1:1–2:4a, you would probably ask the person playing God to stand backstage with a microphone as a disembodied voice. The humans in this story are gifted with fertility, dominion, and the divine image. This account's **cosmology**, or description of the created world, envisions a flat expanse of seas and dry land covered by a domed sky that holds back the waters of heaven. The story also affirms repeatedly that every part of creation was good. Many elements of this religious worldview are repeated in other parts of the Pentateuch. For example, in one version of the flood story the deluge occurs because Elohim opened the windows of heaven to allow the waters above to reclaim the dry land (Gen. 7:11).

A completely different religious worldview dominates the second cosmogony. It features a much more personal and anthropomorphic deity called Yahweh Elohim. A play based on Genesis 2:4b-25 might have an onstage actor or actress portray the creator. The humans in this story seem connected to the earth and face a divinely imposed limitation that they eventually choose to reject. This story's cosmology ignores the heavens and seems extremely concerned with the land's need for caretakers and rain to permit agricultural fertility. Likewise, in the corresponding flood account, the deluge results from too much rain allowed by an anthropomorphic Yahweh, who is "grieved . . . to his heart" over human corruption (Gen. 6:5-7).

The very presence of two creation stories and two flood narratives gives us important information about the nature of the Pentateuch. Duplicated accounts are a common feature throughout the five books of Torah (CD Chart IIA.1). Three separate stories involve a man who pretends that his irresistible wife is really his sister so that a foreign monarch will not kill him to claim the woman for himself (Gen. 12:10-20; 20; 26:1-13). Twice Jacob's name is changed to Israel by the deity (Gen. 32:24-32; 35:9-15). Two separate texts explain how the region Meribah received its name by recounting similar stories in which the deity provides water for the thirsty, complaining Israelites in the wilderness (Exod. 17:1-7; Num. 20:1-13). Such repetition often confuses modern readers who expect to find a seamless narrative.

Another difficulty in reading the Pentateuch involves its numerous inconsistencies. We have already noticed the different orders of creation depicted in the two cosmogonies and the differing instructions concerning how many animals to preserve on the ark. Many other contradictions appear elsewhere in the Torah. When Joseph is sold by his brothers into slavery, the text alternates between identifying the slave traders as Midianites (Gen. 37:36) and as Ishmaelites (Gen. 39:1). Although Genesis 12:4 claims that Abram was 75 years old when he departed from Haran, the preceding genealogy implies that he was at least 135 years old at that time (Gen. 11:26-32).

In addition, varying claims are made concerning when the divine name, Yahweh, was introduced to humanity. One text claims that humans begin to call upon this name during the generation of Enosh, who is depicted as the grandson of Eve and Adam (Gen. 4:26). Yet, Eve refers to Yahweh even before the birth of her grandson (Gen. 4:1). To complicate matters further, when God appears to Moses in Exodus, the name Yahweh is *twice* revealed to him as though for the first time (Exod. 3:13-15; 6:2-3). On the second of these occasions, God tells Moses that the ancestors did not know this name, but Abraham occasionally uses it long before Moses' birth (Gen. 13:4; 14:22; 22:12).

Many additional examples could be added to those offered above, but these suffice to demonstrate that the Pentateuch is characterized by the following difficulties: (1) varying literary genres, (2) varying literary styles, (3) varying sets of vocabulary, (4) varying religious worldviews, (5) duplicated accounts, and (6) inconsistencies. In addition, these features tend to be correlated to one another so that narratives written in a particular literary style typically contain a similar set of vocabulary and a similar religious worldview. Any attempted explanation of the Pentateuch's literary origins or authorship must account for these observations.

The Tradition of Mosaic Authorship (CD Preliminary Exercise IIB.1)

After encountering the primeval history firsthand and reading the above discussion of the Pentateuch's peculiar features, you may be surprised to learn that tradition in both the synagogue and the church attributes authorship of the entire Torah to a single person. The traditional author of this collection is Moses, the person called to lead Israel out of Egyptian slavery and through the wilderness to the brink of the promised land. Certainly Moses is the most dominant character of the Pentateuch aside from the deity. If these books had a single author, then Moses would have been in a better position than anyone else to write about most of these events. The assumption of **Mosaic authorship** may have arisen from several passages in the Torah in which God commands Moses to write down specific things such as an account of a military victory (Exod. 17:14), particular laws (Exod. 21–23; 24:4; 34:27-28; Deut. 31:9), Israel's travel itinerary through the wilderness (Num. 33:2), and a song of his own composition (Deut. 31:19-22). Based on these scattered references, the entirety of the five books of Torah came to be known collectively as "the book of Moses" by the fifth century B.C.E.

Nevertheless, several factors raise doubts that the Pentateuch was actually authored by Moses or, for that matter, any other single person. Early rabbinic scholars realized that the report of Moses' death in the final chapter of Deuteronomy was an obstacle to the theory of Mosaic authorship. They concluded that this report, along with the notice that no one knew the place of his burial "until this day," must have been added by a later editor such as his successor Joshua. Yet even this explanation fails to account for the consistent literary style and vocabulary that run from the first to the last chapter of Deuteronomy.

Furthermore, had Moses really written these stories about himself, we would expect to find references to him in the first person. The text consistently reads "Moses said" and "Moses did" instead of "I said" or "I did." This third-person style makes the Pentateuch sound as though it were written *about* Moses rather than *by* him. Similarly, descriptions of Moses as the most humble man who ever lived (Num. 12:3) must be either blatantly false or written by someone other than the man himself.

Perhaps the most insurmountable problem with Mosaic authorship of the Pentateuch is the occurrence of multiple **anachronisms** scattered throughout the text that reflect events and circumstances that did not exist until long after his death. For instance, the Edomite kings listed in Genesis 36 actually ruled over Edom many years after the lifetime of Moses. These future kings are also described as reigning "before any king reigned over the Israelites," even though a system of monarchy did not develop in Israel until centuries after the exodus. Likewise, the Pentateuch refers frequently to Philistines although they did not appear in Canaan until shortly prior to the monarchic period. Genesis describes the time of Abram with the proclamation that "at that time the Canaanites were in the land," as they certainly continued to be until well after Moses' career. Deuteronomy even opens with a description of Moses standing with Israel "beyond the Jordan," which would be a strange way for Moses to describe the eastern bank of the Jordan River given that he never crossed over to the western bank.

All of these observations cast doubt on the tradition of Mosaic authorship. Neither does this theory nor any other theory that posits a single author account for the six peculiarities, such as inconsistencies and duplication, described in the previous section. We might argue that one author could feasibly vary his or her literary style or even vary vocabulary to some degree. We might also suggest reasons for a single writer to compose stories reflecting alternate religious worldviews. We might even be able to convince ourselves that one person chose to write several different versions of the same story. However, this does not seem very likely. Although it would perhaps be possible to overlook any one of these features in the work of a single author, their cumulative effect makes it difficult to view the Pentateuch as a unified composition.

Preliminary Exercise IIB.1: Could Moses Have Written the Pentateuch?

The Documentary Hypothesis

Since it is difficult to imagine that the Pentateuch is the product of a single author, our alternative is to theorize that two or more authors or editors shaped parts of what eventually became this problematic collection. As mentioned in the previous chapter, scholars use a method called **source criticism** to identify and describe earlier written sources that were eventually combined to produce the biblical text in its present form. Such a process may very well explain the origins of the Pentateuch, and source criticism has proved to be enormously influential on Pentateuchal studies over the last century.

When source critics examine the Torah, they begin with the peculiar features discussed above: (1) varying literary genres, (2) varying literary styles, (3) varying sets of vocabulary, (4) varying religious worldviews, (5) duplicated accounts, and (6) inconsistencies. A close examination of these features suggests that it may be possible to identify four literary strands running through the Pentateuch, each of which demonstrates a unified style and vocabulary and reflects a coherent religious worldview. When these strands are isolated from one another, they do not seem to have internal inconsistencies or unnecessary repetition.

Source critics theorize that these four strands represent originally independent written source documents, each composed at significant moments in Israelite history. By studying the features of each strand in isolation from the rest of the Pentateuch, source critics are able to deduce some information about the authors or editors responsible for it. Although it is doubtful that the names or precise identities of these individuals will ever be discovered, we can infer things such as their interests, historical context, authorial agendas, and perhaps social location (CD Chart IIC.1). The classic statement of this source-critical theory of the

Pentateuch's origin, along with a description of its four sources, is called the **Documentary Hypothesis** (CD Special Topic IIC.1). For over a century, it has remained the standard theory employed to describe the Torah's authorship.

Despite the longevity of the Documentary Hypothesis, it will not necessarily provide the last word on the mystery of the Torah's origin. Biblical scholars continue to critique this theory (CD Special Topic IIC.2) and to provide alternate models of authorship (CD Special Topic IIC.3). Biblical scholarship is an ongoing conversation in which all statements are provisional and no theory is considered inviolable. In recent years, scholars have debated the number and precise dating of the Torah's sources. Compelling evidence has suggested that each source draws upon earlier written and oral material. The so-called authors of these sources also appear to have been compilers and editors of prior traditions.

Although discussion should and will continue around such issues, almost all biblical scholars agree that the Torah can best be appreciated by recognizing its composite nature. We can better understand the Pentateuch in light of the historical and literary process by which it came to exist in its present form. For that reason, our journey through the Torah will be enriched by familiarity with the four sources traditionally associated with the Documentary Hypothesis: the Yahwist, Elohist, Deuteronomist, and Priestly sources.

The Yahwist Source

The earliest of these sources is widely held to be the **Yahwist**. This account of Israel's origins is frequently abbreviated by the letter **J** because the German scholars who first formulated the Documentary Hypothesis noticed that throughout. this source uses the divine name Yahweh (German *Jahwe*). Politically, the Yahwist source appears to be associated with the concerns of the united monarchy during the reigns of David and his son Solomon. For this reason it is usually dated around 950 B.C.E., and its authorship is attributed to a scribe or scribes in the Solomonic royal court in the Jerusalem capital. J may have been intended to provide theological direction and legitimacy for the new monarchy. By selectively gathering and reshaping familiar traditions, the Yahwist writer(s) arranged them into a new theological history tracing the deity's activity from creation through the formation of Israel. The overall message of this history is that Yahweh intended from the very beginning to create this nation and to bring divine promises to fruition through the auspices of the Davidic/Solomonic monarchy.

Many of the stories comprising this source can be better understood in light of its historical origin. When isolated from the surrounding material, the J narrative begins with the second creation account and garden story. The evident concern for agricultural fertility in this account is very much at home in the agrarian society from which the early monarchy emerged. A persistent concern throughout this period was whether Yahweh could provide the rainfall and other conditions necessary for successful crops or whether the people should instead rely upon traditional Canaanite fertility rituals. The story of Noah's insobriety also reflects political interests of the early monarchy. Noah's curse of Canaan and blessing of Shem gives legitimacy to attempts by Israel to dispossess their Canaanite neighbors. Other enemies of the united monarchy, such as the Philistines, Edomites, Moabites, and Ammonites, are featured negatively in later Yahwist stories (Gen. 19:30-38; 25:21-34; 26:12-33; Num. 20:14-21).

The Elohist Source

The **Elohist** is widely believed to be the second oldest source that was eventually incorporated into the Pentateuch. This source is typically abbreviated by the letter **E** because of its preference for the divine name Elohim and its attention to sites in the northern kingdom of Israel. The Elohist ignores primeval history and begins with stories of Israel's ancestors, especially emphasizing Jacob and Joseph, who are associated with northern sites. Yet most of the surviving portions of E describe the exodus and the conditional **Sinai covenant**. Moses, as the central human character in this source, is the first person to learn the divine name Yahweh.

Distinguishing features and concerns of the Elohist lead most source critics to date it around 850 B.C.E. and place it in the northern kingdom shortly after the division of the monarchy. It seems to have been intentionally constructed as an alternate tradition to the Yahwist's southern-oriented account (CD Special Topic IIC.4). The northern kingdom maintained a different understanding of monarchy than did the southern Davidic kingdom. The south had formulated a royal theology in which God established an eternal and unconditional covenant with the Davidic dynasty. This provided divinely sanctioned legitimacy for one ruling family and contributed to the stability of the Davidic lineage. When the northern kingdom rebelled against David's grandson, they rejected this royal theology in favor of the older Sinai tradition of a conditional covenant between God and all Israel. Even the northern king was obliged to uphold the terms of this covenant and could be challenged or deposed if he did not do so.

The Yahwist and Elohist sources were eventually combined into the **JE Epic**. This combination is generally believed to have occurred shortly after the fall of the northern kingdom to the Assyrian Empire in 722 B.C.E. Refugees from Israel would have brought their valued religious traditions with them as they fled southward. An unknown Judean editor, who must have recognized the value of these traditions, integrated E materials into the J source. This editor apparently preferred Yahwist material, since less of E survives in the final form of the Pentateuch.

The Deuteronomist Source

The **Deuteronomist** source, abbreviated **D**, is traditionally understood to be confined to the fifth book of the Pentateuch. Deuteronomy is presented as speeches of Moses to Israel just before they enter the promised land, but several features reveal that it was actually composed centuries later. For example, the description of Israel receiving these words when they were "beyond the Jordan" (Deut. 1:1), the instructions for future Israelite kings (Deut. 17:14-20), and the threat of invasion and exile by a foreign power (Deut. 28:47-57) suggest the perspective of a later author. The source clearly intends for Moses' speeches to address not only the fictional audience of the wilderness generation but also future generations of Israelites (Deut. 5:1-3).

These speeches are designed to encourage covenant obedience by reminding the Israelites of the deity's faithfulness along their journey in contrast to their own past unfaithfulness. Moses calls on the people to make a choice of either obedience, associated with blessing, or disobedience, which brings a curse (Deut. 30:15-20). The positive and negative consequences set alongside these options are characteristic of **Deuteronomic theology**, which holds that national welfare depends upon covenant obedience. The next section of the Hebrew canon, the Former Prophets, adopts this theological outlook to explain the eventual downfall of both the northern and southern kingdoms as resulting from their unfaithfulness.

According to the Documentary Hypothesis, the Deuteronomist source originated in the north and was carried south by refugees following the fall of Israel in 722 B.C.E. Some version of Deuteronomy almost certainly must be identified with the "book of the law" that was reportedly discovered during temple renovations undertaken by King Josiah in 622 B.C.E. and which validated a religious reform in the southern kingdom (2 Kgs. 22–23). The close parallels between the worship-related injunctions in Deuteronomy and the measures taken during **Josiah's Reform** could not be coincidental. Both involve centralizing worship, destroying outlying sanctuaries, prohibiting religious **syncretism**, and celebrating the **Passover** in a particular manner. This provides a firm date for the composition of at least an early form of D by 622 B.C.E. (CD Special Topic IIC.5).

The Priestly Source
The Documentary Hypothesis places the **Priestly** source, abbreviated **P**, in the late exilic or early postexilic period between 550–450 B.C.E. Several prominent themes in this source identify its authors or compilers as priests responding to the tremendous crisis brought about by the experience of exile. Earlier traditions and national covenants based Israel's relationship to her deity on

the promise of land, on the reign of a Davidic monarch, and on pilgrimage festivals to the temple. Stripped of land, king, and temple, the exilic community was in danger of losing its religious identity. Likewise, the experience of defeat and exile by Babylon would naturally be understood by many to mean that Marduk, the Babylonian high god, had defeated Elohim or that Elohim had, at the very least, abandoned Israel.

In response to these fears, the Priestly source reassures its audience that Israel's God had always been and continues to be in control of the world and that history proceeds according to a divine plan. Multiple genealogies provided by the Priestly source reinforce the sense that the deity had directed history toward the formation of Israel. In the absence of a temple and other identity-reinforcing institutions, the Priestly writers give more importance to rituals that did not require a temple cult, such as circumcision, Sabbath, and dietary restrictions. The Priestly writers also provide a program for restoration by compiling and standardizing a catalog of sacrifices for a restored temple (cf. Ezek. 40–48). They attempt to forestall the possibility of another national downfall in Israel's future by providing rituals for repairing breaches in the covenant relationship.

Many of the materials belonging to the Priestly source are better understood against the historical background of the sixth century. The first cosmogony of Genesis, for example, clearly depicts Elohim in complete control of the world being created. This story can also be read as an attempt to demythologize Babylonian creation stories, such as the **Enuma Elish**, by turning their deities into inanimate objects manipulated and ordered by Elohim. The word *deep* (Hebrew *tehom*), for example, is related to the name Tiamat, a dragon-like chaos monster slain by Marduk and used as the raw materials for heaven and earth in the Babylonian myth. Heavenly bodies, such as the sun and moon, as well as animals commonly related to ancient Near Eastern deities, also appear simply as powerless creations of Elohim. The thematic importance of order and classification in Genesis 1 corresponds to the Priestly writers' concern for maintaining purity and appropriate boundaries. Even the seven-day structure of this account, ending with divine rest, serves as an etiology for Sabbath observance.

The Priestly writers collected, arranged, and supplemented many older traditions (including the JE Epic) in order to address the needs of the exilic and early return communities. They chose to begin the Torah with an expansive creation account and to emphasize the exodus event as a prototype of Israel's return from exile. They also decided to end the Torah prior to the fulfillment of God's promises just as the exilic and return communities awaited a complete restoration. It would be difficult to overestimate the significance of their role in giving the Torah its final form.

As we pause for a moment to reflect on our journey through the Torah, we should consider the implications of this widely accepted theory of its literary origins. If readers find in the Documentary Hypothesis a convincing explanation of the features we have so far observed in this collection, we can now conceive of the Pentateuch's formation as a continuous literary process with four important stages. First, oral traditions were selected and arranged by a southern scribe around 950 B.C.E. in order to give direction and legitimacy to the **Davidic monarchy**. Second, an alternate history was formed from oral traditions around 850 B.C.E. to express the northern kingdom's different understanding of its relationship to Israel's deity. These two accounts were merged by a southern editor following the political collapse of the northern kingdom in 722 B.C.E. Third, older written and oral traditions, possibly northern in origin, were used to validate the religious reforms of the Judean king Josiah in 622 B.C.E. Finally, this collection received its final form when earlier sources were supplemented and edited by priests to give hope and direction to the late exilic and early postexilic communities.

Chart IIC.1: The Four Sources of the Documentary Hypothesis
Special Topic IIC.1: The Development of the Documentary Hypothesis
Special Topic IIC.2: Ongoing Critique of the Documentary Hypothesis
Special Topic IIC.3: Alternate Models of the Torah's Origin
Special Topic IIC.4: Who Was the Elohist?
Special Topic IIC.5: Who Was the Deuteronomist?

FAMILY ORIGINS:
THE ANCESTRAL HISTORY

As we resume our journey through the Torah, we next encounter Israel's account of her ancestral origins in Genesis 12–50. In its present form, the **ancestral history** is organized into three major **cycles**, or sagas, each revolving around a major character. The first two cycles, highlighting **Abraham** and **Jacob** respectively, are more episodic in nature and consist of loosely connected narratives that seem to lack a clear linear progression. In contrast, the **Joseph** cycle resembles a short novel as a longer and more unified narrative with more evident plot development.

Biblical scholars vigorously debate the issue of whether these characters represent historical people or legendary figures (CD Special Topic IIIA.1). Some critics of the Documentary Hypothesis view all of these stories as fictional creations of the postexilic period. Other scholars argue that names and customs preserved in the ancestral traditions fit a second-millennium context or that the ancestral journeys can be understood as part of the larger migrations occurring during this period.

Regardless, the freedom biblical authors demonstrate in reshaping these accounts indicates that preserving history was not their primary concern. Rather, these stories of ancestral origins served as formative narratives that created Israel's sense of identity and purpose. Figuratively speaking, stories narrating the travels of Abraham, Sarah, and their progeny served as a compass to guide Israel's own later journey. The nation would frequently look back on its ancestral traditions to find direction as its historical circumstances continually shifted. Biblical writers preserved and edited these stories primarily to inspire their audience rather than to inform them of historical facts.

Like all of the Pentateuch, the ancestral history derived from a complex editing process. The hands of the Yahwist, Elohist, and Priestly writers can all be detected in Genesis 12–50. Source criticism helps us appreciate the contributions that each of these writers made to the stories of Israel's ancestors. Yet the final form of these chapters is more than a random amalgam of sources. Biblical writers who made use of earlier materials did not slavishly copy them. Instead they played a creative role in weaving together and reshaping the traditions they had received. As mentioned in the previous chapter, biblical scholars use a method called **redaction criticism** to examine how biblical authors or redactors edited received traditions to reflect their own particular interests and religious worldview. Redaction criticism assumes that the arrangement of stories and the recurrence of themes or significant details provide clues to the author's intention. Such clues are most evident in the Pentateuch's final form, which was shaped by Priestly writers in the exilic and postexilic periods when a diminished Israel lived precariously under foreign rule.

In the final arrangement of the ancestral narratives, the fulfillment of God's promises to Abraham and his descendants is repeatedly blocked by seemingly insurmountable obstacles (infertility, famine, and so on) that only can be overcome with divine assistance. Through this cycle of promise-obstacle-fulfillment, the Priestly writers emphasize God's ability and willingness to prevail over dire circumstances. They also encourage their audience to hope that God's promises might prove trustworthy even in the crisis of exile. Genesis ends before the promises to Abraham have been fulfilled, just as P's audience continued to await a promised restoration.

The Abraham Cycle (Gen. 12–23; CD Preliminary Exercises IIIA.1 and IIIA.2)

Throughout the primeval history humans had repeatedly disappointed the Creator, and now God once again decides to begin afresh by focusing upon a single man and his family. This time, rather than destroying the rest of the species in a flood, God intends for this chosen man to become a blessing to all other human families (CD Special Topic IIIA.2). The ancestral history begins with the **call** of Abram, later renamed Abraham ("father of a multitude"), who is invited to set out on a journey that lacks a clear destination (CD Map IIIA.1). In return he is given three promises: land, descendants, and a blessing.

Although Yahweh speaks only to Abraham in this opening passage, we later learn that he is accompanied by a nephew (Lot), a wife (Sarai, later renamed Sarah, meaning "princess"), and servants. Although Lot continues to surface throughout the Abraham cycle, the biblical authors carefully distinguish his line from that of his uncle. Lot and Abraham separate because the land cannot support both of their herds together. Because he chooses to settle in the notorious region around Sodom, Lot soon requires his uncle's assistance. A battle with the kings of the east demonstrates Abraham's superiority over his nephew and the inhabitants of Canaan (CD Special Topic IIIA.3).

Later in the cycle, Abraham again intervenes on Lot's behalf, this time against the deity. Having learned that God intends to destroy every inhabitant of Sodom and Gomorrah, Abraham tactfully questions the justice of this act. His words result in part of Lot's family being spared (CD Special Topic IIIA.4). Despite Lot's deliverance from Sodom, he is not to become Abraham's heir and Israel's ancestor. Instead he becomes the ancestor of Moab and Ammon through incestuous encounters with his two daughters. The Yahwist writer introduces this account to provide an embarrassing etiology for two enemies of the Israelite monarchy.

If Lot cannot inherit the covenant promises of Abraham, then who can? We are informed even before Abraham's call that Sarah is barren (Gen. 11:30). The undeniable emphasis of the narrative is upon Israel's male ancestors, or patriarchs, and their relationship to the deity. However, the female ancestors, or matriarchs, also play a crucial role in the story. We eventually learn that not just any woman can bear children who will be included in this covenant; only Sarah can provide the descendants that God has promised.

Sarah's infertility is the first of many obstacles that appear to block any possibility that God's promises might be fulfilled. Another complication arises when Abraham learns that the promised land is already occupied by other people. To make matters worse, a severe drought drives them from this land into the fertile valley of Egypt. There Abraham persuades his wife to pose as his sister so that rivals will not kill him in order to claim her. The matriarch is almost lost to **Pharaoh**'s harem until God intervenes. This wife-sister story from the Yahwist (Gen. 12:10-20) is later repeated in a similar account by the Elohist (Gen. 20). Unlike the earlier version of this tale, the Elohist writer moralistically excuses Abraham's lie as having some basis in fact and is eager to reassure the reader that Sarah's virtue remained intact.

As obstacles continue to mount, Sarah and Abraham grow impatient awaiting the fulfillment of God's promises. Despairing that Sarah will ever bear a child of her own, they attempt to find an alternate solution through the surrogacy of the maid **Hagar**, who becomes Abraham's **concubine**, or secondary wife. Once Hagar conceives a child, tension arises between the two women, whose separate roles and statuses are no longer clearly defined (CD Special Topic IIIA.5). Within the Torah, God intends that Sarah's child rather than **Ishmael** will continue the **Abrahamic covenant**. The deity even orders the pregnant slave to return and submit to her abusive mistress. On the other hand, Hagar is the only woman in the Hebrew Bible who experiences a **theophany**, or an encounter with God, who identifies her unborn child as the ancestor of bedouin Ishmaelites.

Later in the narrative, God miraculously enables the elderly Sarah to conceive her own child, **Isaac**. The fulfillment of this promise brings matters to a head between the two mothers and leads to Hagar and Ishmael's expulsion. Again God appears to the slave woman and promises that her son will also become a great nation. Nevertheless, the Yahwist writer describes Ishmael's future in less favorable terms than Israel's. This nationalistic source carefully excludes the Ishmaelites, like Lot's descendants, from the promises made to Israel's ancestors (CD Special Topic IIIA.6).

Alongside the embedded politics and mounting obstacles of the Abraham cycle runs another theme. God frequently reiterates the covenant promises and offers repeated assurances that these promises will be fulfilled (Gen. 12:1-9; 13:14-18; 15; 17; 22:15-18). Most of these passages derive originally from the Yahwist writer. According to this source, Yahweh forms an **unconditional covenant** with Abraham that foreshadows the later **Davidic covenant**. Even the extent of the land promised to Abraham corresponds to the boundaries of the future Davidic empire (Gen. 15:18-21; 1 Kgs. 4:21).

The Priestly authors retain these Yahwist traditions and insert their own understanding of God's covenant with Abraham. In Genesis 17, Elohim forms a **conditional covenant** with the patriarch that requires the **circumcision** of Israelite males. This story anachronistically defines the rite of circumcision as the mark of covenant membership for all future generations. In actuality, the Priestly writers were investing old customs with new significance to serve as national markers in the absence of land, king, and temple during the exilic crisis and its aftermath (CD Special Topic IIIA.7).

In the final arrangement of the Abraham cycle by Priestly writers, reaffirmation of the covenant becomes a refrain that follows almost every major episode. For P's audience, these repeated assurances would take on added significance. The promises to Abraham became grounds for hope that God was still at work on behalf of the exilic and postexilic communities. Even though the covenant appeared broken in light of defeat and exile, God could overcome these circumstances just as the overwhelming obstacles facing Israel's ancestors had been surmounted.

Abraham eventually witnesses the realization of one of God's promises in the birth of Sarah's son Isaac. The other promises await fulfillment in future generations. Yet the greatest potential obstacle to the Abrahamic covenant occurs after Isaac's birth when God unexpectedly demands that the child be sacrificed. In this episode by the Elohist writer, Abraham's obedience is put to its most stringent test. Until this point in the cycle, Abraham is portrayed as a very human character whose actions often betray a lack of faith despite God's repeated reassurances. When the patriarch now responds without hesitation to the deity's command, God halts the sacrifice and reaffirms the prior covenant (CD Special Topic IIIA.8). As the Priestly writers edited their received traditions and gave the ancestral history its final shape, they chose to place this story near the end of the Abraham cycle. This arrangement might suggest that the patriarch's faith has matured over the course of his journey. He now trusts God's promises despite external appearances and is willing to act in obedience.

> Preliminary Exercise IIIA.1: Point of View in the Abraham Cycle
> Preliminary Exercise IIIA.2: Artists' Renderings of Genesis 22
> Map IIIA.1: Significant Sites in the Ancestral History
> Special Topic IIIA.1: Were Israel's Ancestors Historical People?
> Special Topic IIIA.2: Does the Abrahamic Covenant Include Non-Jews?
> Special Topic IIIA.3: Melchizedek
> Special Topic IIIA.4: Homosexuality in Genesis 19
> Special Topic IIIA.5: Sarah and Hagar
> Special Topic IIIA.6: Abraham in Judaism, Christianity, and Islam
> Special Topic IIIA.7: Circumcision
> Special Topic IIIA.8: Child Sacrifice in Ancient Israel

The Jacob Cycle (Gen. 24–35; CD Preliminary Exercises IIIB.1 and IIIB.2)

Genesis passes briefly over Isaac, who remains a passive figure in most of the accounts that mention him. He is largely overshadowed by his father's knife, his sons' rivalry, and his wife's assertiveness. Isaac's cousin **Rebekah** first appears in Genesis 24 when Abraham sends a servant to arrange a marriage for his son with a near relative. The ancestral traditions prefer this type of marriage as one strategy for remaining separate from the other inhabitants of Canaan (unlike Lot, Gen. 19:12-14). Modern readers might better understand the reasons for this custom if we draw an analogy between Israel's ancestors and contemporary Amish communities whose members likewise try to avoid assimilation into the dominant culture. Parentally arranged marriages were also a common custom in Israelite society since weddings often occurred at a young age. However, Isaac's passive stance at the age of forty is surprising (Gen. 25:20).

In many ways, Rebekah is Isaac's opposite. She is portrayed as a whirl of activity and decides on her own to accept Isaac's proxy proposal (CD Special Topic IIIB.1). After her marriage, the text only briefly mentions her requisite barrenness to demonstrate God's involvement in the conception of the next generation. The story pays more attention to Rebekah's difficult pregnancy, which prompts her to approach the deity for information. She is the only matriarch of Israel to obtain an **oracle,** or message from the deity, through which she discovers God's intentions for her sons. Her preference and advocacy for Jacob is based on this disclosure.

The oracle that Rebekah receives is actually another political etiology from the Yahwist writer (Gen. 25:23). As elsewhere, this source associates characters in the ancestral history either with Israel or with rival groups from the early monarchic period. Rebekah's twins become symbols for two nations. The elder, later identified as **Esau** (or **Edom**), is destined to serve the younger, later identified as Jacob (or Israel). This revelation runs counter to ancient Near Eastern customs guaranteeing the privileges of firstborn sons, but the rights of **primogeniture,** or "first birth," are frequently overturned in Hebrew scripture. Isaac, Jacob, Joseph, Moses, David, and Solomon are all younger sons who somehow surpass their elder siblings. Nonetheless, in the ancestral history, birth order presents another obstacle that temporarily blocks the realization of God's promises. Like Abraham and Sarah before her, Rebekah does not wait for God to remove the obstacle. Instead, she attempts to force the issue herself by manipulating the succession in favor of her younger son.

Jacob also prefers to take matters into his own hands. Like their parents, Esau and Jacob are portrayed as opposites. The twins could not be more different in appearance, ability, and personality. Esau is described as a stereotypically masculine outdoorsman, but not very smart or responsible. Jacob is mild, intelligent, and resourceful, but surprisingly is not depicted as a morally heroic character despite his identification with Israel. Modern readers are often surprised by the Torah's tendency to depict the ancestors of Israel as very fallible humans. Jacob is deceitful and determined to secure his own future at the expense of his brother. He first strips Esau of the **birthright** that represents his legal claim as the elder son to inherit a larger share of the family estate. Then with Rebekah's aid, he steals the deathbed blessing his father had intended for Esau.

Ironically, Jacob and Rebekah's attempts to manipulate the succession produce another obstacle, Jacob's lengthy exile from the promised land. To escape his brother's justifiable rage, he must flee Canaan and seek refuge with Rebekah's family. This development within the Jacob cycle would obviously capture the attention of the Priestly writers' audience. Like Jacob, they too had been driven from the land that God had promised them. At least some members of the sixth-century exilic community understood their situation as a deserved punishment for national sins. They believed that the deported Israelites, like their ancestor Jacob, had brought this fate upon themselves.

Yet, in the final arrangement of the Torah, the Priestly writers emphasize that God provides for Jacob during his exile. He prospers in his uncle's household and becomes the father of a large family. Each of Jacob's sons (with the exception of Joseph) will become an eponymous ancestor of an Israelite tribe. Even in exile, God's promises to Abraham are being fulfilled. The deity ultimately returns Jacob to the land of Canaan, not due to his own merit, but because of God's faithfulness to the Abrahamic covenant. These stories intentionally portray a deity who can and eventually will overcome all obstacles, even exile.

Twenty years will pass, however, before Jacob finally returns to Canaan. During that time this habitual trickster becomes the victim of a more experienced scoundrel in the person of his uncle. Just as Jacob had used deceit to gain an advantage over Esau, **Laban** tricks Jacob into marrying **Leah** before **Rachel** (CD Special Topic IIIB.2). Having posed as Esau to steal a blessing from his blind father, Jacob now blindly consummates a marriage with the wrong sister. In light of Jacob's earlier treachery toward his older brother, Laban's words resound with irony: "This is not done in our country—giving the younger before the first-born" (Gen. 29:26)!

Careful readers should notice the similarities between Jacob's deceit in Genesis 27 and Laban's deceit in Genesis 29. In each text an act of treachery is revisited ironically upon the original perpetrator. Jacob defrauded his elder brother of the birthright but is punished when Leah is granted her right as the elder daughter to marry before Rachel. Redaction critics assume that the parallels between these stories are not coincidental but are used intentionally by biblical writers to link deed with consequence. These stories form part of a larger pattern of trickery that spans across the Jacob and Joseph cycles. Betrayal and revenge become almost commonplace within this dysfunctional extended family. As the treachery continues to escalate through the next generation, the very survival of Israel's ancestors will become uncertain. If Israel is to become a blessed and landed nation, then this pattern of deception and revenge must be resolved.

Israel's future also depends upon Jacob returning to the promised land. That this homecoming would eventually take place is assured even before the patriarch leaves Canaan. In the final form of the Jacob cycle, the story of his exile is bracketed by two theophanies, one at **Bethel** (Gen. 28:10-22) and one at **Penuel** (Gen. 32). The first theophany takes the form of a dream provoked by the holiness of the resting place Jacob had unwittingly chosen for himself. Bethel, the site of an important Israelite sanctuary, is associated with several key events in the lives of Israel's ancestors. In his dream, Jacob sees angels ascending and descending a ladder between heaven and earth. He also meets Yahweh, who renews for a later generation the promises originally given to Abraham. Moreover, the deity pledges to accompany the patriarch into exile and guarantees both protection and a safe return. These promises would have been particularly comforting for the sixth-century exilic community and its descendants. Although this account is usually regarded as a combination of the Elohist and Yahwist sources, the Priestly writers intentionally retain this story and place it at the beginning of Jacob's exile. Yet, Jacob greets the deity's promises with both interest and skepticism. The next morning he transforms God's unconditional promises into a conditional bargain, suggesting that this patriarch still prefers to control his own destiny.

The deity eventually does instruct Jacob to return to the land of his ancestors with his newfound family and wealth. However, Laban is not at all pleased with his son-in-law's abrupt departure or with the apparent theft of his household gods (Gen. 31:19). Scholars debate whether these icons might have been associated with ancestor worship or property rights (cf. 2 Kgs. 23:24). Regardless, Laban's attempts to reclaim them are thwarted by Rachel's ingenuity. He is forced to settle for an uneasy covenant with Jacob that ends the prolonged conflict between these two adversaries by establishing a boundary agreement. As elsewhere, the Yahwist writer uses this story to distinguish between the Israelites, who are descended from Jacob, and the Arameans, whom J associates with Laban (cf. Deut. 26:5 where D links Israelites and Arameans).

Jacob's struggles with Laban end during his homeward journey, but the patriarch still dreads the thought of resuming his struggles with his brother. From before their births, Esau and Jacob had wrestled together in Rachel's womb. They had battled with one another over birth order, over their parents' affection, and over matters of inheritance and succession. Careful readers can easily recognize the overwhelming theme of wrestling within the Jacob cycle. Having cheated and betrayed his brother, the patriarch finally returns to face Esau's anticipated wrath. He anxiously attempts to appease his brother's anger with gifts sent ahead of his party.

Such is Jacob's state of mind when he experiences a second theophany. On the eve of his homecoming, he engages in a nocturnal wrestling match with a mysterious opponent whom the story implies was God (CD Special Topic IIIB.3). As an experienced "wrestler," Jacob holds his own in this skirmish and ultimately wins a blessing and a new identity. Jacob the heel-grabbing supplanter (Gen. 25:26; 27:36) is renamed "**Israel**," making him the eponymous ancestor of the Hebrew nation. Consistent with the wrestling theme, this name is here interpreted as "one who struggles with God." Both the new name bestowed upon Jacob and the wound inflicted upon him suggest that he is fundamentally changed by this encounter. Recognizing that he had seen the face of God, Jacob names the place Penuel.

Having survived a battle with the deity, Jacob is now ready to face his past and his estranged brother. In fact, the reunion between Esau and Jacob is almost anticlimactic in light of the preceding theophany. Jacob remarks ironically that seeing his brother again is "like seeing the face of God" (Gen. 33:10), which had actually happened in the previous chapter. Do these words suggest reconciliation between the brothers or does their relationship remain strained beneath the surface? Readers are allowed to decide for themselves. Despite the absence of bloodshed and the outward friendliness, the reunion is marked by cautious diplomacy and negotiation. Gifts are offered, formally refused, pressed, and accepted as politeness demands. Then the brothers warily part to become the two separate nations that they represent for the Yahwist writer.

Preliminary Exercise IIIB.1: Literary Artistry in the Jacob Cycle
Preliminary Exercise IIIB.2: Jacob on Trial
Special Topic IIIB.1: Literary Conventions and the Betrothal Type-Scene
Special Topic IIIB.2: Leah and Rachel
Special Topic IIIB.3: Jacob's Bizarre Encounter at Penuel
Special Topic IIIB.4: Dinah, Daughter of Israel

The Joseph Cycle (Gen. 37–50; CD Preliminary Exercises IIIC.1 and IIIC.2)

Attentive readers of Genesis 12–50 might notice a difference between the Joseph cycle and previous chapters of the ancestral history. The Abraham and Jacob cycles consisted of loosely connected episodes that obviously had been pieced together by editors to produce a larger story. Often these episodes can be rearranged without disturbing the logic of the account. It makes little difference whether Lot is saved from Sodom before or after Hagar bears Ishmael, for example. Many other stories seem to have had an earlier purpose before they were used in the ancestral history. It is likely that Jacob's wrestling match at Penuel, for instance, was originally a story told to explain a dietary custom (Gen. 32:32).

The "editorial glue" of the Joseph cycle is less visible. Its readers encounter a carefully crafted narrative that introduces a problem that builds up to a climax and then is neatly resolved. Most of the episodes concerning Joseph are inseparable from the larger story in which they are embedded. The one apparent interruption in this tightly woven storyline is the **Judah/Tamar** account of Genesis 38, although even this story is in some ways connected to the larger narrative (CD Special Topic IIIC.1). Because of the Joseph cycle's overall unity, many interpreters have wondered if it might have been the work of a single author rather than a compilation of sources like the rest of the Pentateuch.

However, the hands of the Yahwist, Elohist, and Priestly writers are occasionally evident in these chapters. The account of Joseph's betrayal by his brothers, for example, is clearly a combination of at least two sources. In one version, Reuben attempts to intervene on Joseph's behalf by persuading his brothers to cast him into a pit rather than killing him outright. Meanwhile, Midianite traders discover the lad and sell him to Potiphar in Egypt. Reuben later returns to the pit with the intention of rescuing Joseph only to discover that he is gone. Because Reuben represents a prominent northern tribe, this version of the tale probably belongs to the Elohist source. In the alternate version, Judah is the compassionate brother who intervenes to spare Joseph's life. He convinces the other brothers to sell Joseph to Ishmaelite traders who later sell him to Potiphar in Egypt. Judah's prominence in this version suggests that it belongs to the southern Yahwist source. The same author surely would not claim, on the one hand, that Potiphar purchased Joseph from Midianites (Gen. 37:36) and, on the other, that he bought him from Ishmaelites (Gen. 39:1).

Moreover, the Joseph cycle is not entirely self-contained. In many ways, it is intricately connected to the stories surrounding Abraham and Jacob. The birth of Joseph and his brothers occurred within the Jacob cycle. The sibling rivalry integral to the plot of the Joseph cycle is explained by the maternity of Jacob's sons. It is even difficult to pinpoint precisely where Jacob's cycle ends and Joseph's begins. The betrayal and revenge motif that began with Jacob and Esau continues into the next generation. Likewise, the pattern of promise-obstacle-fulfillment spans Genesis 12–50 from the call of Abraham to the death of Joseph. Whatever the origin of the Joseph cycle, it clearly is now an integral part of the ancestral history.

As this final ancestral cycle begins, the promises made to Abraham have been partially fulfilled by the birth of many children to Jacob, renamed Israel. Up until this point in the ancestral history, the story of each turbulent generation involved the **election** of one potential heir over another. Abraham rather than Lot receives God's initial promises, which are then passed down to Isaac rather than Ishmael. Next, divine election and human intrigue combine to pass the covenant to Jacob rather than Esau. Disqualified persons typically become the ancestors of rival nations and move toward the east, just as Cain had been driven east of Eden (Gen. 4:16, cf. 13:11; 25:1-6, 12-18; 36:6-8). In the Joseph cycle, however, the central character is not elected at the expense of his brothers. Marking an important stage in Israel's journey toward nationhood, eleven of Jacob's twelve sons represent the eponymous ancestors of Israelite **tribes**. Although Joseph himself is not an eponymous ancestor, his two sons (**Ephraim** and Manasseh) each become half-tribes, bringing the total to twelve.

Because Jacob's sons are destined to become a unified nation rather than rival groups, we know that the ongoing discord in his family is a serious problem. Parental favoritism and the resulting sibling rivalry create divisions among the brothers from the moment of their births. Jacob's preference for Rachel establishes her son Joseph as his favorite even though he is not firstborn. Sibling rivalry had rocked this dysfunctional extended family in previous generations when only two prospective heirs vied for succession. With twelve sons, the potential for conflict increases exponentially. This tense situation is further aggravated by Joseph's own behavior. He tattles on his older brothers and brags about dreams that obviously imply his superiority over them.

As in the previous generation, rivalry erupts in betrayal. Joseph's brothers sell him to traders as a slave and then hide their treachery by manufacturing evidence of his death. When Jacob is fooled by his favorite son's torn and bloody robe, attentive readers should recall that he had also fooled his own elderly father with a clothing disguise (Gen. 27). The use of garments for deception is a repeated motif throughout the Joseph cycle (Gen. 37:31-36; 38:12-19; 39:6-20; 41:42–42:8). Redaction critics assume that such details are an intentional means of connecting these stories.

Not only does this story recall previous episodes from the Torah, it also anticipates upcoming events. Joseph's servitude to Potiphar foreshadows the account of Israel's Egyptian bondage found in Exodus. Likewise, after the defeat of 587 B.C.E., the Priestly writers' audience would see Joseph's predicament as a harbinger of their own experience of bondage in a foreign land. The tradition of Joseph's plight would have special significance for an audience that had actually experienced forced deportation and exile from their homeland.

STUDYING THE OLD TESTAMENT

Like Joseph, the exilic community found themselves in vulnerable situations often beyond their control. They would hear with interest the reassurance that God was with the patriarch first in Potiphar's house and then in prison. They would also follow with keen attention the remarkable reversals of fortune that eventually result in his success in the Egyptian court. Like Joseph, the Babylonian exiles and many of their descendants experienced life as outsiders in a foreign land. The story of this patriarch's meteoric rise to power against the odds would provide a hopeful model for later generations in exile. Similarly, the postexilic tales of Esther and Daniel demonstrate ways of negotiating the challenges involved in living on the margins of a foreign court.

The Joseph cycle also introduces another theme that would become important in later postexilic literature: the threat of its hero's assimilation into the dominant foreign culture that surrounds him (Dan. 1–6; Ezra 10:2-4; Neh. 13:23-27). Joseph is given an Egyptian name and marries the daughter of an Egyptian priest. The names that he gives to his children suggest that he prefers to forget his past (Gen. 41:51-52). At least outwardly, he becomes indistinguishable from those around him, so much so that he is not recognized by his own brothers. Their arrival in Egypt forces Joseph to confront his past and reclaim his identity as a son of Israel.

When his brothers unwittingly appear before him believing that he is an Egyptian official, Joseph at first continues the familiar cycle of betrayal and revenge. He accuses them of being spies and liars, frames them as thieves, and threatens them with imprisonment. Only after forcing his brothers to endure a protracted period of mental anguish does Joseph eventually reveal his true identity. First, however, he pressures them to prove that they have reformed since selling him into slavery. Finally, the brothers express remorse for their former treatment of Joseph. Judah even offers to sacrifice himself on behalf of Rachel's second son, Benjamin, who has become Jacob's new favorite child. Joseph's choice to forgive his brothers finally unites this dysfunctional family and resolves the betrayal-revenge pattern of the ancestral history.

Only at this point, near the end of the Joseph cycle, are we given an explanation for the near-absence of God as a character in Genesis 37–50. Alert readers should have noticed that none of Jacob's sons ever speaks to God or receives reaffirmation of the covenant promises made to their ancestors. Dreams requiring interpretation replace direct theophanies. God briefly appears only once in these chapters to the elderly Jacob before he journeys to Egypt to join Joseph (Gen. 46:1-4). In contrast to the involved deity of the Abraham and Jacob cycles, God almost becomes a background presence at the end of the ancestral history.

However, when Joseph finally reveals himself to his brothers, he recognizes that God has been a guiding presence throughout the many changes in fortune that he had experienced (Gen. 45:4-8). This affirmation of God's **providence** reappears when Joseph again forgives his anxious brothers after their father's death (Gen. 50:15-21). Despite the apparent absence of God in this story, in retrospect Joseph can declare that God actually has been present and in control of events all along. As in previous generations, human efforts to manipulate the succession prove to be either ineffectual or counterproductive. Yet God manages to overcome seemingly impossible circumstances that threaten to block the fulfillment of covenant promises. This theological claim would have great significance for later audiences—especially in periods when God's presence and activity on behalf of Israel were not readily apparent.

As the ancestral history concludes, Jacob's descendants have become numerous and are currently safe from famine or threat. Yet the children of Israel are in the wrong place, and only one of the three promises given to Abraham has come to fruition. Joseph's position in Egypt has ensured the momentary well-being of his family, but ironically it also contributes to the creation of an even greater obstacle. While actively promoting Pharaoh's interests, Joseph transforms almost the entire population of

Canaan and Egypt into slaves of the state (Gen. 47:13-26). This ominous note prepares us for the exodus traditions that follow.

Preliminary Exercise IIIC.1: Prominent Themes in the Joseph Cycle
Preliminary Exercise IIIC.2: Joseph on the Catwalk
Chart IIIC.1: Eponymous Ancestors in Genesis 12–50
Special Topic IIIC.1: Levirate Marriage and Genesis 38

NATIONAL ORIGINS: EXODUS, COVENANT, AND WILDERNESS

As we enter the next stage of our journey through the Pentateuch, we leave behind family history and enter an account of national origins. God's promises to Israel's ancestors had begun to be fulfilled among the descendants of Jacob, who, although still in Egypt, are now described as numerous and powerful (Exod. 1:9). Because of Israel's expansion, Egypt's new ruler presses the Israelites into forced labor. The Torah's promise-obstacle-fulfillment pattern reaches its climax in the exodus story and the Sinai covenant that follows. Like the ancestral history, the account of Israel's national origins emphasizes God's fidelity and ability to overcome seemingly impossible circumstances.

The remainder of the Torah can aptly be described as Israel's birth story, a national charter that would form the identity of later generations. The very extent of the exodus and Sinai traditions, which constitute the bulk of the Pentateuch, attests to their central importance. In many ways, this was the most important story that Israel knew. For that reason, successive generations revised and supplemented these traditions to make them speak more clearly to their own historical contexts. Over the course of centuries, this resulted in a long and convoluted account in which many seams and tensions are apparent.

As we explore this composite account of Israel's national origins, we will attempt to appreciate the contributions made by various writers as they reclaimed this birth story for later generations. Like the rest of the

Pentateuch, the exodus and Sinai traditions attained their final form in the context of the Babylonian exile and its aftermath. For this reason, we will especially consider how these traditions would have been received by the Priestly writers' sixth-century audience.

Due to its length and complexity, the remainder of the Torah can be daunting to read from beginning to end. In its present form, the book of Exodus begins with an account of Israel's liberation from slavery (Exod. 1:1–15:19) and closes with their lengthy sojourn at Sinai (Exod. 19–40). Between these sections have been inserted several wilderness wandering traditions that function almost like "travel music" between Egypt and Sinai (Exod. 15:20–18:27). Most of the material in the book of Exodus appears to be a mixture of the Yahwist and Elohist sources, which have been arranged and supplemented by the Priestly writers. In contrast, the voice of the Priestly writers is heard almost exclusively in Leviticus. This book contains an assortment of regulations that deal primarily with issues of purity, ritual, and the priesthood. Numbers, like Exodus, is a mixture of earlier sources heavily redacted by P. This book interweaves legal traditions, census lists, and stories set in the wilderness. In fact, the Hebrew title of the book (Hebrew *bemidbar*) means "in the wilderness." In Deuteronomy, the D writer recaps Israel's exodus, Sinai, and wilderness traditions and provides a theological framework in which they can be understood.

Because this leg of our journey spans four biblical books, it will require stamina. To facilitate our expedition through these complicated traditions, we will organize the remainder of this chapter around the three major themes that dominate Exodus—Deuteronomy: liberation, covenant and law, and wilderness wandering. For each of these themes, we will explore a representative selection of materials without attempting to exhaust the primary text. The distinctive theology of the Deuteronomist will provide a springboard for our journey through the Former Prophets in the next chapter.

STUDYING THE OLD TESTAMENT

Liberation (Exod. 1–15; CD Preliminary Exercises IVA.1 and IVA.2)

God's deliverance of the Hebrew people from bondage in Egypt was the defining memory of the Israelite nation. It profoundly shaped Israel's communal identity as well as her understanding of God and the divine-human relationship. The fundamental importance of this memory is evidenced by its continued centrality. Throughout Hebrew scripture, Israel's life and faith are grounded in the story of the **exodus**. Psalms celebrate this moment as God's supreme act of benevolence toward Israel (Pss. 105:23-45; 106:6-46; 136:10-26). The exodus event provides a rationale for major rituals (Exod. 12:1-20; 13:1-16). Its moral and cultic implications are recognized in legal codes (Exod. 23:9; Deut. 5:12-15) and prophetic literature (Hos. 11:1; Mic. 6:4). Creedal summaries of Israel's faith highlight the deliverance from Egypt as a pivotal moment in the nation's history (Deut. 26:5-10; Josh. 24:2-13). The exodus story is repeatedly cited in Hebrew scripture as evidence that God once had and would continue to intervene in history on behalf of the chosen people (Isa. 43:14-21; Ezek. 20:32-44). Nor does the exodus memory end within the pages of the Hebrew canon; it has been continually reclaimed in both Jewish and Christian communities down to the present day (CD Special Topics IVA.1 and IVA.2).

The overriding importance of this memory for later generations does not necessarily prove that an exodus occurred. Serious problems beset any attempt to determine what, if any, historical basis may lie behind Israel's tales of servitude, deliverance, covenant, and wilderness wandering (CD Special Topic IVA.3). There are few verifiable historical references contained in the Torah, which fails to provide even the proper names of Egypt's pharaohs. Nor do any surviving Egyptian records mention Hebrew slaves or an exodus event.

Regardless, these traditions were preserved, not for their historical value, but as a national birth story. This story was retold generation after generation because it offered a foundation for understanding both Israel's communal identity and the character of Israel's God. The presence of multiple sources in Exodus 1–15 attests to the continued vitality of this narrative for many different audiences. Clearly, however, the oppression-liberation themes of the exodus story would have a special appeal for generations that found themselves in similarly desperate circumstances. Read in light of experienced oppression, the exodus tradition affirms that God hears the cries of the oppressed and sides with them against their oppressors.

Such themes are strikingly relevant to the situation of the exilic and postexilic communities in which the exodus story, along with the rest of the Torah, attained its final form. After 587 B.C.E. the population of Judah had been decimated by invading Babylonian armies, and the temple, the preeminent symbol of God's presence with Israel, lay in ruins. Many of the survivors had been deported to live in captivity in a distant land. Israel was again in bondage in a foreign land and subject to an abusive ruler. Even after Babylon fell to the Persian Empire, the struggling postexilic community continued to live under a foreign imperial power. The ancestral promises, as recalled by Priestly writers, must have seemed profoundly unrealistic. In this context the exodus story was recalled.

The story begins with a description of a dire situation in which an unnamed pharaoh ruthlessly oppresses the children of Israel. Later audiences could identify this pharaoh, who did not know Joseph, with any tyrannical ruler they happened to face. Like their ancestor Joseph, who had also been a slave in Egypt, the oppressed Israelites continue to thrive in their captivity. The apparent absence of God as an involved character in the first two chapters of Exodus also recalls the Joseph cycle. Although readers might wonder whether God is again at work "behind the scenes" (Exod. 1:17-21), these chapters focus on the human situation. **Moses** and Israel survive because the cruel decrees of Pharaoh are defied by five women: two midwives, a mother, a sister, and a daughter. Their actions precede and foreshadow the merciful intervention of the deity.

The perils of Moses' infancy highlight his importance to Israel's story, just as the barren mother theme of Genesis did for the ancestors. In each case, the survival of Israel is not ensured until an overwhelming obstacle has been overcome—be it infertility or threat. Moses' infancy story also resembles a type of **hero legend** that is common in world mythology and literature. In most of these legends, endangered infants of royal birth are preserved and reared by humble foster parents until they eventually reclaim their rightful place. Readers should be familiar with this pattern in both ancient and modern lore such as the stories of the Mesopotamian king Sargon, Roman twins Romulus and Remus, Superman, Luke Skywalker, and even Harry Potter. But the story of Moses actually reverses the typical hero myth since he is born into slavery and reared in Pharaoh's court. For the biblical writers and their audiences, membership in the covenant people is more valuable than royal power and wealth.

Hero legends were often used, as in the case of Sargon, to justify the rise of a commoner to the throne by fictionally claiming that he or she belonged there by birth. Could the biblical writers be attempting to explain with this story how a known Egyptian became leader of the Hebrew people? Although this question cannot be answered with certainty, it does highlight the intriguing ambiguity of Moses' identity. Unlike most contemporary films based on the exodus account, the book of Exodus never discloses whether Moses is aware of his true parentage (CD Special Topic IVA.4). The two short episodes that precede his flight from Egypt could reflect Moses' personal identification with Hebrew slaves, or they could simply indicate a keen sense of justice. In either case, these two disputes foreshadow his future role as mediator as well as the many times the Israelites will challenge his leadership.

Moses' actions in Midian also demonstrate his compassion for the oppressed and foreshadow his future role as deliverer. Marriage to the

Midianite woman **Zipporah** (the daughter of Reuel, Hobab, or Jethro, depending upon the source) further complicates his identity (CD Special Topic IVA.5). Like Joseph, Moses is nearly assimilated into the foreign cultures that surround him. The danger of assimilation and the importance of maintaining a separate identity became very real concerns for exilic and postexilic audiences living outside the boundaries of their homeland.

It is not until the end of the second chapter of Exodus that the deity intrudes upon the scene. Readers are abruptly informed that God has heard the cries of the Hebrew slaves and remembered the covenant with their ancestors (Exod. 2:23-25). From this point forward, the deity dominates the narrative. In contrast to the understated theology of the Joseph cycle, the apparent absence of God in early chapters of Exodus gives way to the deity's direct involvement in human affairs.

The exodus story functions as a vehicle through which Yahweh is made known to Israel, Pharaoh, the Egyptians, and the world (Exod. 5:2; 6:3; 7:17; 8:10; 15:14-15). For this reason, we should pay close attention to its portrayal of Israel's God. For example, God's notice of the Israelite slaves and subsequent call of Moses demonstrate that this deity remembers and keeps promises. Yahweh's fidelity does not depend upon human merit but stems from promises made to the ancestors. Like much of the exodus narrative, this theological affirmation is especially pertinent to exilic and postexilic audiences. God surely seemed absent to those displaced and diminished communities who also had reason to wonder whether the covenant had been nullified. Recalling the exodus story would provide reassurance that God was indeed present, trustworthy, and compassionate. It would offer grounds for hope even when outward circumstances warranted none.

God, rather than Moses, is the primary actor in the exodus event. Moses is called only to function as a mediator between God and Pharaoh. The composite traditions in the book of Exodus actually contain two parallel accounts of Moses' call. The first theophany, which is

STUDYING THE OLD TESTAMENT

a combination of the Yahwist and Elohist sources, takes the form of a burning bush that is not consumed (Exod. 3:1–4:23). Moses is idealized, especially in the Elohist source, as Yahweh's premier prophet. The reluctance that he demonstrates before accepting his call becomes the pattern for future prophetic call stories (Isa. 6:5; Jer. 1:6; Jonah 1). This hesitation recognizes not only Moses' extreme humility, but also the enormous and thankless burden of the prophetic task (CD Special Topic IVA.6).

Priestly writers retained this earlier call story and inserted a second theophany that places more emphasis on the role of **Aaron**, Moses' brother (Exod. 6:2–7:7). For their audience, Aaron represents the **Aaronid priesthood**, which provided leadership for the exilic and postexilic communities after the fall of the monarchy. The P source almost always names Aaron as an actor alongside Moses. This call story also places more emphasis on the promised land as the destination of the exodus community. Exilic and postexilic audiences would have heard these assurances in relation to their own anticipated exodus and return to the land of their ancestors.

Both of these call stories further reveal God's identity by disclosing the divine name Yahweh. In both the Elohist and Priestly sources, Moses is the first person to learn this name. *Yahweh* is sometimes called the **Tetragrammaton** because it is a four-letter word in consonantal Hebrew (*YHWH*). Moses' call stories explain it as a play on the verb "to be" in a form that most scholars believe to be either future ("He will be") or causative ("He causes to be"). This disclosure is rather remarkable, especially in comparison to God's earlier refusal to reveal a name to Jacob (Gen. 32:29). The ability to call upon a deity by name was believed to enable more immediate access. A divine name could also add power to blessings and curses. The potential for abuse and reverence for the divine name led later Judaism to discourage pronouncing the Tetragrammaton (CD Special Topic IVA.7).

Other important aspects of Yahweh's identity are revealed during the deity's prolonged struggle with Pharaoh. Exodus 7–15 is above all a contest between Yahweh, the God of Israel, and Pharaoh, the ruler of Egypt. Kings in the ancient Near East were normally considered divine or, at least, the embodiment of divine power on earth. They also typically sponsored the nation's priesthood and religious cult. For these reasons, the gods could easily be invoked to sustain the privileges of an elite class at the expense of commoners. The exodus story, however, makes the extraordinary theological claim that Yahweh sides with the oppressed and demands social justice. For later audiences, the situation of the Hebrew slaves under Pharaoh became emblematic of any confrontation between the powerless and the powerful.

Yahweh's struggle with Pharaoh on behalf of Israel would be especially significant to exilic and postexilic audiences. It offered hope that, despite external appearances, Israel's God was still in control of historical events. Priestly writers reworked and supplemented the **plague** account to heighten its drama as Israel's God gradually overcomes the powers of Egypt (CD Chart IVA.1). They enhanced the miraculous nature of the tale by adding two episodes (gnats in Exod. 8:16-19 and boils in Exod. 9:8-12) to the earlier account. The ten-plague tradition is a creation of the Priestly writers, whereas the number and order of the plagues vary in earlier versions of the exodus story (cf. Pss. 78:43-51; 105:26-38).

These additions allowed P to develop the role of Pharaoh's magicians. After the second plague, the magicians cannot replicate the works of Israel's God and, after the sixth plague, cannot even stand before Yahweh's messengers. At this point, the reputedly all-powerful Pharaoh even loses control of himself as Yahweh begins to harden his heart for him (Exod. 8:15; 9:12; 9:34–10:2). The final two miracles deliver indirect jibes at Egyptian religion by demonstrating Yahweh's sovereignty over the sun and death. The final plague, which momentarily persuades Pharaoh to capitulate, also recalls his predecessor's decree against Hebrew children (Exod. 1:22). However, Yahweh's total devastation of Egyptian powers is demonstrated by the miracle at the **Red Sea** (Exod. 14).

Israel's most important narrative reveals its people's fundamental understanding of themselves and of God's character and will. The exodus story defines Israel as the former victims of an oppressive regime and the chosen people of a liberating God. It portrays Yahweh as a faithful and responsive deity with an acute sense of social justice and the ability to overcome Israel's enemies. However, the exodus event is only the beginning of Israel's national journey. At Sinai, they learn that with freedom comes responsibility.

Preliminary Exercise IVA.1: A Closer Look at the Exodus Story
Preliminary Exercise IVA.2: Go Down, Moses
Map IVA.1: The Route of the Exodus
Chart IVA.1: The Structure of the Plague Account
Special Topic IVA.1: The Passover in Contemporary Judaism
Special Topic IVA.2: Liberation Theology
Special Topic IVA.3: Did the Exodus Really Happen?
Special Topic IVA.4: Moses in the Movies
Special Topic IVA.5: A Bridegroom of Blood
Special Topic IVA.6: The Prophetic Call Type-Scene
Special Topic IVA.7: The Holy Name of Israel's God

Covenant and Law
(CD Preliminary Exercises IVB.1 and IVB.2)

The Torah follows the exodus story with a journey to Mount **Sinai** (**Horeb**) where the liberated descendants of Abraham enter into a new agreement with their divine benefactor. The Sinai covenant is the only covenant in the Hebrew Bible that consistently appears in a conditional form. God's deliverance and continuing protection of Israel form one half of this agreement. The Israelites, in turn, assent to live in a manner that would define them as the people of God. In its present shape, the Torah contains 613 laws that are associated with Sinai. These laws are presented not as a burden upon Israel but as another of God's gracious gifts to ensure their well-being. Israel's obedience to the law stems from gratitude for the redemption that Yahweh has already accomplished on their behalf.

At this stage of our journey, we encounter a confusing jumble of law and narrative that spans across large sections of four books. Many intrepid readers stumble at this point in the Torah, but those who do miss out on theologically rich covenant and legal traditions. Our appreciation of these materials can be enhanced by approaching them methodically with an awareness of the historical circumstances that produced them. Observant readers might notice that many of these laws presuppose a later situation such as settlement, monarchy, or exile. Israel did not assume that the law was given once for all time. Rather, successive generations reinterpreted and expanded the covenant's requirements to address the nation's changing circumstances. In fact, the Torah contains several distinct legal collections that developed gradually over the course of Israel's historical journey. The Torah's legal traditions do not stand alone but are integrated into the surrounding narrative. Biblical authors situated their new and revised laws against the backdrop of the Sinai account to connect them with Israel's distinctive story of salvation and national origins.

We will organize this leg of our journey around several discrete legal collections found in the Torah: the Ten Commandments, the Book of the Covenant, the Deuteronomic Code, and the Priestly and Holiness Codes. Although we cannot establish precise dates for these collections, certain moments of national crisis or transition led Israel to reflect more systematically upon its ethical obligations and religious duties. These situations gave Israel's covenant and legal traditions their decisive shape.

The Ten Commandments (Exod. 20:1-17; Deut. 5:1-21)

When the Israelites arrive at Sinai in Exodus 19, they prepare themselves for an encounter with their deity. These preparations, which included establishing boundaries around the mountain, accentuate the awesome holiness of God, whose presence is both desired and feared. Inserted into the middle of this theophany are two juxtaposed legal collections, the Ten Commandments and the Book of the Covenant. We

STUDYING THE OLD TESTAMENT

will consider the first of the two collections here and the second in the next section.

The **Ten Commandments**, also known as the **Decalogue** ("ten words"), is the first text that comes to mind for most readers when they think about biblical law. This collection is preserved with slight variations in two places in the Torah (Exod. 20:1-17 and Deut. 5:6-21). As it is preserved in both Exodus and Deuteronomy, the Decalogue presupposes a setting after Israel has become a settled, agricultural society in which one might find towns, servants, houses, and oxen.

Whether the Ten Commandments were written at an early date or composed later as a summary of Israel's covenant obligations, they are the most elemental laws in the Torah. In this sense, other biblical laws are simply an interpretation of these commands. Moreover, the Decalogue in Exodus is the only legal text in Hebrew scripture expressed as God's direct address to Israel. All other legal texts, including the version of the Decalogue in Deuteronomy, are conveyed indirectly through Moses. For these reasons, we should linger at this point on our journey to consider the content of the Ten Commandments.

That the Decalogue is a product of its time is readily apparent in the fact that it addresses a wealthy male audience. It mentions servants, children, and wives only as dependents within the male landholder's household. In Exodus, the wife is even included in a list of her husband's property that should not be coveted! Likewise, its adultery laws assume a double standard in which married men are not obligated in the same way as are married women. Adultery, in the context of the biblical world, meant a sexual relationship between a man and a married woman. If a married man had a sexual relationship with an unmarried woman, it was not considered adulterous. These laws can be seen as attempts to protect the husband's exclusive claim on his wife and to safeguard marriage in a culture that accepted multiple wives but not multiple husbands. Such assumptions and cultural practices are paralleled in other biblical and ancient Near Eastern legal codes.

In other ways, the Decalogue stands out from the law codes known to Israel and her neighbors. Other legal collections in the Torah and the ancient Near East are dominated by **case laws**, which apply only under specific conditions. They usually specify that "if" or "when" certain circumstances take place, "then" this is how the situation should be handled. The Decalogue contains only **absolute laws**, which spell out neither the circumstances of nor the penalties for an offense.

The Decalogue may be roughly separated into two tables. The first table primarily explains Israel's obligations toward God, whereas the second describes obligations within human relationships. Other cultures in the ancient Near East also had clear ideas about how their gods should be worshiped and how people within society should relate. However, they did not generally place these requirements alongside one another. The combination of religious and social obligations in the Ten Commandments and other biblical law codes suggests that Israel considered one's duties toward God and neighbor inseparable and mutually reinforcing.

The first three commands of the Decalogue focus solely upon Israel's obligations toward Yahweh. They require that Israelites give their full allegiance to the God of the exodus and neither represent this God visually nor misuse the divine name. The first command does not deny the existence of other gods. In fact, a firm statement of **monotheism** never appears in the Torah (cf. Isa. 45:5). The Decalogue merely insists that Israel worship only one deity. Read in light of the exodus story, Yahweh's right to claim exclusive allegiance from Israel is clear. Nonetheless, this requirement is very unusual in Israel's polytheistic environment.

The second and third commands continue to assert Yahweh's distinctiveness in relation to other ancient Near Eastern deities. The second command prohibits crafting images of God. Israel's neighbors could visit their deities at shrines where their images were located. Individuals might even own a smaller image as a good luck charm. The elusive Yahweh, however, could not be represented as a localized, controllable object. Likewise, the third command prohibits attempts to control

Yahweh by misusing the divine name. Modern readers often misunderstand this law as a prohibition of vulgar language, but in its cultural context it actually means much more than that. Israel and her neighbors believed that a name held an individual's identity and power. When called upon, a deity's name could be used to invoke a blessing or a curse upon others. The third command warns Israel not to activate God's name for inappropriate reasons. Taken together, the first three commands affirm Yahweh's exclusive right to be worshiped by Israel while remaining free of human control.

The fourth command is an instruction to remember the **Sabbath** by setting it apart as a day of rest. This practice is mandated, not as a special privilege of the social elite, but as the right of everyone (even animals). The democratic impulse behind this law is even more evident in Deuteronomy, where it is linked to Israel's own experience as slaves in Egypt (Deut. 5:12-14). Exodus, on the other hand, encourages Sabbath observance as imitation of God, who also rested on the seventh day according to the Priestly story of creation (Exod. 20:8-11). The practice of Sabbath observance probably predates the Priestly writers, but during the exile it became especially important as a way to remember Israel's distinctiveness as God's people.

The fifth command to honor parents ensures that Israelite values and practices will be transmitted from one generation to the next. It also provides for the well-being of elderly parents who, in the absence of social security, would be wholly dependent upon their adult children. Equal legitimacy is given to the authority of mother and father.

The next four commands, which are more concisely stated, order human relationships in the larger community. The prohibitions of murder, adultery, theft, and perjury all have parallels in the legal traditions of Israel's neighbors. The sanctity of human life, respect for private property, and limitation of personal autonomy were familiar values throughout the ancient Near East. Such principles are indispensable for maintaining a viable community.

As the previous four commands focused on detrimental behaviors, the tenth command targets an attitude that endangers the community's well-being. The unenforceability of the coveting prohibition suggests that the Decalogue was never intended to be implemented as a law code. None of the Bible's legal collections provides exhaustive rules for Israelite society. Rather they offer illustrative principles of correct behavior within the covenant community. In other words, biblical authors compiled these laws to teach what they believed to be Israel's social and religious obligations.

Overall, the Ten Commandments communicate a vision of life within the covenant community that is in some ways paralleled by the legislation of Israel's neighbors and is in some ways distinctive. Most of its social principles are fairly typical of other ancient Near Eastern codes. Yet the prohibition of coveting and the inclusion of outsiders in the Sabbath requirement are somewhat unusual. Even more distinctive is the way the Decalogue understands Israel's obligations toward Yahweh. Not only are these commands virtually unparalleled in the ancient world, they are also presented on the same terms as Israel's social responsibilities. The authority of these laws, at least in their present literary context, rests upon their origin in the God of the exodus.

The Book of the Covenant (Exod. 20:22–23:19)

The **Book of the Covenant**, also called the **Covenant Code**, was probably inserted into the literary context of the Sinai theophany by the Elohist writer (Exod. 20:22–23:19). This legal collection seems to clarify the Decalogue by applying its absolute commands to specific circumstances. Its references to agricultural matters presuppose a time after Israel's settlement in the promised land and prior to her exile from it. The Covenant Code was shaped by the development of monarchic government and other social institutions during this period. It demonstrates a marked ambivalence toward these institutions, which it sometimes attempts to buttress and other times attempts to restrain.

During her preexilic tenure in Canaan, Israel clearly shared many social customs and institutions with her neighbors. The Book of the Covenant contains more parallels with wider ancient Near Eastern legal traditions than does any other biblical law code. Many illustrations can be provided by comparing it to a legal text from Babylon called the **Code of Hammurabi** (CH) (CD Primary Text IVB.1, Special Topic IVB.1). Often the same or strikingly similar cases appear in these two collections. For example, both invoke the *lex talionis,* or principle of retribution, which suggests that an eye should be given in exchange for an eye, a tooth for a tooth, and a life for a life (Exod. 21:24-25, CH 196-203).

Although the Covenant Code borrows fairly liberally from neighboring legal traditions, the selection and treatment of these materials communicates its own particular understanding of Israel's obligations as God's chosen people. To illustrate this point, it is again instructive to compare the Covenant Code to Hammurabi's Code. In general, the latter invokes the death penalty much more frequently than the former. Furthermore, although both codes cite the *lex talionis*, Babylonian law applies this principle only if the victim of a crime is a person of high social stature (CH 116, 198-223, 230-232, 251-252). The Covenant Code cites the *lex talionis* only once and does not use it to reinforce class distinctions (Exod. 21:22-25).

Every ancient Near Eastern society had citizens who, for various reasons, had lost their social standing. In this patriarchal context, widows and orphans were disadvantaged without an adult male advocate. Economic hardship due to natural disasters or social exploitation might force individuals to enter indentured service. Resident aliens lacked rights of citizenship altogether. Many laws in the Book of the Covenant aim to protect the socially marginalized from more powerful members of society (Exod. 21:20-21, 26-27; 22:25-27; 23:1-11). These principles are not applied consistently, nor would the Covenant Code have eliminated social inequities had it been rigorously enforced. Yet this legislation does demonstrate a higher level of concern for socially disad-vantaged groups than is found elsewhere in the ancient Near East. Slavery and other forms of social oppression clearly existed in Israel, but large sections of the Covenant Code attempt to subordinate economic interests to claims of human dignity.

Overall, the Book of the Covenant reflects tension between exploitive social realities and liberating theological ideals. The convic-tion that Yahweh hears and responds to the cries of the oppressed was central to Israel's national identity. The Covenant Code often promotes concern for disadvantaged groups by appealing to the exodus story (Exod. 22:21-24; 23:8-9). Those formerly exploited in Egypt must now become the protectors of the poor and vulnerable in their own society. This notion became a powerful metaphor for social ethics as a check on the social and economic hierarchies that developed under the Israelite monarchy. The Covenant Code struggles, with varying degrees of suc-cess, to work out the ethical implications of the exodus story.

Deuteronomy and the Deuteronomic Code
(Deut. 1; 5–6; 9–12; 15; 17; 28)

In their present literary context, the Decalogue and the Covenant Code seem to provide the stipulations of a treaty created at Sinai between Israel and Yahweh. Exodus 19–26 exhibits many formal similarities with ancient Near Eastern treaties between regional rulers (suzerains) and the local rulers (vassals) who were subject to them. The **suzerainty treaty** provided one of Israel's metaphors for understanding their relationship to Yahweh. This metaphor is even more evident in Deuteronomy's reit-eration of the covenant formed at Sinai (CD Chart IVB.1).

The title Deuteronomy is derived from two Greek words: *deuteros* ("second" or "copy") and *nomos* ("law"). This book purports to be a col-lection of sermons delivered by Moses just before his own death and Israel's entry into the promised land. In it Moses recaps Israel's journey to that point and explains the stipulations of the Sinai covenant for life

STUDYING THE OLD TESTAMENT

in the land. The Deuteronomist borrows and adapts older legal traditions to compile the **Deuteronomic Code** (Deut. 12–26), which is presented as a later interpretation of the original agreement at Sinai. Its existence demonstrates Israel's belief that the requirements of the covenant should be revised and updated as her historical circumstances continued to change.

Despite their professed origin with Moses, Deuteronomy and its legal code appear to have received their decisive shape toward the end of Israel's monarchic period under the reforming Judean king Josiah (2 Kgs. 22–23). In the face of Assyrian rule over Judah in the late seventh century, the Deuteronomic Code calls for resistance to any foreign influence and allegiance to Yahweh alone. This concern is introduced by a repetition of the Decalogue (Deut. 5:6-21) followed by a sermon on the first commandment (Deut. 6–11). The command to have no other gods before Yahweh is restated positively at the beginning of a passage called the *Shema* ("Hear"), which becomes a central statement in later Judaism: "Hear, O Israel: the LORD is our God, the LORD alone. You shall love the LORD your God with all your heart, and with all your soul, and with all your might" (Deut. 6:4-5). Exclusive commitment to Yahweh is also promoted by centralizing worship in a single unnamed location, which would be understood as Jerusalem by Josiah's contemporaries (Deut. 12). Eliminating outlying sanctuaries would enable tighter controls on cultic activities. According to the **Deuteronomic** ideal, all Israel should worship in the same place in the same manner.

Centralization was not the only innovation of the Deuteronomic Code. Both the code and its surrounding sermons express a much more abstract theology than found elsewhere in the Torah by conceiving of Yahweh as an incorporeal deity who cannot be seen. In contrast to Exodus, Deuteronomy always insists that the Sinai theophany was an aural experience rather than a visual one (Deut. 4:12-18, 33; cf. Exod. 24:9-11). Deuteronomic law describes the central sanctuary as the dwelling place of God's name but denies that the deity actually dwells there bodily (Deut. 12:13-14; 26:15). This "name theology" leads to the demystification of cultic objects such as the **ark of the covenant**, which in Deuteronomy is merely a container for the Ten Commandments rather than God's throne (Deut. 10:1-5; cf. Exod. 25:21). Likewise, sacrifices in Deuteronomy are not offered for God's sake (cf. Lev. 1:9, 13, 17), but they are opportunities for celebration and for feeding socially disadvantaged members of society (Deut. 12:12, 18-19).

Socially marginal groups are another special concern of the Deuteronomic Code, which demands that the covenant be lived out in the daily affairs of Israel's social, political, and economic life. By the late seventh century, Israel's increasingly urbanized monarchy had produced pronounced social inequalities. In response, Deuteronomic law advocated severely restricting the authority of the king, limiting his acquisition of wealth, and requiring him to study the Torah on a daily basis (Deut. 17:14-20). The authority of the king was to be balanced by the authority of other public figures including judges, prophets, and priests (Deut. 16:18-20; 17:18; 18:15-22).

Like the earlier Covenant Code, Deuteronomic law reflects a struggle to reconcile liberating theological ideals with oppressive social realities. However, Deuteronomy often shows a greater sensitivity to the ethical implications of the exodus memory by deliberately modifying earlier laws to reflect a more humanitarian ethic. For example, the Covenant Code had limited the indentured service of males to a maximum of six years (Exod. 21:2-11). Deuteronomic law extends that reprieve to female indentured servants on the same terms (Deut. 15:12-17). This law and others encourage kindness and generosity toward socially marginal segments of the population as a sign of covenant obedience (Deut. 15:1-11; 23:19-20).

Although much of Deuteronomy received its present shape in the late seventh century, the Deuteronomic tradition continued well beyond Josiah's premature death in 609 B.C.E. (2 Kgs. 23:29-30). After Judah fell to the Babylonian Empire in 587 B.C.E., the book was supplemented to address the crisis of exile. With the aid of hindsight, it is regarded as inevitable that the Israelites would become complacent toward their covenant obligations and, as a result, be scattered among the nations (Deut. 4:25-28; 31:16-30). The despair of exile is eloquently expressed by the Deuteronomic writers:

> The LORD will scatter you among all peoples, from one end of the earth to the other . . . Among those nations you shall find no ease, no resting place for the sole of your foot. There the LORD will give you a trembling heart, failing eyes, and a languishing spirit. Your life shall hang in doubt before you; night and day you shall be in dread, with no assurance of your life. In the morning you shall say, "If only it were evening!" and at evening you shall say, "If only it were morning!"— because of the dread that your heart shall feel and the sights that your eyes shall see. (Deut. 28:64-67)

Deuteronomic writers reassure the diminished exilic community that they have not been abandoned by God and will be restored to the land if they wholeheartedly renew their commitment to the covenant (Deut. 4:29-31; 30:1-10).

Overall, Deuteronomy views covenant obedience as the sole measure of Israel's success and the only guarantee of her continued well-being. This Deuteronomic theology is powerfully expressed by a list of blessings and curses that outline both the positive consequences of obedience and the negative consequences of disobedience (Deut. 28). As interpreted by the Deuteronomic writers, Israel's covenant obligations could be epitomized by a humanitarian ethic and exclusive allegiance to Yahweh. These two foci set the agenda for Josiah's Reform and later set the conditions for the exilic community's homecoming.

The Tabernacle, Priestly Code, and Holiness Code (Exod. 32–34; Lev. 1; 11–15; 19; 25)

The Priestly writers also reinterpreted the Sinai covenant for a later audience. Their expression of Israel's covenant obligations probably draws upon older traditions and practices, but it received its final form during the exile or shortly thereafter. The Priestly writers made two major contributions to the Torah's Sinai traditions. First, they overhauled the earlier account of this covenant's formation in Exodus, giving this book its final shape. Second, they compiled laws, most of which are now mostly preserved at the center of the Torah in the book of Leviticus. These laws are loosely incorporated into the Sinai account as an additional revelation to Moses at the holy mountain (Lev. 27:34). Other Priestly statutes appear scattered throughout the narrative of Numbers as additional revelations to Israel in the wilderness (Num. 5–6; 15; 19; 28–30; 35).

As Exodus stands, its latter half is dominated by the Priestly writers' description of an elaborately outfitted **tabernacle**, or tent of meeting, in which God would accompany Israel on her journey from Sinai to Canaan. In Exodus 25–31, Moses receives excruciatingly detailed instructions for building this portable tent, which are repeated in full as it is constructed in Exodus 35–40. Although tedious to most modern readers, this twofold repetition signals the importance of God's presence for the exilic community, whose own recent experiences suggested the deity's absence.

The promise of the tabernacle signifies a new way to understand God's presence with Israel. Whereas Deuteronomic tradition advances an abstract name theology, the Priestly writers portray God as actually present in the tent of meeting. There God would be invisibly enthroned on the outstretched wings of two golden cherubim that adorned the lid of the ark of the covenant. In the Priestly source, the ark is not simply a container but is God's portable throne. The deity would no longer meet Israel at special sites but would be a constant and intimate companion wherever their journey led. God could even accompany Israel to Babylon while the Jerusalem temple lay in ruins.

The Priestly writers intentionally arranged earlier sources in Exodus so that a pivotal narrative (Exod. 32–34) fell between these two descriptions of the tabernacle—the construction of a **golden calf** (CD Special

Topic IVB.2). This **apostasy** endangers the covenant even before Israel has departed from Sinai. Yahweh is prepared to renounce Israel, but Moses negotiates a new beginning despite their failure. Renewal of the covenant is possible only because of Yahweh's inordinate mercy and fidelity (Exod. 34:6-7). By framing the earlier account of the golden calf with the tabernacle's promise and eventual construction, the Priestly writers mimic the promise-obstacle-fulfillment pattern familiar from earlier sections of the Torah. They intend to reassure their audience that the unfaithfulness that had resulted in exile did not negate God's presence with Israel or the possibility of restoration.

The Priestly writers also compiled an extensive list of laws that, like the tabernacle, were intended to enable God's presence with Israel. These covenant stipulations, sometimes called the **Priestly Code** (Lev. 1–27), provide a means for bridging the gulf between sinful humans and a holy deity. They begin with a catalog of sacrifices and basic rules for their performance (CD Chart IVB.2). Because the literary setting of Leviticus is Sinai, these sacrifices are described as taking place in the tabernacle (Lev. 1–7). Israel may have practiced such sacrifices in the Jerusalem temple prior to its destruction in 587 B.C.E., but the Priestly writers preserved this catalog in anticipation of reinstituting a sacrificial system in a restored temple (cf. Ezek. 40–48).

The concept of animal **sacrifice** is foreign to modern readers, although the practice was common throughout the ancient Near East. Though the procedure differs somewhat for various types of sacrifices, typically an animal is brought by a worshiper to the sanctuary, where it is slaughtered and its organs are cleansed. Blood is often poured out or sprinkled around the altar before the animal is burned upon it. The smoke ascends to the deity as a "pleasing odor," a common phrase in the Priestly Code (for example, Lev. 1:9, 13, 17). Whatever part of the animal is not burned is consumed by the priests or the worshipers. This ritual was believed to consecrate the sacrifice by transferring it from the mundane to the sacred realm as a gift to the deity.

Torah: The Journey Begins   83

Such sacrifices provided a visible, tangible means for the worshiper to offer thanksgiving, commune with the deity, and redress sin. Atonement, or the redressing of sin, is an especially prominent motivation for sacrifice in the Priestly source. The word *atonement*, which appears over fifty times in the Priestly Code, suggests deliverance from sin by means of a substitute. Leviticus develops this idea further in relation to the **Day of Atonement** (Yom Kippur), when the accumulated sins of the community necessitated the cleansing of the sanctuary (Lev. 16). As part of this ritual, the high priest selects two goats. One goat is sacrificed as a sin offering, and its blood is placed on the ark of the covenant. No one could enter the temple's Holy of Holies where the ark was housed except the high priest on this day. The priest sends the other goat out into the desert bearing the sins of the community (CD Special Topic IVB.3).

The Priestly Code limits Israel's priesthood to Aaron and his male descendants, who alone are charged with presiding over sacrifices in the tabernacle (Lev. 8–9). Whereas Deuteronomy considers any male from the tribe of Levi a legitimate priest (Deut. 18:6-7), the P source reflects the postexilic ascendancy of certain priests claiming Aaronid descent and demotes other **Levites** to supportive roles (Num. 1:47-53). Nevertheless, the account of Aaron's two sons, who are consumed for offering an "unholy fire," cautions against anyone approaching the deity in a careless manner (Lev. 10).

The Priestly Code also governs the sanctity of everyday life outside the cult. These laws begin with the assumption that Yahweh is unapproachably different from humans. To make communion with this deity possible, the people of Israel either had to avoid objects and actions that were designated as **unclean** or follow prescribed rituals to restore **cleanliness** (Lev. 11–15). Cleanliness does not necessarily correspond to morality nor does uncleanliness indicate immorality. Some natural and beneficial activities, such as sex and childbirth, result in defilement. Neither does cleanliness automatically render a person or object holy, although it is a prerequisite for entering the sacred realm. Many attempts have been made to explain the purity guidelines in priestly law, none of which are entirely satisfactory (CD Special Topic IVB.4). However, these regulations clearly reflect a desire to maintain appropriate boundaries in many areas of life. This anxiety is especially understandable in the context of exile, where such practices would help Israel maintain a distinctive communal identity.

Israel's distinctive identity also finds expression in another series of laws addressed to the entire community (Lev. 17–26). These chapters are sometimes called the **Holiness Code** because of their repeated demand that Israel imitate Yahweh's holiness (Lev. 19:2; 20:26). This originally independent collection was edited by the Priestly writers who inserted it into its present literary context. Some of its laws, such as the prohibition of garments made from different materials (Lev. 19:19), are products of a distant culture and might sound strange to modern readers. In other places, the Holiness Code eloquently expresses a more familiar ethic. Its demands for social justice rival even those found in Deuteronomic law. For example, **Jubilee** observance includes a periodic restoration of property to original owners who had been forced to sell their land due to financial hardship (Lev. 25). The Holiness Code's understanding of Israel's moral responsibilities may be epitomized by the command to love one's neighbor as oneself (Lev. 19:18), a requirement that applies even if one's neighbor is not Israelite (Lev. 19:34).

In summary, the Torah's complex account of the Sinai covenant and its requirements emerged gradually over the course of Israel's historical journey. Although impossible to date, the Ten Commandments articulate the basic values of the covenant community. The formation of monarchy and the development of a hierarchical society with "haves" and "have nots" led to more systematic reflection on Israel's moral obligations in the Covenant Code. Generations later, Assyrian hegemony and the increasing impoverishment of a segment of Israel's population generated an impassioned call for covenant loyalty and social justice in

Deuteronomy. Finally, the crisis of exile prompted the Priestly writers to reflect on the possibility of divine presence in a situation marked by God's apparent absence. The end result is a theologically rich, if somewhat convoluted, document.

Preliminary Exercise IVB.1: Israel's Legal Codes
Preliminary Exercise IVB.2: Murder and Capital Punishment
Primary Text IVB.1: The Code of Hammurabi
Chart IVB.1: Parallels between Hittite Treaties and the Sinai Covenant
Chart IVB.2: Sacrifices in Leviticus 1–7
Special Topic IVB.1: Comparing the Covenant Code and Hammurabi's Code
Special Topic IVB.2: The Golden Calf Heresy
Special Topic IVB.3: The Scapegoat and Azazel
Special Topic IVB.4: What Makes Something Clean or Unclean?
Special Topic IVB.5: Is the Sinai Account Historically Accurate?

Wilderness Journey (Exod. 15:22–18:27; Num. 11–14; 16–17; 20–26; CD Preliminary Exercises IVC.1 and IVC.2)

Interwoven with the Torah's covenant traditions are several narratives set in the desert **wilderness** between Egypt and Canaan. As these stories are now arranged, they comprise a two-stage journey. Its first leg takes the exodus community from Egypt to Sinai (Exod. 15:22–18:27), whereas its second leg carries them from Sinai to the eastern bank of the Jordan River (Num. 10:11–36:13; cf. Deut. 1:19–3:29). Several attempts have been made to reconstruct Israel's circuit through the wilderness. However, like the rest of the Torah, these traditions were preserved for theological rather than historical reasons.

Biblical writers remember the wilderness sojourn as a time of transition when Israel was tested, disciplined, and forged as a nation. Later generations would return to these stories when they themselves faced precarious circumstances, often reading their own experiences back into these earlier memories. As the Torah's wilderness traditions were shaped by their retelling, they came to center on several crises that threatened Israel's continued well-being. We will approach Israel's wilderness tradi-

STUDYING THE OLD TESTAMENT

tions under these headings: (1) a crisis of faith, (2) a crisis of leadership, and (3) a crisis of identity. Then we will consider why these issues might have held special importance for the covenant community.

A Crisis of Faith

The first crisis concerns Israel's relationship with the deity. Elsewhere in the canon, the wilderness sojourn is sometimes remembered as a "honeymoon period" for Yahweh and the recently liberated Israelites (Hos. 2:15; Jer. 2:2-6). Yet in the Torah's wilderness traditions, the divine-human relationship is often so rocky that divorce seems more likely! The deity's actions on behalf of Israel contrast sharply with the young nation's ungrateful response. Despite daily miracles of provision and protection, they repeatedly fail to trust God's ability to sustain them.

As these stories are now arranged, this crisis of faith becomes an increasingly problematic issue as Israel's journey toward Canaan progresses. Within Exodus, Israel's complaints are tolerated by a gracious deity. After the covenant community leaves Sinai, however, their rebelliousness begins to provoke Yahweh's anger. The book of Numbers frequently portrays God violently lashing out at the unfaithful Israelites, killing many of them with plagues and natural disasters (CD Special Topic IVC.1). The emergent nation seems poised on the brink of failure.

Two episodes particularly illustrate Israel's chronic lack of faith in God's ability to provide for their physical needs and to defeat their enemies. The first incident, which is set before Sinai, is triggered by anxiety over the food supply (Exod. 16). The people have apparently forgotten the signs and wonders that accompanied their deliverance, and they now long for a return to Egypt where food was plentiful. The story emphasizes that God hears Israel's complaint (an assertion repeated four times) and immediately responds by sending quail and bread from heaven. This bread is at first an enigma to them though it is to become the basis of Israel's diet in the wilderness. Their initial question "What is it?" (Hebrew *mān hû*) leads to its popular name, **manna**.

Food comes with conditions that test Israel's trust in God as a provider. They are not permitted to collect more than a single day's supply of bread, except on the sixth day, when they are instructed to gather food in advance for the Sabbath. They are warned that no manna will fall from heaven on the seventh day. Twice members of the community fail to heed these instructions. First, some attempt to gather a surplus of manna only to discover that it spoils overnight. Perhaps because of that experience, some of the Israelites do not prepare for the Sabbath by collecting extra bread on the sixth day. When they vainly seek manna on the seventh day, God bemoans Israel's stubborn disobedience. The deity also requires that a measure of manna be stored as proof to future generations of God's ability to sustain life in an environment inhospitable to it.

A second episode demonstrates Israel's lack of confidence that Yahweh would be able to deliver the promised land. In this story, representatives of each of the twelve tribes are sent to reconnoiter southern Canaan in preparation for an invasion (Num. 13–14). After forty days, the spies return with a large cluster of grapes borne on a pole between two men and tales of a land flowing with "milk and honey." Yet all but two of the spies caution against invasion because of the size and military strength of the land's inhabitants. Joshua and Caleb alone insist that conquest would be assured by Yahweh's support.

This time Israel's lack of faith evokes Yahweh's wrath in the form of a plague that consumes the skeptical spies. Moreover, the deity determines that Israel is not yet ready to receive the land. Only after the exodus generation dies in the wilderness will the promise be fulfilled for a new generation. Exceptions are made only for Joshua and Caleb, who had demonstrated faith in Yahweh (CD Special Topic IVC.2).

A Crisis of Leadership

A second crisis that characterizes the Torah's wilderness traditions is the problem of ensuring appropriate leadership for the covenant commu-

STUDYING THE OLD TESTAMENT

nity. Along the way to Canaan, the Israelites repeatedly question who might legitimately speak for God and who should provide guidance for God's people. As later generations returned to these stories, they too sought answers to these questions. Especially during periods of instability, such as the wilderness sojourn, it becomes critical for the community to discern whose voice is authoritative and trustworthy.

Even the leadership of Moses is questioned. Despite his role in the exodus, the Israelites repeatedly doubt the legitimacy of his authority during their journey through the wilderness (Exod. 15:24; 16:2-3; 17:2-7; Num. 14:2; 20:2-5; 21:5). Whenever difficult circumstances arise, he is accused of leading them into the wilderness in order to kill them. In the face of these accusations, several wilderness episodes confirm Moses' authority over against any potential rival. His relationship to the deity is described as unique (Num. 7:89; 12:8), and challenges to his leadership are presented as tantamount to testing Yahweh (Exod. 17:2). On one occasion, the Israelites' complaints against Moses actually evoke a plague of biting serpents (Num. 21:4-9; CD Special Topic IVC.3).

Although God often defends Moses' exclusive prerogatives, the man himself is portrayed as humble and more than willing to share the burden of leadership (Num. 11:29; 12:3). At the suggestion of his father-in-law, he introduces a tiered court system (Exod. 18:13-27). Judges are selected from among upstanding men in the community and trained by Moses to arbitrate minor grievances. In a similar episode, elders of Israel are temporarily endowed with a portion of Moses' spirit, which allows them to prophesy (Num. 11:11-17, 25-30). When Moses' supporters become jealous on his behalf, he declares his wish that every Israelite would receive this ability. Both judges and elders would play important leadership roles in preexilic Israel. These wilderness stories legitimate their authority by illustrating that it is derived from and sanctioned by Moses.

Miriam and Aaron also provide leadership for the covenant community. Yet the final form of the Torah only hints at Miriam's importance, while portraying Aaron ambiguously. In Numbers 12, the two appear as allies against Moses, whom they criticize for marrying a Cushite woman (Zipporah is elsewhere described as Midianite). They also challenge his exclusive leadership rights by asking, "Has the LORD spoken only through Moses? Has he not spoken through us also?" (Num. 12:2). In this episode, God clearly takes the side of Moses and subordinates both Miriam and Aaron to him (CD Special Topic IVC.4).

In other wilderness episodes, Aaron appears alongside Moses as an equally legitimate, or perhaps an even more legitimate, intermediary between God and Israel (Exod. 16:2-3; Num. 14:2-5; 16–19). Just as the deity elsewhere defends Moses' unique leadership credentials, God comes to the defense of Aaron's authority as a priest. Aaron is first challenged by his cousin **Korah**, who represents other members of the priestly Levite tribe (Num. 16). A contest demonstrates God's preference for Aaron and his descendants over other Levites. This story was likely used in the postexilic period by Aaronids to justify their ascendancy within the priesthood. Korah and his supporters become examples of what will happen to anyone who challenges their authority (CD Special Topic IVC.5). Grumbling against Aaron continues in the next chapter until a second contest reaffirms the divine election of his line out of all twelve tribes (Num. 17). Each of these accounts provides visible signs (an altar cover and a blooming staff) as "proof" of Aaron's authority and deterrents to future challenges.

A Crisis of Identity

A third crisis evident in many of the wilderness narratives is how Israel should interact with outsiders while maintaining a distinctive identity. This concern persists in Israel during much of its historical journey. Once settled in the land, they are continually tempted to adopt the gods and customs of their neighbors. Eventually, the Israelite monarchy is forced to submit first to Assyrian and then to Babylonian hegemony. Deportation later creates an exilic community in the midst of outsiders. Even return from exile only results in life under Persian rule. It is not surprising that this concern is read back into the wilderness traditions as they are recalled and shaped by later generations.

Neither is it surprising that Israel's wilderness stories affirm God's preference for her over other nations. In these accounts, the deity vanquishes many foes before the covenant community (Exod. 17:8-16; Num. 21). The wilderness traditions emphasize that victories are due to Yahweh's support rather than Israel's own strength and prowess. Military skirmishes in the wilderness also foreshadow the eventual conquest of Canaan in the book of Joshua.

Israel's advance alarms the king of Moab, who hires the prophet **Balaam** to utter a curse against God's people (Num. 22–24). The non-Israelite prophet is presented in a relatively positive light in this folk story, which even features a talking donkey! Balaam tries to obey God, who one minute permits and the next minute forbids him to accept the job. The deity's inconsistency in the story, along with the alternation of the divine name, may lead readers to suspect the presence of multiple sources. In its final form, the story emphasizes God's control over the prophet and protection of Israel. Ultimately, the king of Moab is frustrated by Balaam's inability to bestow anything other than a blessing upon the Israelites. Like the donkey, Balaam also defies his master and becomes an unexpected spokesperson for God.

Observant readers will notice an ambivalent attitude toward non-Israelites in the wilderness traditions. Some stories suggest that foreigners could befriend Israel and even assimilate into the covenant community. Others portray outsiders as a polluting influence and advocate a strict separatist policy. Even the same individual or group can be approved in one text while demonized in another. Balaam, for example, is later killed as an enemy of Israel (Num. 31:8, 16).

The Torah's attitude toward the Midianites is similarly inconsistent. In Exodus 18, Moses' Midianite father-in-law (variously called Jethro, Reuel, and Hobab) offers praise and sacrifices to the God of the exodus. Before he returns to his own country, he offers advice on the administration of justice, which his son-in-law gratefully accepts. In Numbers, Moses even begs his father-in-law to remain with Israel and guide them through the wilderness to the promised land (Num. 10:29-32).

Elsewhere in Numbers, Midianite and Moabite women tempt Israel to commit apostasy by worshiping a deity called Baal Peor (Num. 25). When an Israelite man engages in sexual relations with a Midianite woman at the entrance of the tabernacle, Aaron's grandson, Phineas, impales them both with a single spear (CD Special Topic IVC.6). The story implies that God approves of this violent act when it ends a plague that had been evoked by Israel's apostasy. In response to their role in the Baal Peor incident, Moses later declares a war against the Midianites (his in-laws!) in which only virgin women are spared as potential wives and concubines for Israelite men (Num. 31).

In brief, the Torah describes the wilderness sojourn as a time when Israel chronically lacked faith in God's providence, often rebelled against divinely chosen leaders, and occasionally flirted with other nations and their gods. God graciously continued to provide sustenance, protection, and leadership for the covenant community. Yet their rebelliousness sometimes provoked the deity's anger and produced negative consequences. With the exceptions of Joshua and Caleb, the exodus generation was barred from experiencing the fulfillment of God's promise. The book of Numbers is suitably framed by two census lists, one listing the exodus generation as Israel left Sinai (Num. 1–10) and one numbering a new generation as Israel prepared to enter Canaan (Num. 26). The unfaithful generation died in the wilderness, but their descendants will inherit the promised land.

The three crises evident in the wilderness tradition—faith, leadership, and identity—would be valid concerns at almost any point of Israel's historical journey. However, they take on a special urgency during the Babylonian exile and in its aftermath, during which the Torah received its final shape at the hands of Priestly writers. Older stories were transformed and supplemented to address the devastating events of

587 B.C.E. and their consequences. Just as Egypt became a cipher for Babylon (Isa. 40:1-5; 43:13-17) and the exodus for Israel's anticipated homecoming (Deut. 28:64-68), the wilderness also assumed symbolic importance for the exilic community.

Like the wilderness sojourn, exile was a tumultuous and uncertain time that necessitated the community's utter dependence upon Yahweh. Faith in the covenant promises had been severely tested. The failure of former leaders raised the question of who could now be trusted to speak for God. Contact with foreigners was a daily reality for the exilic community, one that was not greatly affected by return to a land under Persian hegemony. Under such conditions, the boundary between outsider and insider could easily become blurred for the covenant people.

These concerns left a lasting impression on the Torah's wilderness traditions. For the Priestly writers' audience, these stories affirm that trust in Yahweh is a necessary prerequisite for life in the land. They also confirm the authority of the Aaronid priesthood and the importance of maintaining a distinctive identity among outsiders. Most important, they provide assurance that God's promises are delayed only by Israel's own mistrust and apostasy. A new faithful generation can inherit the land despite the sins of their ancestors.

Preliminary Exercise IVC.1: Crises of Faith, Leadership, and Identity
Preliminary Exercise IVC.2: A Cinematic Wilderness
Special Topic IVC.1: God as Destroyer
Special Topic IVC.2: The Sin of Moses and Aaron
Special Topic IVC.3: Moses' Bronze Serpent
Special Topic IVC.4: Miriam
Special Topic IVC.5: Korah's Rebellion
Special Topic IVC.6: The Phineas Priesthood
Special Topic IVC.7: Are the Wilderness Traditions Historically Accurate?

The Journey Continues

As the Torah's story of origins draws to a close, Israel finds herself at the beginning of a new journey. Standing on the plains of Moab, she is poised at last to inherit the promised land. Deuteronomy provides a momentary pause for Israel to reflect on the road behind and to anticipate challenges to come. This final book of the Torah emphasizes the need for Israel to remember her experiences with God, to learn from her past, and to pass this knowledge on to future generations (Deut. 4:1-40).

As readers, we too can pause momentarily to reflect upon the completed form of the Torah and gather perspective for the next leg of our journey through Hebrew scripture. The Torah, with its many loose ends, leaves readers with both apprehension and hope for the covenant community. God's promises to Abraham are never completely fulfilled within its pages. Conquest is deferred, and Israel's later journey will be taken over by other storytellers in the Former Prophets. Deuteronomy's final chapters hint at the negative course that will be charted by future generations, and Deuteronomic theology provides the interpretive framework for the books that follow. The death of Moses is also unsettling (Deut. 34). Biblical writers seem to despair over Israel's chances of ever finding another leader who knows God so intimately. Yet the uncertain future is full of possibility. The first five books of Hebrew scripture were intended to provide a compass for Israel's continuing journey.

CHAPTER THREE

FORMER PROPHETS: A NATION'S JOURNEY

In the last chapter, we learned that the Torah resulted from a long process of literary growth before finally attaining its present form during or shortly after the Babylonian exile (587–539 B.C.E.). As we now have it, the Torah presents the beginning of Israel's story and preserves the foundational traditions that shaped the nation's faith and identity. The ancestral promises, the deliverance from Egyptian bondage, and the covenant relationship between God and Israel are presupposed in the books that follow. In this sense, the rest of Hebrew scripture is simply an expansion and clarification of the Torah.

Nevertheless, the story of Israel continues beyond the Bible's first five books. In the next section of the canon, Abraham's descendants finally gain a foothold in the promised land. Readers might expect that this long-anticipated accomplishment will signal a happy ending, but we soon discover that life in the land will be more complicated than the ancestral promises had anticipated. We learn in the book of Joshua that the promised land is already occupied by other peoples, most of whom are unwilling to yield before Israel's theological claim. Disturbingly violent conquest traditions portray the Israelites seizing Canaan by force. Even after rival claimants have supposedly been annihilated, conflicts over the land continue throughout Judges and the books of Samuel.

While struggling to become a viable nation within Canaan, Israel also wrestles with her communal identity. Traditional tribal structures prove inadequate for the challenges posed by life in the land, leading Israel to adopt a monarchic government like her ancient Near Eastern neighbors. We will find that many biblical traditions express serious misgivings about kingship. Israel was to be ruled by Yahweh, not by a human king! Was political accommodation possible without theological compromise?

Israel experiments tentatively with monarchy under the reigns of Saul and David but becomes a true state under David's son, Solomon. The stories that reflect these developments also reflect a struggle to reconcile the older Mosaic covenant with an emerging royal theology centered on the Davidic house. Tension between these two covenant traditions contributes to the division of the Israelite monarchy into two separate kingdoms, Israel and Judah. As the histories of these twin kingdoms are recalled in 1 and 2 Kings, almost every ruler is judged inadequate. Ultimately, Israel is decimated by Assyrian forces. After a disappointing attempt at revival, Judah falls to Babylon and suffers the ignominy of exile.

The books that narrate Israel's tragic national journey constitute a part of the **Prophets** (Hebrew *nevi'im*) within the Jewish canon. This is the second of three canonical divisions represented by the three consonants of the acronym Tanakh (*torah, nevi'im, ketuvim*). Allusion to "the Law and the Prophets" in the Apocrypha demonstrate that this division of the Bible was recognized as early as the second century B.C.E. In the Middle Ages, a further distinction emerged between the **Former Prophets** (Joshua, Judges, 1–2 Samuel, and 1–2 Kings) and the **Latter Prophets** (Isaiah, Jeremiah, Ezekiel, and the Book of the Twelve). Although a discussion of the Latter Prophets will be postponed until chapter 4, it is important for us to recognize that this division is late and artificial. While obvious differences do exist between the books assigned to the Former and Latter Prophets, both collections are an essential part of Israel's prophetic tradition.

What does it mean to say that these books are prophetic? Modern readers tend to link **prophecy** with either social critique (for example,

Martin Luther King, Jr.) or prediction (for example, Nostradamus). Neither of these assumptions is entirely wrong, but both are inadequate. Prophetic literature does not focus solely upon social ills, but measures *both* Israel's society *and* worship life against the requirements of the covenant with Yahweh. Whether through narrative (which dominates the Former Prophets) or direct address (which is typical of the Latter Prophets), social and cultic abuses are condemned as contrary to the values of the covenant community. Moreover, since God is assumed to be active in historical events, everything that happens to Israel is interpreted as a result of her relationship to the deity. On this basis, prophetic literature often offers a preview of the sort of consequences Israel might expect should she refuse to repent and uphold the covenant requirements. Yet these consequences are avoidable, and Israel's future always remains fluid. The ultimate goal of prophecy is not to predict the future, but to inspire covenant fidelity. Hence, the Former Prophets should be understood as prophetic testimony to God's involvement in the course of Israel's history.

While the Jewish canon places Joshua, Judges, 1–2 Samuel, and 1–2 Kings with the prophets, Christian canons traditionally class them with other so-called **historical books**. Such an arrangement could lead to misperceptions about the fundamental nature of this literature, largely because modern readers tend to think of "history" as an objective and reliable report of past events. Upon reflection, however, the process of writing history is actually much more complicated. Any account of the past is necessarily a selection of certain moments and personages at the expense of others. Also, historians do not simply catalog selected events, but they generally offer interpretive judgments about cause and significance. To some extent, political and cultural biases inevitably affect both what is included in a historical account and how it is interpreted. Realizing this fact, most modern historians carefully evaluate their sources and their own prejudices. Ancient historians, however, did not take such a critical stance toward themselves or their sources.

So in what sense might the Former Prophets be considered historical literature? Scholars disagree over the historical value of the traditions contained within these books. Yet they do tend to agree that preserving a complete and accurate record of Israel's past experiences was not their authors' primary intention. These traditions are highly selective, treating certain periods in great detail yet passing over others. Neither do they make any pretense of objectivity. At times, an interpretive outlook is explicitly voiced within the text. On other occasions, the authors communicate their convictions more subtly by arranging the text to highlight repeated themes or patterns. Most important, this account of Israel's past is completely theologized. Its authors identify the God of Israel as the driving force behind historical events. These books clearly do not chronicle history for its own sake, but rather offer an interpretive theological commentary on the nation's journey from conquest to exile.

Recognizing the nature of this literature should shape our expectations as readers. As our journey through Hebrew scripture proceeds into the Former Prophets, we should *not* expect to discover there a complete and objective historical report. Instead, we should expect these books to be thoroughly saturated with the ideology of their authors or editors. Rather than forcing this literature to serve as a straightforward account of Israel's past, we will appreciate its attempt to create a sense-making narrative out of her national traditions.

THE ROAD TO CANAAN

The book of Deuteronomy envisions Israel standing collectively on the plains of Moab poised to cross the Jordan River and inherit the land promised to Abraham. Crossing the Jordan would signal a significant transition. The wilderness journey had ended, and another kind of journey was about to begin. How would they negotiate the unfamiliar terrain of a settled, national existence? Deuteronomy provides direction and encouragement for this undertaking, but the story of Israel's national journey actually begins in the books of Joshua and Judges. As we have them, these two books narrate the appearance and early tenure of Israelites in the land of Canaan.

The importance of this land in Hebrew scripture can hardly be overestimated. More than real estate, it is a concrete expression of Israel's covenant with Yahweh. Anticipated throughout most of the Torah, the land represents the promise to their ancestors, the goal of their wilderness wanderings, and the place of their anticipated rest. As such, it is consistently affirmed as highly desirable—a "good land" with abundant resources (Deut. 8:7-10; Josh. 23:13-16), a "land flowing with milk and honey" (Exod. 3:17; Josh. 5:6). These affirmations take on even more significance when we realize that the Torah was finalized in the context of exile and that the story of Israel's national journey will end with expulsion from that good land.

Israel's contested territorial claims figure prominently in Joshua and Judges. Both of these books understand the land as an inheritance from Yahweh, who, as sovereign over the earth, would have the right to assign or reassign any portion of it at will. The Israelites do not receive this land through their own efforts but only as an undeserved gift from a generous deity. The very designation "land of Canaan" serves as a reminder that this territory originally belonged to others. This point is reinforced by formulaic lists of peoples whom Israel will displace, including the Canaanites, Hittites, Amorites, Perizzites, Hivites, and Jebusites (Josh. 3:10; 9:1; 11:3; 12:8; 24:11; Judg. 3:5). Throughout Joshua, Yahweh appears as a decidedly partisan deity who typically sides with Israel against other nations. While the Israelites cooperate in military endeavors, it is ultimately Yahweh who subdues rival claimants to enable the takeover of Canaan.

Joshua and Judges repeatedly illustrate that Israel's continued residence in Canaan depends on Yahweh's good graces. The former book functions primarily as a positive object lesson. In Joshua, Israel is usually the model of obedience and, as a result, meets with amazing success. In Judges, we find almost the opposite scenario. The fortunes of Israel rise and fall with her inconsistent allegiance to Yahweh. Apostasy and other covenant violations inevitably lead to military defeat at the hands of enemies. Although received as a free gift, the land could be retained only through obedience. This Mosaic principle, established so vividly at the beginning of the Former Prophets, anticipates the eventual outcome of Israel's tragic national journey.

The Conquest Tradition (Josh. 1–12; CD Preliminary Exercises IA.1 and IA.2)

Joshua begins as Deuteronomy ended—with the death of Moses. Although brief, this obituary notice for the "servant of [Yahweh]" is incredibly significant. This title for Moses, drawn from Deuteronomy 34:5, is repeated so often in Joshua that it almost becomes a part of his name. Moses looms over Israel's formative Torah traditions, which depict him leading the exodus from Egypt, mediating the covenant at Sinai, and guiding Israel through the wilderness for forty years. Readers of the Torah are left asking how anyone could fill this void (Deut. 34:10-12), and the Former Prophets begin by answering this question.

God immediately confirms the choice of Joshua, son of Nun, as Israel's new leader and promises to be with him through the task ahead. Because the conquest will be accomplished by Israel's deity, not her general, the instructions given to Joshua are decidedly non-militaristic. He is required only to meditate upon and scrupulously obey the "book of the law" that had been recorded by Moses (cf. Deut. 31:9-13). God's pep talk is followed by a conversation between Joshua and the eastern tribes. Although their territory had already been won under Moses' leadership, these eastern tribes had pledged their support until the conquest was complete (Num. 32; Deut. 2:24–3:17). When Joshua reminds them of their continued military obligations, they pledge to obey him just as they had Moses. The task that one had begun, the other would complete.

Careful readers will observe that the effort to portray Joshua as Moses' rightful successor continues throughout the book. Many of Joshua's experiences clearly echo those of his mentor. Like Moses, he also parts a body of water before Israel (Josh. 3–4). Both men experience a theophany in which they are instructed to remove their sandals as they stand upon holy ground (Josh. 5:13-15). Israel was able to defeat Amalek in the wilderness because Moses had held his hands aloft during the battle (Exod. 17:8-16). Similarly, Joshua must stretch out his sword during the battle at Ai to ensure Israel's success (Josh. 8:18-26). When the completed conquest is reviewed, their military feats are juxtaposed (Josh. 12:1-24). As Moses had mediated the Sinai covenant, his successor mediates a reaffirmation of the relationship between Israel and Yahweh (Josh. 24). Finally, at the end of his career, Joshua is also granted the title "servant of [Yahweh]" (Josh. 24:29). The overall effect of these parallels is to portray Joshua as Moses-in-miniature.

Despite his importance in Israel's conquest traditions, Joshua is never made an equal to his predecessor. Moses' mighty deeds outstrip those of his apprentice in both number and magnitude. Joshua intercedes on behalf of the people less often and with less eloquence. His prayer following the setback of Ai sounds more like Israel's murmuring in the wilderness than Moses' more eloquent pleas (Josh. 7:7-9; cf. Num. 14:13-19). Perhaps most tellingly, Joshua speaks less often on the deity's behalf. He receives no new word from Yahweh that had not already been delivered to his mentor. Instead, Joshua is charged with obedience to the recorded words of Moses, the lawgiver.

In his first act as general, Joshua mimics Moses' military strategy by sending advance scouts into the land of Canaan (cf. Num. 13–14; Deut. 1:19-36). For unexplained reasons, espionage brings these spies to the house of a prostitute named Rahab (CD Special Topic IA.1). This story resonates with several biblical traditions involving clever tricksters who get the better of more powerful figures. Not only does Rahab misdirect representatives from the king of Jericho, she also places Joshua's spies in a compromising situation where they could hardly refuse her request for asylum. Moreover, Rahab utters an eloquent declaration of faith in Yahweh that heralds the imminent conquest. On the lips of a non-Israelite resident of Canaan, her words serve to validate Israel's claim upon the land.

Satisfied with his espionage, Joshua prepares to cross the Jordan (CD Map IA.1). This significant act is marked by rituals and supernatural assistance. Like the Red Sea, the Jordan River is not just a geographical marker. It is also a symbolic boundary indicating a change in status. The Israelites passed through the Red Sea to freedom, whereas crossing the Jordan will lead to settled nationhood. The ark of the covenant, mentioned no less than sixteen times in this chapter, plays a key role in the Jordan crossing, just as it will in the battle for Jericho. Throughout Israel's conquest tradition, the ark symbolizes God's presence with Israel and agency on her behalf.

The ritualistic Jordan crossing is followed by more rituals. Readers may begin to wonder when the battle will finally begin! First, Joshua circumcises the males who had been born in the wilderness. Although a dubious undertaking for troops facing battle (cf. Gen. 34), circumcision indicates Israel's commitment to the covenant's requirements. Unlike their disobedient parents, this generation will be allowed to inherit the land because of their faithfulness to the law. Israel then celebrates the first Passover in Canaan and begins to eat of the land's produce. The cessation of manna, Israel's wilderness diet, anticipates Israel's transition to a settled life in the land Yahweh has promised to provide. These rituals remind Israel that the conquest will not be accomplished by military might but through faith and obedience. That message is reinforced by a theophany in which Joshua encounters the angelic commander of Yahweh's army.

When the invasion finally begins, the siege of Jericho is just as ritualistic as preparations for war had been. The battle of Jericho stands at the center of Israel's conquest stories and functions as a paradigm for the conquest as a whole. The hallmark of this story is Israel's obedience to Yahweh. The deity issues detailed commands that Joshua relays and the people follow. This threefold repetition of the battle plan makes the account rather tedious for readers, but it also underscores the fidelity of Joshua and Israel. The battle is won not by military superiority or stratagem but by a divine act on behalf of an obedient people. Israel's forces simply promenade around the city with the ark of the covenant and seven trumpet-blowing priests. The excessive repetition of the number seven in this story accentuates the ritual nature of the siege. After the procession is enacted seven times on the seventh day, a shout brings down the city walls, allowing Israel to charge ahead without resistance.

Joshua commands that the captured city of Jericho along with its inhabitants and their possessions be "devoted to [Yahweh] for destruction" (Josh. 6:17-19). Modern readers may be disturbed by the claim that Yahweh took sides in a military conflict and enabled the wholesale slaughter of Jericho's population. This account presupposes an ideology of **holy war** that envisions God as a divine warrior who leads Israel in battle (CD Special Topics IA.2 and IA.3). Such a perspective is even more evident in other conquest stories. For example, one later report actually portrays Yahweh hurling deadly hailstones upon Israel's enemies (Josh. 10:8-14).

The biblical conquest tradition assumes that, although Israel cooperates in battle, it is Yahweh who gives the victory. For that reason, spoils of war rightly belong to the deity. A practice of holy war called the **ban** (Hebrew *herem*) requires the total eradication of an enemy population and, at times, the dedication of its captured wealth to the deity. Once dedicated to Yahweh, these items would be forfeited by the victors and removed from common use. These rules of holy war are spelled out in Deuteronomy 20, which recommends a strict application of the ban during the conquest of Canaan.

The book of Joshua reinforces the seriousness of this requirement with the story of Achan, who violates the ban at Jericho by retaining part of the spoil for himself (Josh. 7). Achan's sin has consequences for all of Israel. Joshua's forces suffer an embarrassing setback in the next battle even though reconnaissance had suggested that Ai would prove an easy target. Whereas obedience to the laws' requirements had led to victory against the might of Jericho, disobedience resulted in defeat in a lesser battle. The story of Achan provides an object lesson in the results of lawbreaking. The invasion of Canaan cannot resume until the offender has been discovered and eliminated, along with his family and possessions. Achan's household is subjected to the ban he had violated.

Readers may well be confused when a few chapters later the Israelites are allowed to keep livestock and spoil with no dire consequences (Josh. 8:2, 27). Strangely, they are permitted to do the very thing for which Achan had just been executed! Outside of the Jericho/Ai account, the ban is limited to human captives (Josh. 11:14), and even this rule is not rigorously enforced. The asylum extended to Rahab certainly violated the terms of the ban as it is strictly interpreted in Deuteronomy 20. Rahab, the faithful outsider, saves herself and her household, whereas Achan, the faithless Israelite, is executed along with his family. Not only did Rahab demonstrate faith in Israel's deity, the crimson cord used to mark her window recalls the symbolism of Passover (Josh. 2:18). Danger bypasses the inhabitants of her house because of the crimson cord, just as the Israelites who marked their doors with blood were spared the devastation of the tenth plague. Rahab essentially becomes a new Israel.

Another exception to the ban is made for the inhabitants of Gibeon, who trick Israel into sparing their lives. The rules of holy war allow the formation of treaties with people from distant towns, who would then become Israel's servants. However, no treaties may be formed with the inhabitants of Canaan, who must be annihilated lest they tempt Israel to sin (Deut. 20:10-18). The Gibeonites fool Joshua by disguising themselves as well-worn travelers from a distant land. Once the truth of their origin is discovered they, like Rahab, are protected by the terms of a sworn oath. Ultimately the fates of Rahab and Gibeon are determined by their professions of faith in Yahweh and their willingness to submit to the inevitability of Israel's conquest. In contrast, resistant outsiders and even disobedient insiders (like Achan) are eliminated under the ban.

The remaining conquest stories describe defensive campaigns against two coalitions of kings, one in the south (Josh. 10) and another in the north (Josh. 11). Because these kings and their subjects offer resistance, Joshua leaves no survivors. Chilling refrains insist that Israel's invading force left "no one who breathed." In language recalling the exodus account, the narrator even attributes their resistance to Yahweh's design. Their hearts, like the heart of Pharaoh, are hardened so that they would face Israel in battle where they could be mercilessly annihilated (Josh. 11:20).

Modern readers may be disturbed by the almost gleeful violence of Israel's conquest tradition. This reaction can be eased, at least in part, by the realization that the Former Prophets are not straightforward historical reports. We must remember that the writers and editors of the conquest stories were not primarily concerned with preserving a record of past events. In fact, most scholars agree that the conquest traditions *do not* accurately represent the process of Israel's emergence in Canaan (CD Special Topic IA.4). As we shall see in the next section, tensions and outright contradictions in the biblical account should make us question the historical accuracy of these texts. To better understand the conquest tradition preserved in Joshua, readers should consider who would tell such stories and for what purpose—questions to which we shall return in the Interlude of this chapter.

Preliminary Exercise IA.1: A Closer Look at the Conquest Tradition
Preliminary Exercise IA.2: Conquest and Holy War
Map IA.1: Significant Sites in the Conquest Tradition
Special Topic IA.1: Rahab (Josh. 2; 6:15-25)
Special Topic IA.2: Religion and War
Special Topic IA.3: The Idea of America as a "New Israel"
Special Topic IA.4: Was the Conquest a Historical Event?

Land and Covenant Renewal (Josh. 13–15; 22–24; CD Preliminary Exercise IB.1)

Most readers notice an abrupt change of tone and subject matter between the twelfth and thirteenth chapters of Joshua. Whereas the first twelve chapters were organized around the themes of preparation and conquest, the second half of the book is occupied with apportioning the land among the Israelite tribes (CD Map IB.1). Later chapters also reveal a dramatically different perspective on the conquest of Canaan from that found in chapters 1–12. Chapter 12 drew the account of conquest to a triumphant close by listing the kings defeated by Moses and Joshua. Although selective, this summary of the invasion reinforces the book's earlier claim that the Israelites had captured the whole land, leaving no survivors aside from Gibeon and Rahab (Josh. 11:19-23). With these words still ringing in our ears, chapter 13 comes as a bit of a surprise. Here we discover that large regions within the borders of Canaan are *not* under Israelite control. The list of unconquered territories in chapter 13 contrasts ironically with the catalog of defeated kings in chapter 12.

As Canaan is divided among the tribes, many details continue to undermine the description of conquest found in Joshua 1–12. For example, the region around Hebron is given to Caleb as a reward for his earlier faithfulness (Num. 13–14; Deut. 1:35-40). Yet, strangely, this territory is still occupied by the Anakim, whom Caleb must drive out using his own forces (Josh. 14:6-15; 15:13-19). He later offers his daughter in marriage to anyone who can defeat the inhabitants of Debir. Attentive readers might well wonder how these cities had survived Joshua's invasion intact, especially since the conquest tradition had reported that the Anakim had already been wiped out in both Hebron and Debir (Josh. 11:21-22). Moreover, why does Caleb seem to command his own independent forces when all of Israel was supposedly still united under Joshua's military leadership?

Similar references to surviving non-Israelites and independent tribal warfare appear throughout these chapters (Josh. 13:13; 15:63; 16:10; 17:12-13). In fact, the tribe of Dan faces so much resistance that it cannot settle in its assigned territory and must relocate from the coastal plain to the far north (Josh. 19:40-48). In stark contrast to Israel's unqualified success in the conquest tradition, the allotment texts suggest a somewhat unsuccessful attempt at conquest and a persistent lack of unity among the Israelite tribes.

That impression is reinforced by an intertribal conflict between Israelites living on either side of the Jordan (Josh. 22). The eastern tribes construct a large altar beside the Jordan on its western shore, an action interpreted by the western tribes as a blatant violation of Mosaic law. They charge the altar builders with worshiping Yahweh in the wrong place, a concern that echoes Deuteronomy (Deut. 12:1-11; 14:23-26; 16:5-6). Civil war is averted only by careful negotiations between the eastern tribes and an investigative team led by Phineas, grandson of Aaron.

In their defense, the offending tribes deny any intention of sacrificing upon this altar. Instead, they claim that it was built as a memorial to remind the western tribes of their common bond. The need for such a reminder is apparent within the story itself. Observant readers might notice several details suggesting that the eastern territory and its Israelite inhabitants are not regarded as a legitimate part of Israel. For example, the narrator often refers to this region as "the land of Gilead" in contrast to "the land of Canaan." The altar is described as standing on the frontier of Israelite territory even though it is actually between the eastern and western tribes. Moreover, the tribes who take offense at the altar are called "the people of Israel" and "the whole assembly." The delegation of Phineas even goes so far as to suggest that the eastern side of the river might be unclean (Josh. 22:19). This internal crisis hints that the tribes of Israel are not as unified as Joshua 1–12 had suggested.

Although Joshua is conspicuously absent from the Phineas delegation, he does dominate the last two chapters of the book that bears his name. The book concludes with Israel's now aged general delivering a farewell address (Josh. 23) and presiding over a covenant renewal ceremony (Josh. 24). In contrast to chapters 1–12, Joshua's farewell speech assumes that indigenous Canaanites still exist within the land. He interprets their continued presence as a test of Israel's loyalty to Yahweh and warns that apostasy, intermarriage, and compromise will stall the continued conquest effort. Conversely, obedience to the covenant will make Israel invincible. Readers can easily recognize these twin claims as an expression of Deuteronomic theology. Israel's tenure in the land depends upon their continued fidelity to the covenant expressed in the law of Moses.

Joshua next convenes a covenant ratification ceremony at Shechem. After rehearsing the mighty acts that God had already performed on behalf of Israel, he calls on the people to choose between allegiance to Yahweh and service to other gods. No compromise between these two options will be allowed. The text emphasizes that Israel freely chose to serve Yahweh even though they were clearly warned that transgressions would have dire consequences. Readers are thus prepared for the twists and turns that Israel's journey will take in the books that follow.

The book of Joshua ends with three short notices. The first and last of these appendices are obituaries for Joshua and Eleazar, son of Aaron. Although the death of the priest receives the last words within the book, Joshua's obituary is more elaborate. Upon his death, Israel's general is at last honored with the Mosaic title "servant of [Yahweh]" and praised for faithful administration. Between these death notices, the narrator reports the burial of Joseph's bones in the land of Canaan. This detail reminds readers that Israel finally possesses (more or less) the land promised to their ancestors. However, framing the burial of Joseph's bones with the obituaries of Israel's trusted leaders introduces a note of uncertainty. Once again Israel faces an unknown future, bereft of human leadership.

Preliminary Exercise IB.1: Inconsistencies in the Biblical Depiction of Conquest
Map IB.1: Tribal Territories in Canaan

The Judges Period (Judg. 1–21; CD Preliminary Exercises IC.1 and IC.2)

Many readers of the Former Prophets either skim through or skip over the rather tedious allotment texts that we discussed in the previous section. The book of Judges takes these readers by surprise. Joshua 1–12 depicted the conquest as a rapid and totally successful military operation completed by unified Israel under the leadership of one general, but Judges presents a radically different perspective. This book begins by emphasizing Israel's failure to conquer all of the land. Throughout Judges, individual tribes are engaged in ongoing struggles to claim and maintain their footholds in Canaan long after the career of Joshua. In contrast to the smooth transition of authority from Moses to Joshua, no clear successor will emerge in Judges. Instead this book depicts the chaos that results from the absence of reliable leadership. If the allotment texts had suggested a lack of unity among the tribes during Joshua's lifetime, Judges gives the impression of almost total disarray after his death.

Observant readers might be surprised to discover that Joshua actually dies twice in the opening chapters of Judges (1:1; 2:6-9). This awkward repetition suggests the presence of two separate introductions that may have originated with different authors. As the book now stands, readers first encounter a military survey reviewing the exploits of several individual tribes (Judg. 1:1–2:5). Much of this material is borrowed and adapted from the allotment texts of Joshua 14–19. In Judges, however, clear preference is shown for the southern tribe of Judah, which receives more attention and meets with more military success than the other tribes until finally outmatched by Canaanites equipped with iron chariots.

As the narrator's gaze moves northward, tribes meet with less and less success against their enemies. Each campaign is depicted as a greater failure than the last until the survey ends with an embarrassing rout of

Dan at the hands of Amorites. In all, the narrator identifies twenty-one towns in Canaan that remained unconquered. Whereas the allotment texts in Joshua had usually attributed military failures to inability ("they could not drive them out"), Judges suggests that the northern tribes were simply unwilling to complete the conquest ("they did not drive them out"). This impression is reinforced by repeated claims that Canaanites were pressed into forced labor, suggesting that the Israelites could have driven them out of the land had they chosen to do so.

Overall, Judges' first introduction depicts a progressive deterioration of the conquest effort after Joshua's demise. Although the arrangement of the text places a larger share of the blame on the northern tribes, the survey concludes with a judgment against all of Israel voiced by the angel of Yahweh. The angel contrasts Yahweh's unfailing fidelity with Israel's willful failure to complete the conquest. As a result of their accommodation and compromise, they are doomed to be continually tempted by these surviving nations and their gods.

The book's second introduction focuses on Israel's penchant for worshiping other gods (Judg. 2:6–3:6). Whereas the military survey had distinguished *geographically* between relatively successful southern tribes and less successful northern tribes, this text distinguishes *temporally* between the faithful generation of Joshua and the faithless generation that follows. The failings of the post-Joshua generation are described as following a cyclical pattern, often called the **judges cycle**. This repeated sequence of events involves five crucial elements, which readers will recognize again and again in the chapters that follow:

1. Apostasy: Israel does what is evil in the sight of Yahweh by worshiping other gods.

2. Punishment: Yahweh becomes angry with the Israelites and allows them to be overrun by their enemies. In accordance with Deuteronomic theology, unfaithfulness to the covenant results in national defeat.

3. Cry and Response: When Israel "cries out" on account of their oppression, Yahweh takes pity and raises up a deliverer to rescue them. Deuteronomic theology is here tempered by divine mercy, which provides an unmerited second chance.

4. Deliverance: The deliverer, or **judge** (CD Special Topic IC.1), unites the tribes in a defensive campaign to oust the oppressor and restore the people to worship of Yahweh.

5. Momentary Rest: During the lifetime of a judge, Israel remains faithful and the land has rest from war. When the judge dies, the Israelites revert to apostasy and the cycle begins again.

Judges' double introduction provides readers with an interpretive lens for viewing the book as a whole. The juxtaposition of these texts connects the stalled conquest effort (the *external* symptoms) to Israel's infidelity to Yahweh (the *internal* problem). The double introduction also sets readers' expectations for the shape of the book as a whole. When read on its own, the military survey conveys a steady decline in Israel's fortunes (Judg. 1:1–2:5), and the indictment of the post-Joshua generation suggests a cyclical pattern (Judg. 2:6–3:6). The combined introduction creates an impression that the young nation is caught in a downward spiral, an impression that will be confirmed in the chapters that follow.

These chapters contain accounts of twelve individual deliverers—six **major judges,** who are featured in extended narratives, and six **minor judges**, who appear only in brief notices (CD Chart IC.1). Attentive readers will observe a gradual decline in the quality of Israel's leaders throughout the book. Early judges are models of success and faithfulness under whose leadership Israel remains loyal to the covenant and safe from external threats. As the storyline progresses, however, so-called deliverers increasingly begin to pursue personal vendettas and self-interests. Later accounts tend to focus less on the deity and more on the life of the judge. At the same time, the judges cycle itself begins to break down (CD Chart IC.2). The nation's apostasy becomes more determined, the resulting period of oppression becomes longer and more severe, and God appears less and less inclined to provide a deliverer. Later judges are either unable or unwilling to unite the tribes in defensive warfare. Internal conflicts increase until, near the end of the book, the nation is locked in devastating civil war.

The first judge whom readers encounter (Judg. 3:7-11) does exactly what a deliverer is supposed to do according to the expectations set by the judges cycle. Having been raised up and empowered by the deity, Othniel mobilizes and successfully leads the tribes in defensive warfare against Cushan-rishathaim (meaning "dark, double wicked"). The rather unlikely name of this villain cautions against reading the story as a historical tale. In fact, the compact narrative of Othniel is little more than a minimal elaboration of the basic judges cycle that combines formulaic phrases with a few extra details. Yet this stereotypical account plays a crucial role in the book. Othniel provides the standard by which later judges are to be evaluated. The period of oppression in this account is limited to a mere eight years, God's response to Israel's cries is immediate, and the peace Othniel establishes endures for a respectable forty years.

The narratives of the other major judges are much more elaborate. Clearly, editors have attempted to fit inherited stories into the predetermined mold of the judges cycle by adding formulaic phrases to the beginning and end of each account. In their original form, these stories likely celebrated the exploits of local heroes rather than an unbroken succession of national leaders. It is easy to imagine that the entertaining adventures of Ehud, for example, would have been recited with gusto within the tribe of Benjamin long before this account was incorporated into the book of Judges.

The well-told tale of this left-handed Benjaminite warrior lingers with relish over ambiguous words and grotesque details. Ehud himself is an unlikely hero because the ancient world viewed left-handed people as misfits (*Benjamin* ironically means "son of the right hand"). Nevertheless, he cleverly assassinates the Moabite king and leads a successful assault against Israel's disoriented enemies. Ehud tricks the obese Eglon (whose name is related to the word *ēgel*, meaning "fatted calf") by claiming to deliver a divine *dābār* (an ambiguous Hebrew term that can mean either "word" or "thing"). Eglon expects a divine message, but he instead receives a "thing" in the form of a two-edged sword that is engulfed by his corpulent body. The royal guards do not immediately discover the dead king because the contents of his colon release upon death. The resulting smell leads them to believe that he is simply taking his time on the toilet. This undignified description of the Moabite king surely would have delighted Israelite audiences!

The story of Deborah actually appears twice in Judges, first in narrative form and then as a poetic victory song (CD Special Topic IC.2). Like the left-handed Ehud, the female Deborah is an unlikely deliverer in the context of the ancient world. In fact, none of the characters in this story exactly fits the model of a judge-deliverer. The narrator describes Deborah as both a judge and a prophetess, while the storyline portrays her as an arbiter of disputes. Rather than leading Israel into battle herself, she calls Barak to act as general and accompanies him only at his (cowardly?) insistence. Yet the final victory over Israel's enemy goes to neither of them, but to an even more unlikely person—Jael, the wife of a foreigner, who slays the Canaanite general Sisera. Because these three characters share the usual functions of a judge, none of them dominates the story at the expense of the deity.

Yahweh continues to dominate the narrative in the beginning of the Gideon account. This time the cries of the oppressed Israelites evoke divine frustration instead of immediate deliverance. Yet God still provides a deliverer for this wayward people. Gideon's call story, which appears to be modeled on the call of Moses, raises readers' expectations that he might prove to be a judge who can wield Mosaic authority.

However, this expectation is quickly thwarted. Like Moses, Gideon is in hiding when called to deliver Israel, protests his worthiness, and is reassured by miracles. However, unlike Moses, Gideon's reluctance and need for reassurance continue even after he accepts his call (Judg. 6:27, 36-40; 7:9-14).

Later in the story Gideon begins to act out of self-interest. He introduces the battle cry "For [Yahweh] and for Gideon!" despite Yahweh's concern that victory not be deemed a human achievement (Judg. 7:2-8). After delivering Israel, Gideon pursues the Midianite kings across the Jordan to repay a personal vendetta and even exacts retribution against the inhabitants of two Israelite towns who had refused to supply his army. If the narrative suggests that Gideon has overstepped his authority as a military leader, it even more clearly depicts his religious failings. At the end of his career, he crafts a golden cult object for the Israelites to worship.

Although he piously refuses an offer to establish a dynasty (Judg. 8:22-23), Gideon does act like a king in many ways. Not only does he collect both wives and gold in direct contrast to the Deuteronomic ideal of kingship (Deut. 17:14-20), he also names one of his many sons Abimelech, meaning "my father is king." Readers are left wondering whether Gideon's public rejection of monarchic power was sincere. After his death, his worst qualities are embodied and magnified in this half-Canaanite son, who conspires to seize the kingship his father had refused. Liberally shedding blood to consolidate his power and defend his personal honor, Abimelech provides a cautionary tale about the dangers of monarchy. Suspicion of kings is eloquently expressed in Jotham's fable (Judg. 9:7-15), which suggests that anyone who desires the office cannot be worthy of it! The narrator revels in Abimelech's ignoble death and views it as just retribution for his unrestrained lust for power.

In the overall structure of Judges, Gideon functions as a transitional character who is in some ways effective and in other ways unsuccessful

STUDYING THE OLD TESTAMENT

and unappealing. The remaining two judges—Jephthah and Samson—have few if any redeeming qualities and neither are able to establish lasting peace. As the quality of Israel's leaders deteriorates, the judges cycle itself begins to collapse. At the beginning of Jephthah's story, Israel is accused not simply of apostasy but of worshiping almost every god other than Yahweh (Judg. 10:6). As the nation's sin worsens, the deity's patience continues to wear thin. Before Yahweh decides to act, the people of Gilead appoint their own unlikely deliverer.

Jephthah is portrayed as the son of a prostitute, the family outcast, and the leader of a band of outlaws. His motivation for delivering Gilead, a desire for personal power, is reminiscent of Abimelech. Although Jephthah eventually receives God's spirit and defeats the Ammonites, in the course of battle he utters a rash and unnecessary vow obligating him to sacrifice whomever or whatever he meets first when he returns home. Tragically, that sacrifice turns out to be his daughter and only child.

Despite his initial military success, Jephthah is not portrayed as a sympathetic character or an able leader. Unlike earlier judges, who had at least limited success uniting Israel in defensive warfare, Jephthah leads only a single clan within the tribe of Manasseh. Intertribal conflict had been narrowly averted under Gideon (Judg. 8:1-3). Because of Jephthah's lack of diplomacy, civil war now erupts between Gilead and Ephraim, resulting in the deaths of forty-two thousand Israelites. The basis for identifying the enemy in this conflict is a slight difference in regional dialects (Judg. 12:5-6).

By the time readers meet Samson, it has become clear that Israel is in an era of decline. In this final round of the judges cycle, the stubbornly disobedient Israelites do not even cry out to the deity. Nevertheless, the angel of Yahweh announces the birth of a deliverer to an elderly childless couple. As Gideon's call had echoed the call of Moses, this annunciation recalls the story of Abraham and Sarah. Again the expectations of readers are raised. Will this birth signify a new beginning for Abraham's descendants? Once more, such hopes are disappointed.

Samson flaunts almost every expectation of a righteous judge that readers bring to this story. As a Nazirite, he is consecrated to Yahweh and obligated to abstain from wine, unclean foods, and haircuts (Num. 6:1-21). Yet he systematically breaks every one of these vows. Nor does Samson demonstrate any concern for the deliverance of Israel. Rather than uniting his people in a defensive war against their enemies, he moves from one romantic/sexual entanglement to another, often with Philistine women. When he does strike out against the Philistines, he does so on his own for personal vengeance. His dalliances eventually lead to his capture and death when he stupidly betrays the secret of his strength to his overtly treacherous paramour, Delilah.

The colorful story of Samson can be read as a comment on the state of Israel at the end of the Judges period. As Israel claimed descent from Abraham and Sarah, Samson was also born to elderly, barren parents. Both Israel and Samson are obligated by an agreement that Yahweh had formed with a previous generation. Yet Samson violates the requirements of his Nazirite vow, just as Israel rejected the requirements of their covenant with the deity. Just as Samson becomes entangled with a series of foreign women, Israel continually "lusts after" other gods. Readers are left wondering whether it is too late for Israel and if, like Samson, the nation will also meet with a tragic end.

The concluding chapters of Judges do nothing to alleviate readers' apprehensions. Like the book's introduction, the conclusion also consists of two parts, but the ending moves from the internal problem (religious corruption) to its external symptoms (civil war and social chaos). The tale of Micah (Judg. 17–18) illustrates the extent of Israel's apostasy in which even a Levite priest is implicated (CD Special Topic IC.3). Likewise, the violence perpetrated on another Levite's concubine and its intertribal consequences (Judg. 19–21) illustrate the extent of Israel's social decline (CD Chart IC.3). At the beginning of Judges, unfaithfulness had resulted in Israel's inability to oust a foreign enemy. At the book's conclusion, the enemy is now internal—increasing tribal disunity results in civil war and social chaos.

The concluding chapters of Judges are punctuated by a repeated refrain: "In those days there was no king in Israel; all the people did what was right in their own eyes" (Judg. 17:6; 21:25; cf. 18:1; 19:1). Biblical editors clearly intended these words to shape readers' perception of the Judges period. Yet modern interpreters often disagree over what this refrain might mean. In light of the antimonarchic sentiments expressed in the Gideon story, it is possible to read the refrain as a positive statement that Israel is governed by God rather than a tyrannical monarch like Abimelech. However, this interpretation seems out of touch with the more pessimistic tone of the book as a whole. Given Judges' overall structure and rather chaotic ending, the refrain more likely represents a negative evaluation of the period. Readers are left wondering whether Israel would not be better off with a king after all.

Preliminary Exercise IC.1: The Judges Cycle
Preliminary Exercise IC.2: The Dating Game
Chart IC.1: The Twelve Judges
Chart IC.2: The Disintegration of the Judges Cycle
Chart IC.3: Women in Judges
Special Topic IC.1: What Is a Judge?
Special Topic IC.2: The Song of Deborah (Judg. 5)
Special Topic IC.3: Micah and the Danites (Judg. 17–18)

INTERLUDE:
THE LITERARY ORIGINS
OF THE FORMER PROPHETS

The Nature of the Text
(CD Preliminary Exercise IIA.1)

Now that we have observed a significant portion of the Former
Prophets firsthand, we should pause to consider possible clues
about the literary origins of this material. We have seen that the
story of Israel's national journey does not proceed seamlessly from
beginning to end any more than did the Torah. The Former
Prophets also contain diverse traditions that sometimes conflict
with one another. In some stories, Israel faces her enemies as a
united nation and meets with unqualified success. Elsewhere, the
tribes battle independently, sometimes even fighting one another,
and achieve limited success at best. Some traditions claim that
the previous inhabitants of Canaan are utterly exterminated,
leaving the land uncontested. Other texts depict Israel surrounded and outmatched by competing groups. Given these
observations, it is tempting simply to guess that, like the Torah,
these books are also composed of several once-independent documents. However, before jumping to any such conclusion, we
should examine the evidence more closely.

One important clue to the literary origins of the Former
Prophets should be obvious to any attentive reader. From time to
time, the narrative actually refers by name to outside sources,
advising readers who want more information to look there. This
happens infrequently at first but increases in frequency in 1–2
Kings (for example, Josh. 10:13; 2 Sam. 1:18; 1 Kgs. 11:41; 14:19,
29; 15:7, 23, 31; 16:5, 14, 20, 27). The Book of Jashar, the Book
of the Acts of Solomon, and the Annals of the Kings of Israel
and Judah have not been preserved, but we know that they
existed because they are mentioned here. This evidence suggests

that at least part of the Former Prophets was created by one or more compilers who relied upon and pieced together inherited traditions.

This often appears to be the case even when an outside source is not explicitly cited. For instance, in Judges we observed that a recurring narrative pattern (the judges cycle) is imposed, sometimes with difficulty, on diverse stories about local leaders. This suggests that these stories were inherited, rather than composed, by the editor(s) of Judges. Elsewhere, thematically linked blocks of material may also indicate inherited traditions that have been secondarily incorporated into their present context. The conquest tradition (Josh. 1–12), the ark narrative (1 Sam. 4–6), the rise of David (1 Sam. 16–31), and the succession narrative (2 Sam. 9–20; 1 Kgs. 1–2) are a few of the materials that compilers assembled into this longer account of Israel's journey from conquest to exile.

Because these diverse traditions represent various perspectives, compiling them produced tensions that are still apparent in the text. The opposition between total and partial depictions of the conquest has already been noted. Likewise, conflicting attitudes toward kingship are juxtaposed in Judges and Samuel. Some accounts within these books view monarchy as an unnecessary accommodation to non-Israelite customs and a rejection of divine authority (Judg. 9:7-20; 1 Sam. 8). But other traditions view monarchy as a practical necessity meeting with divine approval (Judg. 21:25; 1 Sam. 9:15-17; 2 Sam. 7).

An even more fundamental tension results from the combination of Mosaic and Davidic covenant traditions. The Mosaic or Sinai covenant, especially as it is interpreted in Deuteronomy and the Former Prophets, makes Israel's security in the land conditional upon her continued fidelity to Yahweh and observance of the law. This perspective is presupposed throughout much of the Former Prophets and is cited to explain the eventual tragic outcome of Israel's national journey (2 Kgs. 17; 21:10-15). In contrast, the Davidic covenant promises unconditionally that David and his descendants (called **Davidides**) will forever sit upon the throne in Jerusalem (1 Sam. 7). This guarantee is repeatedly cited in 1–2 Kings to explain why David's descendants retain the throne despite the fact that almost all of them commit apostasy or otherwise worship inappropriately. Any adequate theory of literary origins must account for how and why these two conflicting covenant traditions were combined in the Former Prophets.

In spite of the tensions that are still apparent in the final form of the text, readers can easily trace a coherent storyline across these six books. Editor(s) successfully crafted a new interpretive account of Israel's history by selecting and shaping diverse inherited materials. This is no small literary accomplishment! Attentive readers can still detect much of the literary "glue" that the editor(s) used to hold together these assorted traditions. A prophecy-fulfillment schema, for example, stretches across this sprawling account (CD Chart IIA.1). Prophets frequently arise who pronounce God's judgment on disobedient Israel or her sinful leaders. They also warn of the consequences of continued disobedience that are presumably avoidable through repentance (1 Kgs. 21:27-29; 2 Kgs. 17:13-14). Yet these warnings are rarely heeded. Later texts confirm that the words of the prophets were indeed trustworthy and reinforce the impression that Israel's history is driven by God's will.

The prophetic word fails in only one case throughout these six books as they now stand. The unconditional promise of an eternal Davidic dynasty is guaranteed by the prophet Nathan (2 Sam. 7:14-16) and repeatedly confirmed by claims that less worthy successors retained the throne of Judah "for David's sake" (1 Kgs. 11:12-13; 15:4; 2 Kgs. 8:19). Yet the reign of David's house ultimately does end at the conclusion of 2 Kings. Any adequate theory explaining the literary origins of the Former Prophets must account for the presence of this one great failure of the prophetic word.

Another form of literary glue holding together the Former Prophets is a series of reflective pauses that summarize Israel's history-so-far and offer theological commentary (CD Chart IIA.2). These pauses are strategically placed at critical junctures of the storyline to mark significant events or transitions between

STUDYING THE OLD TESTAMENT

historical eras. They often take the form of speeches placed on the lips of an Israelite leader or the deity (Josh. 1; 23; 1 Sam. 12; 1 Kgs. 8:14-61) but may also appear as the words of a narrator (Josh. 12; Judg. 2:11-23; 2 Kgs. 17:7-23). Common to all of these speeches and narrative summaries are assurances of divine blessing contingent on obedience and warnings of dire consequences for disobedience. Readers should easily recognize these twin claims as an expression of Deuteronomic theology.

In fact, the book of Deuteronomy appears to stand in a special relationship to the Former Prophets, with which it shares many characteristic expressions and concerns (CD Chart IIA.3). The book of Joshua begins at precisely the point at which Deuteronomy had ended, and both books are preoccupied with the succession and legitimacy of Joshua. Likewise, the procedures for holy war, the limitation of kingly prerogatives, the importance of prophecy, and the imperative of centralized worship are derived from Deuteronomy and further developed within the Former Prophets.

Perhaps the most significant motif linking Deuteronomy with the Former Prophets is the book of the law of Moses. Deuteronomy depicts Moses recording the laws of the covenant in a book that is deposited by the ark for safekeeping so that it can periodically be read aloud to the people. In Joshua, Israel and her leaders are repeatedly charged with strict obedience to a Mosaic law book. Explicit references to this book then become rare until it is dramatically rediscovered near the end of 2 Kings and becomes the basis of Josiah's Reform. Because this reform mirrors the concerns of Deuteronomic law, scholars have long believed that the book of the law rediscovered by Josiah was actually an early form of the book of Deuteronomy. Especially emphasized in both Deuteronomic law and Josiah's Reform are the requirements of exclusive fidelity to Yahweh and centralized worship. Throughout 1–2 Kings, almost all rulers of Israel and Judah are condemned for failing to meet these two requirements.

The parallel histories of the twin kingdoms culminate in two climactic events, the fall of Israel (2 Kgs. 17) and the reform of Josiah (2 Kgs. 22:1–23:25). Readers can hardly be surprised by the first climax, given the uniformly dark picture that the Former Prophets paint of the northern kingdom. Israel's fall to Assyria is attributed to repeated apostasy and the "sin of Jeroboam" (worshiping at Dan and Bethel rather than Jerusalem). Although Judah is presented more favorably than Israel, its history is also marked by rulers who tolerate apostasy and noncentralized worship. Readers might expect a similar fate for the southern kingdom were it not for the Davidic covenant and its promise that a Davidide would always rule in Jerusalem. When Josiah appears, rediscovers the Mosaic law book, and begins his reform, it appears that disaster has been averted for Judah. Yet in an awkwardly explained lapse of Deuteronomic theology (2 Kgs. 23:26-27), the faultless obedience of Josiah does not result in divine blessing and security in the land. The Former Prophets end, not with the upbeat climax of Josiah's Reform, but with the somber anticlimax of Judah's inevitable fall. Any adequate theory of literary origins must account for the importance this history attaches to Josiah's short-lived and ultimately unsuccessful reform.

To summarize, our observations as careful readers of the Former Prophets suggest that one or more editors intentionally selected, arranged, and shaped diverse inherited traditions to form this history. These traditions are often, but not always, cited explicitly. Such a theory of literary origins would account for the presence of diverse materials that often stand in tension with one another. Attentive readers can also detect the literary glue its editor(s) used to unify inherited traditions, including a prophecy-fulfillment schema and strategically placed reflective pauses. Furthermore, readers should recognize that a close relationship exists between Deuteronomy and the Former Prophets, which share distinctive vocabulary, interests, and theological perspective.

Our observations have also raised several questions that any adequate theory of the Former Prophets' literary origins should be able to answer. How and why were the conflicting covenant traditions associated with Moses and David combined within this history? Why do these books, which normally stress the reliability of the prophetic word, also include its one great failure—

Nathan's unfulfilled promise of an eternal, unconditional Davidic dynasty? And finally, why does this account of Israel's national journey attach so much importance to Josiah's short-lived and ultimately unsuccessful reform?

Preliminary Exercise IIA.1: Clues of Literary Origins
Chart IIA.1: A Prophecy-Fulfillment Schema
Chart IIA.2: Reflective Pauses in the Former Prophets
Chart IIA.3: Deuteronomy and the Former Prophets

A Deuteronomistic History

We are now ready to consider specific theories that attempt to explain the literary origins of the Former Prophets. Readers should be forewarned that this is perhaps the most highly debated topic in all of biblical studies! Yet, for over half a century, this debate has been dominated by a single theory, the **Deuteronomistic History** hypothesis. Nevertheless, we should keep in mind that biblical scholarship is an ongoing conversation in which no theory is sacrosanct but all are subject to ongoing critique and refinement. The value of any hypothesis dealing with the literary origins of a text rests in its ability to make sense of observations made by careful readers.

Readers had long noticed the prevalence of Deuteronomic language and theology throughout the Former Prophets. In 1943, a biblical scholar named Martin Noth offered a new theory to explain the obvious connections between Deuteronomy and the books that follow. Noth suggested that Deuteronomy, Joshua, Judges, Samuel, and Kings comprised a single literary unit produced by one individual. He coined the terms Deuteronomistic History to describe this unit and **Deuteronomistic Historian** (in shorthand, **Dtr**) to describe its producer.

Noth also noticed that Deuteronomic features were most prevalent in passages containing narrative summaries and reflective speeches by major characters (for example, Josh. 1; 12; 23; Judg. 2; 1 Sam. 12; 1 Kgs. 8; 2 Kgs. 17). He viewed these texts as original compositions by the Deuteronomistic Historian that were intended to unify the storyline and guide readers in interpreting it. Noth also believed that Dtr authored significant parts of Deuteronomy, setting the legal code now found at its center in the context of a speech delivered by Moses. According to the Deuteronomistic History hypothesis, the book of Deuteronomy is both the preface and interpretive key to the Former Prophets.

Although Noth argued that the Deuteronomistic History was the work of a single individual, he also recognized the many tensions within these books. Why would a single author describe the conquest as both complete and incomplete? Why would Dtr both favor and oppose monarchy? These observations led him to view the Deuteronomistic Historian as both an author and a compiler of inherited traditions. Noth assumed that Dtr altered inherited materials as little as possible, allowing conflicting traditions to stand side by side.

According to this hypothesis, the majority of this history was constructed from diverse materials that were carefully selected and arranged to form a continuous story. Dtr divided the story into four major periods: (1) the generation of Moses, (2) the generation of Joshua, (3) the era of judges, and (4) the era of the kings. This extended account begins with the triumphs of an obedient people and ends with the exile of a stubbornly disobedient nation. In the overall shape of the Deuteronomistic History, Noth discovered what he believed was its ultimate purpose: to explain the nation's tragic fate as the result of her willful and repeated disobedience to the covenant. According to Noth, this was a pessimistic account of unrelieved and irreversible doom that held out no hope for a brighter future.

Noth reasoned that the author/editor of this account must have lived during the exile. More specifically, he assumed that Dtr worked in Babylon shortly after the last event that the history relates, the release of Jehoiachin from Babylonian prison around 561 B.C.E. (2 Kgs. 25:27-30). Having recently witnessed the devastation of the temple and the end of the Judean monarchy, Dtr attempts to explain why these events had occurred. From the perspective of this exilic historian, the present dilemma was the culmination of the nation's ever-intensifying decline and a deserved punishment from a just deity.

In the ongoing discussion that is biblical scholarship, the Deuteronomistic History hypothesis has been lauded for explaining many features of the Former Prophets. Yet, although some aspects of this theory gained widespread acceptance, other elements have generated dissension and debate. For instance, many biblical scholars question whether this history was constructed for an entirely negative purpose. Why would anyone go to the trouble of composing a history of Israel simply to illustrate that the exiles had gotten what they deserved? Did not the very act of creating an account of the nation's past presuppose that Israel also had a future that might benefit from the lessons of history? Some scholars sought evidence for a more positive intention within this work.

Gerhard von Rad (1947), for example, argued that alongside the undeniable theme of judgment ran a counterbalancing theme of grace. Noting the overarching prophecy-fulfillment schema in these books, he interpreted the entire history as a lesson in the reliability of Yahweh's word. Not only had the deity proclaimed judgment against Israel and Judah, Yahweh had also guaranteed an eternal and unconditional dynasty to David (2 Sam. 7). Von Rad contended that this promise was still valid for Dtr despite the reality of exile and that such optimism was evident in the way the history ended (2 Kgs. 25:27-30). The brief report of the Davidide Jehoiachin's release from Babylonian prison could be understood as an implicit source of hope for the exiles.

Hans Walter Wolff (1961) also argued that the history held out hope for Israel, but he did not find that hope in the Davidic covenant or in Jehoiachin's release as had von Rad. Wolff assumed that Yahweh's promises to David had been voided by Israel's disobedience to the Mosaic covenant. Instead, he highlighted the pattern of apostasy, punishment, repentance, and deliverance that recurs throughout these books. Wolff suggested that the history was composed to illustrate this pattern in Yahweh's previous dealings with Israel and to show the exilic community where they currently were in the cycle. Thus, according to Wolff, Dtr indirectly offered the possibility that repentance could once again result in deliverance.

Other scholars critiqued the Deuteronomistic History hypothesis for ignoring or inadequately explaining particular characteristics of the Former Prophets—most notably, the presence of the Davidic covenant and the prominence of Josiah. Why would an exilic historian, who had recently witnessed the end of the Judean monarchy, choose to accentuate the eternal, unconditional promise of a Davidic dynasty? Moreover, why would that exilic historian place so much emphasis upon the relatively short reign of Josiah and his ultimately unsuccessful reform? These questions suggested that the literary origins of the Deuteronomistic History were not as simple as Noth's hypothesis had originally supposed. More recent scholars have proposed more complex models of authorship and editing (CD Special Topic IIB.1).

One such proposal, offered by Frank Moore Cross (1973), began with the prominent role that Josiah plays in this history. Cross noted that this king receives more attention from the Deuteronomistic Historian than many others who reigned longer and accomplished more. Of all the rulers in Israel and Judah (including David), only Josiah is evaluated in wholly positive terms. Moreover, this relatively insignificant king is the only person in the whole biblical narrative who is anticipated by name in a prophetic oracle centuries before his birth (1 Kgs. 13:1-2). All of this suggested that Josiah was more than simply one important character within these books. Rather, much of the history seems to have been crafted with Josiah in mind and with the expectation that his reign would be longer and more successful than it actually turned out to be.

In light of such observations, Cross proposed that the bulk of the Deuteronomistic History was compiled during Josiah's reign (640–609 B.C.E.). This early edition of the history, which Cross labeled **Dtr**[1], reflected the optimism generated by Josiah's Reform and served as propaganda for his policies. However, when Josiah met with an unexpected fate (2 Kgs. 23:29-30) and Judah soon after fell to Babylon, this positive account no longer reflected the nation's experiences. Cross argued that a revised and updated edition of this history (**Dtr**[2]) was produced in the context of exile.

To the exilic edition he attributed the final chapters of 2 Kings and several earlier passages that he identified as later insertions (CD Chart IIB.1). The purpose of these revisions was to temper the optimism of the original Josianic edition and suggest that Judah's downfall had always been inevitable.

The revisions proposed by Cross to the classic Deuteronomistic History hypothesis have been widely, though not universally, accepted. The theory that this history was produced in two editions retains the strengths of Noth's original hypothesis while better explaining other features of the text. Not only has Cross accounted for the prominent role that Josiah plays in the Former Prophets, he has also explained the presence of one great prophetic failure in a collection that generally stresses the reliability of prophecy. Nathan's guarantee of an eternal, unconditional Davidic dynasty would have been included in the Josianic edition before that promise failed. The exilic edition could only attempt, however inadequately, to explain why the Judean monarchy ended in spite of this promise.

If Cross has provided a convincing explanation of literary origins, then we can conceive of the composition of Deuteronomy and the Former Prophets as a literary process with at least three important stages. The first stage reflects the formation of oral and written traditions that provide the building blocks of this history. At the second stage Josianic editors gathered and selectively arranged these traditions to form a positive account of Israel's national history culminating in Josiah himself. Finally, exilic editors updated and revised this account in light of Josiah's death and Judah's ultimate defeat (CD Special Topic IIB.2). We have already discussed the tragedy of exile, which also provided the context for the final editing of the Torah. Before we resume our journey through the Former Prophets, we should pause to examine more closely the historical circumstances surrounding Josiah's Reform.

Chart IIB.1: Insertions by Exilic Historians (Dtr[2])
Special Topic IIB.1: Other Models of Literary Origins of the Former Prophets
Special Topic IIB.2: Was Jeremiah the Deuteronomistic Historian?

A Closer Look at Josiah's Reform
(2 Kgs. 18:1–23:25)

Conscientious readers know that it is imperative to understand the historical and cultural circumstances in which a text took shape. If an early edition of the Deuteronomistic History was created during Josiah's reign as a deliberate attempt to legitimate his policies, then this historical context is critically significant for the interpreter. A basic outline of Israelite history was presented in chapter 1. In this section, we will take a closer look at Josiah's reign (ca. 640–609 B.C.E.) so that we can better appreciate the imprint on biblical literature left by his reform. This discussion will provide context for our continued journey through the Former Prophets.

Since the fall of the northern kingdom in 722 B.C.E., the southern kingdom had been controlled by the mighty Assyrian Empire. Judah, as a petty vassal state, was required to pay homage and tribute to these foreign overlords. Although David's descendants still occupied his throne, they were obliged to show loyalty to Assyrian emperors. Statues of Assyrian deities were displayed in the Jerusalem temple as symbols of Judah's political subjugation (2 Kgs. 16:7-18). As a small part of a large empire, Judah's population was pressured to adopt elements of Assyrian culture.

We can assume that most people did not welcome foreign domination. Any perceived Assyrian weakness led to revolts throughout the empire. For example, the death of the emperor Sargon II in 705 B.C.E. sparked a series of insurrections from Babylon to Egypt. This event likely provided the impetus for Josiah's great-grandfather Hezekiah to fortify Jerusalem, secure its water supply, and institute some politically motivated religious reforms (2 Kgs. 18:1-8, 16, 22; 20:20). Many parts of his reform program prefigure policies later pursued by Josiah. Like his great-grandson, Hezekiah is also recognized in 2 Kings for removing outlying worship centers (called **high places**), refurbishing the Jerusalem temple, and purifying the cult.

Strangely, the Deuteronomistic History downplays **Hezekiah's Reform**, which is reported in much greater detail in the postexilic book of Chronicles (2 Chr. 29–31). Readers of Kings are required to piece together the details of this early reform, which are scattered throughout a larger account of Assyrian reprisal. Once Sennacherib, the son of Sargon II, had secured his father's throne, he embarked on a campaign to suppress rebellions and stabilize his empire. Sennacherib's campaign wreaked havoc across the Fertile Crescent but met with only partial success in Judah. He captured several fortified cities and besieged Jerusalem but apparently failed to capture the Judean capital. Although Assyrian and biblical records make conflicting claims about this confrontation, they agree that Hezekiah paid an exorbitant ransom to the Assyrian emperor (2 Kgs. 18:14-16). A Josianic editor of the Deuteronomistic History may have intentionally downplayed Hezekiah's Reform to avoid associating Josiah with his well-intentioned but largely unsuccessful ancestor.

Hezekiah's policies were overturned by his two immediate successors, Manasseh and Amon. Second Kings spares little effort in detailing the great sins of Manasseh, who reintroduced the religious practices that Hezekiah's Reform had abolished. Although the Deuteronomistic History presents these kings as amoral, their policies may have been dictated by necessity arising from increased Assyrian control. The volatile situation behind the biblical record is evident in the murder of Josiah's father, Amon (2 Kgs. 21:23-24). One Judean party assassinated the king while another avenged his death and installed his eight-year-old son on the throne in his stead. Clearly, Josiah inherited an unenviable legacy from his predecessors. The nation was not only controlled by a foreign oppressor, it was also beset by competing internal factions.

Second Kings suggests that Josiah's policies resulted from the discovery of a law book during temple repairs (2 Kgs. 22:3–23:4). Yet his reforms would not have been possible had they not coincided with the beginning of a civil war in Assyria. The resulting decline in Assyrian power again prompted many of the petty states across the Fertile Crescent to reassert their independence. It seems likely in this context that his reform was politically as well as religiously motivated.

In many ways, Josiah's activities echoed those pursued by his ancestor Hezekiah. Like his great-grandfather, Josiah removed a variety of cult objects from the Jerusalem temple and destroyed outlying sanctuaries in the Judean countryside. By purifying the temple of foreign influences, Josiah was making a nationalistic, anti-Assyrian declaration. Moreover, temple building and renovation were commonly considered marks of a successful monarch in the ancient Near East. Josiah's actions were an attempt to reclaim kingly authority following a century of foreign domination over his royal house. Likewise, centralizing worship greatly enhanced the prestige of the Jerusalem temple, which was, after all, the national shrine of the Davidic dynasty. A policy of centralization allowed Josiah to exercise greater control over the priesthood and encouraged national unity under Davidic rule.

In addition to reinstating Hezekiah's policies, Josiah's Reform also attempted to reclaim land that had once belonged to the fallen northern kingdom. By conducting religious purges in the towns of Samaria, Josiah was asserting royal authority over this region (2 Kgs. 23:19-20). The Davidic house had lost control of this territory centuries earlier, largely because Solomon's social and economic policies had alienated his northern subjects. Jeroboam, who led the northern rebellion and subsequently became the first ruler of the northern kingdom, had established national shrines at Dan and Bethel to replace Jerusalem as a place of worship (1 Kgs. 12). As reported in the Deuteronomistic History, this act was tantamount to apostasy. Josiah's desecration of the altar at Bethel is presented as the climax of his reform and the fulfillment of prophecy (1 Kgs. 13; 2 Kgs. 15–18).

During Josiah's reign, the northern territory was inhabited in part by descendants of those who had survived the destruction of Israel and resisted deportation. Josiah's Reform would force them to travel to Jerusalem to perform sacrifices. Yet because the ten northern tribes had renounced Davidic rule, they likely harbored distrust of the southern monarchy. In addition, the northern territory was occupied by defeated peoples from other parts of the Assyrian Empire who had been forcibly resettled there. The

STUDYING THE OLD TESTAMENT

diversity of this northern population would present yet another challenge to Josiah's royal ambitions.

To assert Judean independence and to expand his territorial holdings, Josiah would need to unify northerners and southerners. No doubt religious centralization, the elimination of foreign influences, and the strongly patriotic tone of the reform all played important roles in creating a coherent national identity. Many biblical scholars believe that Josiah also crafted a new national history (Dtr[1]) to support his policies. The prominence given in the Deuteronomistic History to Israel's two most important religious traditions—the Mosaic and Davidic covenants—would appeal equally to northerners and southerners. As a Davidide who champions the Mosaic law, Josiah is portrayed as both the legitimate successor of the Davidic throne and the rightful bearer of Mosaic authority. Had another empire not arisen to fill the void left by Assyria, perhaps the Deuteronomistic History would have retained its happy ending.

THE ROAD TO STATEHOOD

Now that we possess a working model for the literary origins of the Former Prophets (and Deuteronomy), we are much better equipped to continue our journey through this literature. Persuasive evidence suggests that these books consist of diverse traditions selected, compiled, and shaped by editors to form a theologized account of Israel's history in Canaan. Two historical contexts left a deep imprint upon this editorial activity: Josiah's Reform and Babylonian exile. Careful readers should be able to discern these stages of literary growth and remain attuned to the significance of these texts for Josianic and exilic audiences.

Thus far on our journey through the Former Prophets, we have encountered a positive object lesson in the book of Joshua. In the conquest tradition, the Israelites experienced almost total success in claiming the land promised to their ancestors. Foreign influences were ruthlessly eliminated, with the exception of foreigners, like Rahab, who supported Israel's manifest destiny. The book of Joshua shows us what happens when Israel is unified under one leader (be it Joshua or Josiah) who promotes obedience to Mosaic law.

We have also encountered a negative object lesson in the book of Judges, which shows us what happens when Israel lacks unity and stable leadership. Through the continuous repetition of the judges cycle, readers are given the impression that noncentralized, charismatic leadership is a temporary solution at best. Such a situation leads to covenant disobedience and military defeat. Leaders deteriorate in quality, apostasy abounds, and the nation slides ever deeper into social and political chaos. Israel clearly needs a more permanent solution, yet the practical necessity of monarchy competes with the ideal of Yahweh's kingship.

The story of Israel's transition from charismatic leadership to monarchy continues into Samuel. Here also we discover competing attitudes toward kingship. Blended pro- and anti-monarchic traditions may reflect different stages in the literary growth of this book. They could also very well reflect disparate opinions that coexisted within different factions in Israel. Regardless, in the final form of the text, the juxtaposition of these voices reflects Israel's struggle between covenant faithfulness and accommodation to surrounding cultures.

Kingship was the most common model of political organization in the ancient Near East. Kings offered the prospect of order, security, and prosperity in return for their subjects' loyalty and subservience. Monarchic power was buttressed by religious ideology depicting the king as the earthly representative, the offspring, or even the incarnation of a deity or deities. The benefits of monarchy were countered by the potential abuses of such absolute, divinely legitimated authority. Even benevolent kings usually maintained a standing military and central bureaucracy requiring taxation, forced labor, and land seizure that would burden their subjects and contribute to increased social and economic stratification.

Such an institution contrasts starkly with the ideals of the exodus story. This tension is clearly visible in Deuteronomic law (Deut. 17:14-20), which idealistically recommends that Israel's king eschew all of the abuses typical of ancient Near Eastern monarchies and engage instead in constant study of the law under the tutelage of priests. Was it possible for kingship to exist in Israel alongside older Mosaic covenant traditions? The texts depicting Israel's transition to monarchy reflect an attempt to reconcile the practical needs of the nation with the claims of the covenant. Editors have shaped these traditions to suggest the guiding hand of a just and benevolent deity behind the all-too-human machinations that shaped Israelite statehood.

A Time of Transition (1 Sam. 1–6; CD Preliminary Exercises IIIA.1 and IIIA.2)

The account of Israel's transition to monarchy begins with the story of one family. The tale of Hannah, Peninnah, and Elkanah primarily serves to introduce Samuel, who will play the crucial role of kingmaker in the chapters ahead. This pivotal birth story echoes motifs from the ancestral narratives in Genesis while anticipating the dramatic transformation that lies in the nation's near future.

Again we encounter a family with rival co-wives, one of whom is barren. In a society where women are valued for bearing children, Hannah's situation is bleak despite the affection of her husband. Her desperate prayer for a child introduces the character of Eli into the narrative, and the ensuing conversation begins to acquaint readers with a more far-reaching problem. Eli's lack of perception, which allows him to mistake a pious gesture for drunkenness, hints that Israel's current leaders are less capable than one might hope. In answering the prayer of Hannah, Yahweh is also raising up a new leader for Israel. Samuel's miraculous birth to a barren mother signifies God's backstage role in the rise of monarchy long before the people ask for a king.

The theological centerpiece of this story is a song that Hannah offers in gratitude following the birth of her son (1 Sam. 2:1-10). In some ways inappropriate for this particular occasion, Hannah's song is actually a national psalm of thanksgiving like many others in Israel's hymnic tradition (CD Special Topic IIIA.1). By placing this psalm on her lips, our historians have connected a blessed event within an individual family with the fortunes of the larger community and the future of Israel.

The theological affirmations in Hannah's song also provide an interpretive lens through which readers are invited to view the episodes that follow. The song first praises God for enabling a victory over powerful unnamed enemies. While Hannah's "enemy" was the haughty Peninnah, the sentiment applies equally well on a national level to the Philistines, the Assyrians, or even the Babylonians for later audiences. Like the birth of Samuel, the future of Israel depends upon God's gracious intervention. Hannah's song affirms that God is both willing and able to intervene on behalf of the powerless to transform hopeless situations. The song also celebrates several dramatic reversals of fortune in which the oppressed are exalted and the proud humbled. This theme will continue throughout these books as the lad Samuel replaces the priest Eli and later young David outstrips King Saul. The placement of this psalm at the beginning of Samuel suggests God's providential involvement in the events ahead, an impression underscored by the prescient reference to Yahweh's **anointed** king several chapters before such a king exists (1 Sam. 2:10).

Hannah's vow places her son in priestly service at Shiloh under the tutelage of Eli. The piety of Hannah and the growing spiritual discernment of Samuel contrast starkly with the ineptitude of the older priest and the vices of his sons. Alert readers should recognize that the religious corruption that plagued Israel at the end of Judges still poses a problem. As Samuel increases in ability and stature, two episodes express God's judgment against the house of Eli. First, a nameless **man of God** (a common expression for a prophet) proclaims divine judgment against the Elide priesthood. As part of the prophecy-fulfillment formula unifying the Deuteronomistic History, this condemnation of Eli's house anticipates later developments (1 Sam. 22:18-23; 1 Kgs. 2:26-27). David's son Solomon will eventually banish the one surviving Elide priest (the rest having been killed by Saul), giving control of the Jerusalem temple to the Zadokite priesthood. In part, this episode justifies later historical realities.

A second episode serves to enhance Samuel's prestige while simultaneously undermining Eli. Even though Eli had just received a prophetic oracle, readers are informed that the word of Yahweh was rare in those days. This makes it all the more remarkable when young Samuel experiences a nighttime theophany while sleeping before the ark of the covenant. Once the inexperienced Samuel and his inept tutor realize what is happening, an oracle reaffirms God's intention of dispensing with Eli's house. As the elder priest accepts his fate ("It is [Yahweh]; let him do what seems good to him"), his priestly apprentice gains a reputation for prophecy (1 Sam. 3:19–4:1a).

Strangely, Samuel disappears from the story for several chapters following this theophany. Biblical editors followed these traditions about Samuel with what was probably a once separate narrative concerning the ark itself. As the text now stands, Israel's internal leadership crisis (1 Sam. 1:1–4:1a) is paralleled by an external crisis posed by the growing Philistine threat (1 Sam. 4:1b–7:1). This threat is dire indeed! After suffering one rout at the hands of the Philistines, the Israelites decide to bring out the big guns. They send for the ark, Yahweh's portable throne, so their deity can defeat the enemy for them (cf. Josh. 6). This time Israel is defeated even more soundly, and the ark itself is captured by the Philistines. Eli's sons are killed in battle and the old priest dies upon receiving the news. Even more poignantly, word of the ark's capture sends Eli's pregnant daughter-in-law into labor. Before dying in childbirth, she bears a son whom she names Ichabod (meaning "where is the glory?") and declares that the glory has departed (literally "been exiled") from Israel.

The ark's capture would seem to signify that Yahweh has been defeated by the Philistines or, more properly, by the gods of the Philistines. Yet in a humorous turn of events, Yahweh's throne proves too much for Israel's enemies to handle. The story of the ark's escapades plays upon two words with double meanings in Hebrew, "hand/power" (Hebrew *yad*) and "heavy/glory" (Hebrew *cavod*). First, when placed in the temple of Dagon in Ashdod, the ark twice causes a statue of Dagon to fall to the ground. When their deity loses his head and hands, the Philistines complain that Yahweh's hand has been heavy upon them. Next the heavy hand of Yahweh triggers a plague of tumors in Gath. Clearly, the **ark narrative** assumes that Yahweh's power and glory are associated with the ark and undeterred by the Philistines and their gods. Therefore, Israel's defeat had resulted, not from God's weakness or absence, but from God's will. Yahweh can neither be manipulated by Israel nor contained by her enemies (CD Special Topic IIIA.2).

When the troublesome ark is shifted to yet another Philistine town, its panicked inhabitants decide to get rid of the dangerous object. After placating the ark/Yahweh with gifts, they devise one last test to determine whether it actually caused all of this mayhem. They place the ark in an empty cart drawn by cows whose calves are confined behind them. When the cows move away from their calves toward Israelite territory, the Philistines conclude that the ark/Yahweh must be propelling them (1 Sam. 6:7-12). It is as if Yahweh is driving the cart home! The ark had allowed itself to be captured and now it had decided to return from its self-imposed exile. It retains control over its own destiny and remains dangerous for either Philistines or Israelites to handle (1 Sam. 6:19–7:1).

These first chapters of Samuel introduce internal and external crises that hasten the development of Israelite monarchy. For a Josianic audience, these episodes demonstrate God's providential involvement in the rise of kingship long before such an institution existed. Yahweh's guidance of events is indirectly evident through the miraculous birth of

Samuel, the kingmaker, and prophetic oracles that foreshadow developments within the Davidic court. God's activity is more directly visible in the exploits of the ark, a narrative that concludes many chapters later when David safely transports Yahweh's throne to Jerusalem (2 Sam. 6). Readers should infer that the self-determining ark chooses to reside in the Davidic capital as a sign of divine blessing upon this ruling house.

The theme of God's providential care for Israel would be just as significant in the eyes of a later exilic audience but for different reasons. No longer would these stories point triumphantly toward the establishment of an eternal Davidic dynasty. Read in the context of exile, these stories would provide hope that Yahweh continues to intervene on Israel's behalf even in difficult times of transition. As corrupt leaders are judged, simultaneously new leaders can arise who still hear the word of Yahweh. The ark's capture and Shiloh's destruction (Jer. 7:12-14; 26:6-9) become symbolic precursors for the fall of Jerusalem and destruction of the temple by Babylonian forces. Yet apparent defeat, destruction, and deportation do not necessarily indicate that the glory has departed from Israel. Yahweh can enable a return from exile.

Preliminary Exercise IIIA.1: Does Israel Need a King?
Preliminary Exercise IIIA.2: God's Magical Ark
Special Topic IIIA.1: Hannah's Song (1 Sam. 2:1-10)
Special Topic IIIA.2: The Ark of the Covenant in Film

The Creation of Monarchy (1 Sam. 7–15; CD Preliminary Exercises IIIB.1 and IIIB.2)

The next chapters of Samuel depict the emergence of a monarchy from the loose confederation of tribes that had constituted Israel during the Judges period (CD Special Topic IIIB.1). These episodes offer a theological interpretation of the institution of kingship, its origin, and its relationship to older covenant traditions. Samuel, the kingmaker, abruptly reappears in the storyline following the ark narrative to serve as a guiding force through this national transition. Readers are also introduced to Saul, the first Israelite king, who within the space of a few chapters first gains and then loses favor as Yahweh's anointed one. Although he remains the *de facto* monarch throughout 1 Samuel, readers are soon alerted that another, better king waits offstage.

Observant readers will notice a "Jekyll and Hyde" quality to this story, which seems to alternate between celebration and condemnation of kingship. First, Samuel vehemently opposes the creation of monarchy, and then he appears as the principle supporter of this transition. At one moment he plays the role of a nationally recognized leader and the next an obscure small-town **seer**. At times he seethes with righteous indignation, while elsewhere he seems rather petty. Alongside these odd permutations of Samuel's character, Saul also appears in various guises. One minute he cowers among the baggage and the next he bravely leads Israel into battle. To make matters even more complicated, Saul is proclaimed king on three separate occasions and rejected as king twice.

The present shape of the text obviously results from the blending of traditions with differing assessments of monarchy. Traditionally, scholars have separated these chapters into a **pro-monarchic tradition** and an **anti-monarchic tradition**, although the history of these materials is probably more complex than such a simple division would seem to imply (CD Primary Texts IIIB.1, IIIB.2, and IIIB.3). In the final form of the story, as we now have it, these two viewpoints are carefully intertwined (CD Chart IIIB.1). Editors have left both positive and negative appraisals clearly visible in the text, although anti-monarchic traditions dominate the beginning and end of the tale (1 Sam. 7:1–8:22; 15:1-35).

At the beginning of this blended account, Samuel appears in yet another leadership role. While earlier chapters portrayed him as a priest and a prophet, he is now cast as the last of Israel's judges (1 Sam. 7:6-17). Although Samuel is described as more of an arbiter than a military leader, the standard judge formula concludes this chapter, bringing the era of judges to an official close. The heaping of honorific titles upon

STUDYING THE OLD TESTAMENT

him indicates his remembered importance as a leader at a critical juncture of Israel's history.

Samuel embodies Israel's inherited system of leadership and covenant traditions, whereas monarchy represents a significant departure from both. In the anti-monarchic tradition, Samuel vigorously resists the elders' request for a king (1 Sam. 8). First, kingship is described as a rejection of Israel's distinctive covenant identity in favor of becoming more "like other nations." Second, it is condemned as a form of apostasy leading to the rejection of Yahweh's sovereignty. Although the request is grudgingly granted, the consequences of this decision are made painfully clear. Samuel describes a king as someone who does nothing but take from his subjects. In essence, the "ways of the king" are very similar to the ways of Pharaoh.

Saul first appears in a pro-monarchic tradition that depicts him as a handsome and dutiful son seeking his wealthy father's lost donkeys (1 Sam. 9:1–10:16). In this episode, Samuel is merely a local seer who is completely unknown to Saul and apparently expects payment for his services. This tradition seems oblivious of the elders' request for a king or Samuel's objections to monarchy. Likewise, the deity no longer appears affronted by the prospect of a human ruler. In fact, the idea actually seems to originate with Yahweh as a means of delivering Israel from the Philistines. The deity reveals this plan to Samuel in a dream, directs him to **anoint** Saul, and verifies this choice through signs (CD Special Topic IIIB.2). This tradition carefully avoids the ideologically charged term *king* in favor of the more ambiguous term *ruler*. It also presents the new institution as a more beneficial and less drastic change for Israel. The description of the new ruler's role does not differ significantly from the role of a judge.

Alert readers should be struck anew by Samuel's split personality when he summons the people to Mizpah and once again denounces monarchy as a rejection of Yahweh (1 Sam. 10:17-25). Samuel's ability to address and command all of the tribes suggests that he is more than a local fortune-teller in this episode. Once again Saul is designated for national leadership, although this time the potentially offensive word *king* is actually used. Whereas the previous chapter had identified Saul through a divinely inspired dream, this anti-monarchic tradition singles him out by the less auspicious method of casting lots (CD Chart IIIB.2). Although still tall and handsome, Saul on this occasion seems cowardly and less than eager to assume his new role—a role carefully limited by Samuel, who writes down the rights and duties of kingship.

If readers have not yet developed whiplash, they soon will! When we next meet Saul, he acts boldly to deliver the inhabitants of Jabesh-gilead from a hostile enemy (1 Sam. 11). Like the earlier judges, Saul is imbued with Yahweh's spirit and uses a traditional means of summoning the tribes to unite in warfare. Following a decisive victory, Samuel suddenly reappears to make Saul king for the third time.

Chapter 12 plays a pivotal role in this blended account as the farewell speech of Samuel, which strangely appears thirteen chapters before a report of his death (1 Sam. 25:1). Although he will continue to guide events in the chapters that follow, Samuel speaks to the assembled Israelites as if he were retiring from public life. Like many other speeches in the Former Prophets, this one seems to have been composed by Deuteronomistic editors as an interpretive summary of Israel's past and a glimpse into her future. Samuel first defends the faithful guidance that both he and Yahweh have provided for Israel in the past. Once again, he presents monarchy as a concession to the will of the people and an aberration of traditional Yahwistic faith. Yet an attempt is made to reconcile old and new institutions by subordinating kingship to the Mosaic covenant (1 Sam. 12:13-15). According to the Deuteronomistic understanding of history, both the people and their king are obligated to obey Yahweh's commands or risk being swept away.

Following this pivotal speech, a regnal formula (1 Sam. 13:1) announces the official beginning of a new era, Israel's **united monarchy** (CD Chart IIIB.3). Yet Israel's first king seems doomed to failure by both the lingering presence of Samuel and the hovering specter of David. The optimism generated by early military success quickly fades before vastly superior Philistine forces. Saul finds himself with a fearful and rapidly shrinking army. When Samuel fails to show up on the appointed day of sacrifice, the king understandably chooses to proceed without him rather than delaying the battle. Yet Samuel is far from understanding when he conveniently appears just after Saul has offered the sacrifice himself. Sounding jealously protective of his own authority, Samuel declares that Yahweh has rejected Saul's kingship in favor of an unnamed "man after his own heart" (1 Sam. 13:13-14). After this episode, Saul is presented less sympathetically, especially in contrast to his son Jonathan.

A second account of Saul's rejection depicts his failings in a more negative light (1 Sam. 15). At Samuel's command, the king pursues a holy war against the Amalekites to avenge wrongs committed against a previous generation of Israelites (Exod. 17:8-16; Deut. 25:17-19). Yet, against orders, he chooses to spare from the ban the best livestock and the Amalekite king. This time his disobedience is not motivated by necessity despite the excuses he utters (or invents?) when he is caught with the goods. Yahweh and Samuel tolerate no compromise from Saul, whose authority is subordinate to old covenant traditions. Israel's king is not free to interpret commands issued by Yahweh's prophet/priest but must simply obey. Samuel again declares that God has rejected Saul and will give the throne of Israel to someone more worthy (CD Special Topic IIIB.3).

At the end of these chapters, an Israelite monarchy exists but rests upon a rather shaky theological foundation. The predominance of anti-monarchic traditions suggests that this new institution will be grudgingly tolerated only so long as it stands under the authority of the Mosaic covenant and its representatives. Israelite kings are to be carefully monitored by Israelite prophets. However, readers have been alerted that a better king is coming—one who may be able to reconcile inherited religious traditions with new political ideologies.

The Rise of David (1 Sam. 16:1–2 Sam. 5:5; CD Preliminary Exercises IIIC.1 and IIIC.2)

As we have seen, Samuel contains two stories in which Saul is rejected and told that someone better will be replacing him as king of Israel. Thus, before David ever appears onstage, readers are prepared to attribute his usurpation of the throne to divine design rather than human ambition. As elsewhere in the Deuteronomistic History, we are not dealing with objective historical reports but with partisan literature. Unlike the "Jekyll and Hyde" story of monarchy's creation, the account of David's ascent to power has a single, unifying perspective. From beginning to end, this story is unquestioningly supportive of a David, who can do no wrong, and just as condemning of a Saul, who does everything wrong.

Nevertheless, David is not presented as a boy scout in these episodes, many of which actually celebrate his bawdiness and cunning. Instead readers encounter a likeable upstart who quickly matures into a roguish leading man. On the run from Saul during much of this story, this resourceful renegade does what he must to survive and elude the powerful monarch who insanely pursues him. Although the narrator frequently denies David's ambition and attributes his success to God's providential care, hints beneath the surface of the text suggest that David has a hand in engineering his own ascent to power. He marries well, gathers supporters, extorts "protection" money, and builds a base of influence in his native tribe of Judah. People who stand between David and the throne conveniently die while he stands by—always with an ironclad alibi!

Given the partisan nature of this literature, readers would do well to approach it as they would a series of campaign ads during an election year. Most voters do not take a candidate's assertions and self-presentation at face value but interpret them within the context of that candidate's desire to be elected. Although biblical Israel was never organized as a democracy, almost all rulers attempt to cultivate popular support to maintain their power. When these episodes are interpreted as David's political propaganda, their agenda becomes clear to modern readers. No wonder that David is valorized in terms of his abilities, character, and faith, whereas his competition is portrayed as negatively as possible. Similarly, no wonder that these stories humanize David by presenting him as a person who is able to identify with commoners and understand the hardships they experience. Alert readers can easily recognize this pro-Davidic "spin."

Such an agenda is immediately evident in the Cinderella-like episode that introduces David (1 Sam. 16:1-13). Samuel, who has been sent to Judah to anoint a replacement for Saul among the sons of Jesse, is not allowed to settle upon any of David's seven elder brothers. In Cinderella terms, the slipper just does not fit them! God insists that this time the choice of a king will not rest on age or height or appearance, but rather on the heart. David is finally summoned as a last resort from the flock that he has been tending while his elder brothers attend sacrifices. Immediately, he is judged to have the appropriate heart—although, luckily enough, he happens to be handsome as well. David is anointed by Samuel, and Yahweh's spirit rushes upon him.

When readers learn in the next episode that Yahweh's spirit has abandoned Saul, they already know where it has gone. To make God's preference for David complete, Saul is not merely left spiritless but is plagued by an evil spirit. David is first introduced into the royal court as a musician who plays soothing music for the tormented king (1 Sam. 16:17-22). Yet the Goliath story also introduces David to Saul as though for the first time (1 Sam. 17:55-58). The juxtaposition of these two traditions illustrates the composite nature of the Deuteronomistic History, but both episodes valorize David at Saul's expense.

When Israel again finds herself outmatched and intimidated by Philistines, the reactions of the two characters are starkly contrasted. David rises successfully to the challenge of the Philistine champion Goliath, while Saul and his army remain paralyzed by fear (CD Special Topic IIIC.1). Whereas Saul is heavily armed, David takes on Goliath with only with a sling, five stones, and his faith. The disparity between David and Saul (as well as that between David and Goliath) recalls the thrust of Hannah's song (1 Sam. 2:1-10). Like Hannah, David affirms that God will enable the victory of the humble over the powerful.

The next several episodes undermine Saul's authority by describing the great admiration that his people and even his own children develop for David. Imagine a political contest in which one candidate's children publicly align themselves with the opposing side! Depicting Jonathan as one of David's greatest supporters also prevents readers from sympathizing with the soon-to-be-displaced rightful heir. When an adoring Jonathan gives David his robe and armor, he is symbolically handing over his future kingdom (1 Sam. 18:1-4).

Marriage to Saul's daughter Michal, also a David fan, conveniently places him in line for the throne of Israel. While their union could be viewed as a sign of David's ambition, the story's emphasis is upon the king's paranoid insanity. Saul slyly suggests that David marry one of his daughters in exchange for military service. He holds out first Merab and then Michal as bait, hoping that his prospective son-in-law will be killed by a Philistine arrow. Saul treacherously reneges on their deal with Merab, but he is forced to surrender Michal when David delivers the outrageous bride-price of one hundred Philistine foreskins.

When the king's mad jealousy finally forces David to flee the royal court, he demonstrates resourcefulness as a fugitive. He cunningly persuades a priest to provision him and escapes the Philistines by feigning insanity. In the hands of the narrator, David becomes a biblical Robin Hood, an admired outlaw opposing an increasingly oppressive and unpopular regime. He gathers supporters who have been marginalized under Saul's reign and uses this force to defend Israelite cities. Meanwhile, Saul seems more interested in chasing David than fighting the Philistines. His mad pursuit will apparently stop at nothing, even the massacre of priests. When David offers refuge to Abiathar (the one surviving Elide) he gains a conduit to God, while Saul the priest-killer is left without a traditional means of consulting the deity (CD Special Topic IIIC.2).

The king's violent abuse of his power stands in stark contrast to David's nonviolent restraint. Two separate accounts place a defenseless Saul at his mercy, but David twice resists harming his father-in-law against the urging of his men (1 Sam. 24; 26). In the first story, Saul stops to relieve himself in the very cave in which the band of outlaws is hiding. The king is ignobly portrayed performing a private bodily function while he ineptly fails to recognize the nearness of his supposed enemy. Although Saul is quite literally exposed, David refuses to harm Yahweh's anointed one and merely cuts off the edge of his skirt. In the second story, Saul is surrounded by his army and apparently well protected. Yet David still gets within striking distance and again exercises restraint. In each account, when faced with evidence of his enemy's mercy, Saul admits David's innocence and the inevitability of his ascension. David, for his part, declares that any harm that might one day befall Saul will come from Yahweh rather than him.

Between these two accounts lies a third story in which David spares the life of another person. This arrangement allows editors to use the character of Nabal (the "fool") as a literary symbol for Saul (CD Chart IIIC.1). Neither Saul nor Nabal is portrayed in sympathetic terms, although both could be seen as simply trying to protect what is rightfully theirs. After all, Nabal's only crime (other than rudeness) is a refusal to pay "protection money" to David's private army. Nevertheless, readers are encouraged to sympathize with David, who is once again tempted to take vengeance on an enemy. On this occasion, his hand is restrained not by his own resolve but by the shrewd intervention of Nabal's lovely wife. Abigail shows the hospitality that her husband had refused and tactfully urges David to keep his hands clean. Sure enough, he has no need to act on his own. Yahweh smites Nabal, who conveniently dies within days, leaving David to claim his widow and wealth for himself. Readers are left with the impression that David's success is providential and that his enemies (including Saul) should beware.

Most of the episodes describing David's ascent to power focus on his amazing feats, irreproachable character, and divine favor. All of these themes contribute to the pro-Davidic slant of the story. However, the last few chapters of 1 Samuel deal with a potentially scandalous situation (1 Sam. 27–31). These chapters recall that David spent several years living among and fighting for the Philistines, Israel's greatest enemy. Doubtless this tradition was too well-known to be denied or ignored. Instead, the pro-Davidic narrator places the blame once again on Saul, who had apparently chased poor David right out of Israel! The story also deflects criticism from David by portraying him as a type of double agent. Although the Philistine king Achish believes that David has switched sides, in reality he is being deceived. The narrator also provides him with an airtight alibi during the Philistine-Israelite battle in which Saul and Jonathan die. David, who was not allowed to accompany the Philistine army, was elsewhere chasing Amalekite raiders.

Although David publicly laments Saul and Jonathan and avenges their deaths, he also moves quickly to claim the vacated throne for himself. He is first declared king by Judah, his ancestral tribe in which he had already curried favor (1 Sam. 30:26-31). Then he engages in open war over the kingship with Saul's son, Ishbaal (CD Special Topic IIIC.3). The account of this war focuses on behind-the-scenes power struggles rather than battles. When Ishbaal's general, Abner, attempts to switch loyalties, he is killed by David's general, Joab, over a matter of personal vengeance. Because Abner is disloyal and openly ambitious, David is actually lucky to have him out of the way. Yet again he performs a lament over a fallen enemy and adamantly denies any involvement in his death. Likewise, when Ishbaal's bodyguards murder him and deliver his severed head, David avenges his death as well. Once everyone impeding his progress toward the throne has conveniently died, he easily becomes king over all Israel.

As the body count in the story rises, readers might begin to feel suspicious of David's protestations of innocence. For our historians, however, his success has been preordained by God, who is ultimately responsible for bringing this humble shepherd boy to the throne. This account serves to justify the transition from King Saul to King David and to defend the latter from any allegations of wrongdoing in his ascent to power. In the larger context of the Deuteronomistic History, it also introduces readers to the founder of Josiah's royal line. Moreover, the story of David's ascension offers a provisional response to an ongoing question—how to reconcile the nation's need for a king with the ideal of divine sovereignty. The striking absence of monarchic critique in the account of David's rise suggests that he is a king who can pull this off. However, as we will see, few other kings ever live up to this Davidic ideal.

Preliminary Exercise IIIC.1: David's "Campaign" for the Kingship
Preliminary Exercise IIIC.2: Politics and Propaganda
Chart IIIC.1: Parallels among the "Sparing Stories" (1 Sam. 24–26)
Special Topic IIIC.1: Who Really Killed Goliath? (1 Sam. 17)
Special Topic IIIC.2: The Medium of Endor (1 Sam. 28)
Special Topic IIIC.3: Ishbaal or Ishbosheth? (2 Sam. 2–4)

THE ROAD TO EXILE

On the previous leg of our journey through the Former Prophets, we witnessed an ideological struggle occasioned by the rise of Israelite monarchy. The Mosaic covenant, which proclaimed the absolute sovereignty of God, competed with the practical need for a human sovereign. Although the various sources combined within 1–2 Samuel assume different attitudes toward monarchy, readers are left with the overall impression that kingship is a regrettable compromise of Israel's religious identity. A king would be grudgingly tolerated in Israel only if that office remains subject to the requirements of old covenant traditions (1 Sam. 12). When Saul is rejected for transgressing these limitations, God seeks out a better king and guides him to the throne.

David provides a temporary resolution to this ideological tug-of-war. But was the limited kingship espoused by Samuel sustainable? Readers will soon encounter a prophetic announcement that contradicts Samuel's earlier limitation of kingship (2 Sam. 7:5-17). Nathan, a prophet associated with the royal court, declares God's intent to establish a Davidic dynasty that will continue in perpetuity regardless of the reigning king's actions. This unconditional guarantee resembles the religious legitimation given to other ancient Near Eastern kings and represents a significant departure from Israel's older religious traditions. Could the very different claims of the Davidic and Mosaic covenants be reconciled?

In the final editorial arrangement of Samuel and Kings, the positive account of David's ascent to power is followed by a very human portrait of the new king. David's own sins lead to violence within his house as his sons compete to succeed or depose their father. Solomon, who eventually gains the throne, elicits only qualified approval. His royal policies sow seeds of dissension that lead to the division of the kingdom after his death. The northern tribes reject Davidic rule and break away to form a separate monarchy. David's house will continue to reign, but over a greatly diminished realm.

The storyline now must alternate between the northern kingdom (Israel) and the southern kingdom (Judah) as their parallel histories are narrated. A critique of unlimited monarchy continues in the books of

Kings in two ways: (1) through prophetic narratives and (2) through explicit evaluations of kings by Deuteronomistic editors. First, prophets arise whenever a king acts in ways that conflict with requirements of the Mosaic covenant. Although they sometimes support the royal administration, more often these prophets serve as the king's conscience and challenge royal policies. Second, Deuteronomistic editors evaluate a king's success based on whether he promotes exclusive worship of Yahweh in Jerusalem (cf. Deut. 12). All northern kings fail this test by supporting other shrines in place of the Davidic capital, a practice cited by editors to explain Israel's eventual destruction. Yet, surprisingly, most of the southern kings also fail to meet this criterion. Although several of David's descendants receive qualified approval from our historians, only Josiah is wholeheartedly endorsed. The Davidic and Mosaic covenants are momentarily reconciled in this king. But following Josiah's untimely death, the story of Judah's historical journey takes a sudden and tragic detour toward exile.

The Fall of David (2 Sam. 5:6–1 Kgs. 2; CD Preliminary Exercises IVA.1 and IVA.2)

When David at last occupies the thrones of Judah and Israel, he retains the astuteness that led him to power. Knowing that his popularity is weaker in the north, which had not enthusiastically embraced his kingship after Saul's death, he sensibly chooses to move his capital from the southern town of Hebron to a more central location. The Jebusite city of Jerusalem, which David conquers and renames for himself, is politically neutral territory. He also wisely placates any remaining supporters of Saul's house by reuniting with Saul's daughter Michal and extending mercy to a crippled son of Jonathan named Mephibosheth (CD Special Topic IVA.1).

At the same time, readers should detect clues that David's regime will assume a much grander scale than that of Saul. A series of wars extends the nation's borders much farther than ever before (CD Map IVA.1). Although David devotes most of the wealth he captures in battle to the deity, he does keep one hundred horses and chariots for himself. He can also boast a larger harem and royal court than Saul had possessed (2 Sam. 3:2-5; 5:13-15; 8:15-18). These factors customarily increased the prestige of a ruler in the ancient Near East, but they stand in tension with the Deuteronomistic ideal of kingship (cf. Deut. 17:14-20; 1 Sam. 8:10-18).

David attempts to resolve this tension by making a place for the old covenant traditions within his regime. He first relocates to his new capital the most important symbol of Israel's faith, the ark of the covenant. The ark represented Yahweh's portable throne, which had traveled with Israel through the wilderness and into the promised land. Its mobility symbolized the deity's freedom as so aptly illustrated by the ark narrative (1 Sam. 4–6). At the end of that earlier account, the ark had been left in an obscure village because, like Israel's deity, it had proved unmanageable. In the final form of Samuel, David's recovery of the ark forms the belated conclusion of this narrative. Although not without difficulty, the ark allows itself to be transported to Jerusalem, signifying Yahweh's blessing upon the Davidic regime.

With the ark in his capital, David becomes the sponsor of Israel's worship life. Such blurring of the line between divine and human kingship paves the way for the development of a **royal theology** in Israel. Most ancient Near Eastern kings built official state temples adjacent to their royal palaces where the gods could live under their patronage. David's desire to build a temple should be understood in this context. Now that he has a house of cedar built by King Hiram of Tyre (2 Sam. 5:11), David wonders whether the time has arrived to build a house for Yahweh and the ark.

After initially approving of this plan, the court prophet Nathan retracts his endorsement and delivers a lengthy oracle playing upon various meanings of the word *house* (2 Sam. 7:1-17). The king wants to build Yahweh a house (that is, "temple") because he himself lives in a house (that is, "palace"), but God declines this offer and instead declares the intention of building an eternal house (that is, "dynasty") for David. Any transgressions committed by a Davidide would be punished, but this royal house would rule in perpetuity. The bond between the deity and Davidic king is even described as a father-son relationship (cf. Pss. 2; 89).

Nathan's oracle subordinates the conditional Mosaic covenant to an unconditional Davidic covenant. It also explains why it is Solomon, rather than David, who builds the great temple in Jerusalem. The obvious reference to Solomon, among other factors, suggests that at least part of this oracle was written long after the conversation it supposedly describes. Surely such radical ideas did not develop overnight! Nathan's speech probably represents a relatively late, fully developed form of Davidic royal theology. An earlier form might be preserved in Psalm 132, which actually describes the Davidic covenant in conditional terms:

> If your sons keep my covenant
>   and my decrees that I shall teach them,
> their sons also, forevermore,
>   shall sit on your throne. (Ps. 132:12; cf. 1 Kgs. 2:4)

Like the ancestral promises in Genesis, the Davidic covenant attaches the deity to a single family and immediately raises the question of succession. Which son will follow David in this perpetual dynasty? For this reason, the next discernible unit of the Deuteronomistic History is often labeled the **succession narrative** whereas other scholars prefer to call it David's **court history** (2 Sam. 11–20; 1 Kgs. 1–2). Regardless of title, these chapters portray a sudden reversal of fortune for the king. Whereas the story of his rise to power had depicted him as the recipient of divine blessing, the story of his reign presents David under a curse.

Most readers will notice an abrupt change in tone when they reach the story of David and Bathsheba (2 Sam. 11). Suddenly, the man who could do no wrong commits several blunders in one short paragraph! Although it is the season when kings lead their armies into battle, David remains at home in the royal palace while Joab leads Israel's forces in his stead. Not only is the king apparently shirking his duties, he is also coveting the wife of another man. Whether David's intercourse with Bathsheba constitutes rape or adultery we do not know. Her thoughts and words are not reported by the narrator save a terse report of the resultant pregnancy (CD Special Topic IVA.1). The notice that she had been purifying herself after her period leaves no doubt as to paternity. It also raises the possibility that David has violated purity laws (Lev. 15:19-24) in addition to the custom of celibacy during battle (1 Sam. 21:1-5).

David's first thought is to hide his crime by pretending the child belongs to Bathsheba's husband. Ironically, Uriah the Hittite functions as a positive foil to the king of Israel. Unlike David, he must be called from the battlefield and piously refuses to engage in a sexual dalliance during wartime even with his own wife. When one scheme fails, the king concocts another. Unable to cover up paternity, David arranges Uriah's murder in the confusion of battle and then marries the pregnant widow as a spurious act of charity. Whereas the account of David's rise had always denied his involvement in treachery, this story openly reports it.

Not until the very end of the account do we learn that Yahweh disapproves of David's deeds. Again Nathan appears, but this time the prophet is sent to critique rather than affirm. He cleverly begins by telling David a judgment-eliciting parable that parallels the situation at hand (cf. 2 Sam. 14:1-17). When the king responds to the story with righteous indignation, he incriminates himself. In contrast to many later kings, David does then confess his guilt and accept prophetic judgment. Yet he has violently abused royal power to indulge a personal whim and conceal his guilt. Surely his actions equaled or exceeded any of Saul's sins! This is the first test of the Davidic covenant. Readers must wonder whether the deity would now reject David from being king over Israel. We soon discover that, within the limits of the eternal promise of a

Davidic dynasty, Deuteronomic theology is still in effect. David's punishment does not negate God's promises concerning his house, but his sins will have negative effects on those closest to him in the tragic episodes that follow.

Perhaps mimicking the behavior of his father, David's eldest son Amnon rapes his half-sister Tamar. Because their father fails to react, Tamar's brother Absalom murders the rapist and flees the country. When at last Absalom and David are reunited (CD Special Topic IVA.2), the son conspires to seize his father's throne. The near success of this rebellion demonstrates a startling level of dissatisfaction with David among his subjects that foreshadows the eventual division of his kingdom. The king is forced once again to flee Jerusalem until his supporters finally put down the uprising for him. The stunningly human portrait of David in these chapters climaxes in his concern over the fate of his rebellious son. Having urged his soldiers to deal gently with Absalom, he loses control of himself upon learning of his son's death: "O my son Absalom, my son, my son Absalom! Would I had died instead of you, O Absalom, my son, my son" (2 Sam. 18:33b). David's impotence as a father suggests a waning ability to perform his public functions. Although he manages to put down yet another rebellion and recover the loyalties of the tribes, he has clearly become a mere shadow of his former self.

The succession narrative continues in the first two chapters of Kings. With David clearly on the decline, the struggle for succession focuses on two of his remaining sons, Adonijah and Solomon. The eventual triumph of the latter echoes a common biblical theme in which younger sons are chosen over elder brothers (David, Moses, Joseph, Jacob, Isaac). Like the young David, Solomon does not actively seek kingship for himself. His success is attributed in part to providence (2 Sam. 12:24) and in part to palace intrigue involving a plot between his mother, Bathsheba, and the prophet Nathan (1 Kgs. 1:11-27). Once in power, however, the new king ruthlessly executes Adonijah and eliminates his supporters at the earliest opportunity. Joab is killed in accordance with the deathbed wishes of David. Abiathar, the last surviving Elide priest, is exiled to the town of Anathoth, leaving the Jerusalem priesthood in the hands of Zadok (cf. 1 Sam. 2:27-36).

This court history justifies the succession of Solomon to his father's throne. It also suggests that the promise of an eternal Davidic dynasty could not be annulled by the ruling monarch's sins. A violation of the conditional Mosaic covenant might have negative consequences, but it would not result in the total rejection of a Davidic king. For Josiah, the Davidic covenant provided legitimacy for his rule over Judah, while his devotion to Mosaic law gave him legitimacy in the north. Later exilic audiences were all too painfully aware that the Davidic house had fallen, but the hope remained that God's promises were eternal and ultimately could not be revoked.

Preliminary Exercise IVA.1: The Davidic Monarchy
Preliminary Exercise IVA.2: Artists' Renderings of Bathsheba
Map IVA.1: Israel under David
Special Topic IVA.1: Sex and Politics in the United Monarchy
Special Topic IVA.2: Wise Women (2 Sam. 14:1-24; 20:15-22)

The Reign of Solomon (1 Kgs. 3:1–12:24; CD Preliminary Exercises IVB.1 and IVB.2)

Readers next encounter several traditions concerning Solomon, the last king to rule over a united Israelite monarchy (1 Kgs. 3–11). These traditions appear to be drawn from diverse sources, including popular legends and court records. Deuteronomistic editors have collected and arranged these sources to create a deeply paradoxical portrait of Solomon. At the beginning of his reign, God rewards the humble piety of the young king with the gift of unsurpassed wisdom. Near the end of his life, he is criticized for self-indulgence, apostasy, and divisive policies that have alienated most of his subjects. While David's rise and fall were clearly demarcated, it is difficult to determine a precise "turning point" in the career of Solomon.

No clear censure of the king appears before the very end of his reign, and many Solomonic traditions are quite positive. Not only is this king offered any desire of his heart, but God is so pleased with his request for understanding that wealth and honor are granted as well. Solomon's ability to solve riddles while both executing justice (1 Kgs. 3:16-28) and showing off for foreign dignitaries (1 Kgs. 10:1-13) illustrates his great wisdom (CD Special Topic IVB.1). Several passages also celebrate the economic success and international renown of his regime, creating the impression of a golden age in Israel.

In the eyes of biblical editors, Solomon's greatest achievement is the construction of the Jerusalem temple, which had been foreshadowed in the succession narrative. Several chapters are devoted to describing the temple and its trappings in lavish detail (1 Kgs. 5–7). This account climaxes in an elaborate ceremony during which the ark of the covenant is installed in an inner sanctum of the completed structure. Readers might wonder whether the king now "owns" the deity who resides in the royal shrine.

Any such notion is offset by Solomon's eloquent prayer of dedication that reflects theologically on the temple's function (1 Kgs. 8:22-53). This prayer, which was probably written by Deuteronomistic Historians, describes the temple as a place of prayer rather than sacrifice. While clearly connected with the temple, Yahweh is also enjoined to "hear in heaven" the petitions of worshipers whether they are offered within the structure itself or merely aimed in its general direction. Solomon's prayer counteracts the impression that the temple is God's residence by affirming both divine immanence and transcendence. God would be with Israel in the temple but not limited to that structure. This idea would have enormous significance for an exilic audience after the temple's destruction. Interestingly, the prayer also raises the possibility that sincere repentance could result in divine forgiveness even for people in exile.

Although many such traditions are positive toward Solomon, hints of this ruler's dark side are discernible from the beginning. We are informed early on of his marriage alliance with Egypt (1 Kgs. 1:3). Although our historians note with apparent pride Solomon's world-renowned wisdom and wealth, readers might wonder at the excessive lavishness of his court and his close ties with foreign nations. In many ways, Solomon's kingdom appears to be modeled upon other ancient Near Eastern monarchies.

He creates a large bureaucracy to administrate this kingdom, appointing eleven high officials in Jerusalem and provincial officials to oversee twelve newly formed administrative districts across the nation (1 Kgs. 4:1-19). Several important details should catch our attention in this text (CD Chart IVB.1). First, each administrative district is expected to subsidize royal expenses for one month each year. Readers should recognize that Samuel's earlier warning about the ways of a king is now embodied by Solomon's administration (1 Sam. 8:11-18). Second, most of these districts do not correspond to tribal territories. This would be comparable to an American president suddenly deciding to redraw state boundaries! Solomon's economic policy displaces tribal leadership and disregards long-standing traditions. Third, Solomon's policy is distinctly biased toward Judah, his own ancestral tribe. Not only does Judah appear exempt from taxation, but most of the officials appointed over the other districts are close associates of the Davidic house. In other words, Solomon places southerners in positions of authority over northern tribes.

The king's building projects required labor as well as funding. He meets this need by organizing the men of Israel (as opposed to Judah?) into rotating teams of forced labor (1 Kgs. 5:13-18). A month of labor for the king would be followed by two months at home to support their own families. That a later text denies this practice illustrates the composite nature of these traditions and increases the paradoxical presentation of Solomon (1 Kgs. 9:15-23). Whether or not Solomon uses forced labor, his involvement in so many building projects is a typical practice for successful ancient Near Eastern monarchs. Significantly, the construction of his own palace takes six years longer than the construction of the adjacent temple (1 Kgs. 7:1-8).

Solomon's gradual decline is clearly evident in his four encounters with the deity. In the initial dream-theophany at Gibeon (1 Kgs. 3:5-15), Yahweh is prepared to offer him anything he should ask. The deity next speaks to the king, presumably through an unnamed prophet, while temple construction is underway (1 Kgs. 6:11-13). This passage presupposes that a dynastic promise has been extended to David, but here that promise contains an "if" statement. Although this text likely preserves an earlier conditional form of the Davidic covenant, as the Former Prophets now stand, it seems to qualify Yahweh's promise to David. Perhaps this is intended as a warning that temple-building cannot replace obedience. When Solomon later experiences another dream-theophany, the conditional "if" becomes even more explicit (1 Kgs. 9:1-9). Not only is a lasting dynasty dependent upon obedience, but the consequences of disobedience are spelled out in no uncertain terms. If the king disregards Mosaic commandments, the temple will be reduced to a heap of ruins and the people expelled from the land. This warning was likely added by a writer who had witnessed Judah's exile.

The final word from Yahweh reaches Solomon near the end of his reign. Readers are first informed that Solomon has collected an excessively large harem of foreign wives and concubines. Our historians now condemn the king openly by citing the Deuteronomic prohibition against marriage with foreigners (Deut. 7:1-4; cf. Deut. 17:14-20). As often happens in biblical texts, liaisons with foreign women led to the worship of foreign deities. In anger, Yahweh declares to Solomon that most of the kingdom will be torn away from the Davidic house after his death.

For the remainder of Solomon's rule, he is beset by both foreign adversaries and internal rebellion. Whereas the prophet Nathan had conspired to place Solomon on the throne, the prophet Ahijah incites an uprising against him. Ahijah dramatically illustrates what will happen to Solomon's kingdom by tearing his own garment into twelve pieces and giving ten of them to Jeroboam. It is probably no coincidence that both of these men are northerners. Their rebellion likely stemmed, at least in part, from the ongoing preferential treatment shown to Judah by Solomon's regime. This north-south tension is surely exacerbated when the king sells twenty northern cities to pay his building debts (1 Kgs. 9:10-14).

Although Solomon successfully weathers Jeroboam's rebellion, his son cannot retain the northern tribes' loyalties. Foolishly relying on the advice of his younger associates, Rehoboam declares his intention to increase the burden on these tribes rather than lighten it (1 Kgs. 12:1-15). Our historians attribute this imprudent lack of discretion to providence. God intends to fulfill the pronouncement of Ahijah that Israel would become a **divided monarchy** after the death of Solomon. The Davidic covenant is not nullified, but David's descendants will retain only a small portion of the kingdom.

 Preliminary Exercise IVB.1: King Solomon in All His Glory
Preliminary Exercise IVB.2: Solomon—The Movie
Chart IVB.1: Solomon's Twelve Administrative Districts (1 Kgs. 4:7-19)
Special Topic IVB.1: The Legendary Wisdom of Solomon

The Divided Monarchy (1 Kgs. 12:25–2 Kgs. 25; CD Preliminary Exercises IVC.1 and IVC.2)

As we continue our journey into the book of Kings, readers will find the intertwined histories of the **northern kingdom (Israel)** and the **southern kingdom (Judah)**. Our historians shift from one nation to the other as nine dynasties rise and fall in the north and Davidides come and go in the south (CD Charts IVC.1 and IVC.2; Map IVC.1). Again, we do not find a simple historical report in this account of the divided monarchy, which glosses over several significant persons and events that are known to us from other sources (CD Special Topic IVC.1). Our historians unapologetically include only material that pertained to their own theological interests. Readers seeking historical information are referred to other sources that, unfortunately, have not survived (1 Kgs. 14:19, 29).

Kings introduces each ruler by a standard formula that provides basic information, varying slightly for northern and southern monarchs (CD Chart IVC.3). Each king is evaluated by the Deuteronomistic criterion of success: worshiping exclusively Yahweh only in Jerusalem. Our historians assign passing marks to only a few Judean monarchs, but the bulk of their criticism is directed toward Israel. All northern kings are guilty of continuing in the sin of Jeroboam, the northern kingdom's first monarch, who established religious centers at Dan and Bethel. Jeroboam placed at each of these sites a golden calf that was probably intended as a pedestal for Yahweh similar to the ark and cherubim in Solomon's temple (CD Special Topic IVC.2). Because our historians disapprove of any worship outside of Jerusalem, they depict these calves as idols and associate them with the golden calf built by Aaron at Mount Sinai (1 Kgs. 12:28; Exod. 32:4).

Unsurprisingly, our historians emphasize prophetic condemnation of Jeroboam. First, he is criticized by an unnamed man of God from Judah who disapproves of these breaks from Judean practices. Addressing the altar at Bethel, the man of God predicts that a southern king named Josiah would rise up three centuries later to smash it (1 Kgs. 13:1-2). Because biblical prophets typically do not offer such specific long-range predictions (see chapter 4), this oracle was likely shaped by Josianic editors to support his reform efforts in northern Israel. The surprising death met by this man of God illustrates what our historians view as the consequences of deviating from divine commands. If a prophet dies because he is tricked into disobedience, what fate might await Jeroboam?

Ironically, the second prophet to condemn Jeroboam is his former supporter Ahijah. Apparently disappointed in the king he had designated, he now declares that Jeroboam's dynasty will be short-lived (1 Kgs. 14:1-18). Ahijah is the first of several prophets who announce or instigate royal coups in the northern kingdom (1 Kgs. 16:1-4; 19:16;

21:17-29; 2 Kgs. 9:1-10). As opposed to the relative stability of Judah under the Davidic dynasty, Israelite kings claimed the throne based upon a mixture of dynastic succession and prophetic designation. Most of the prophets in Kings embody the principles of the Mosaic covenant and protest flagrant abuses of royal power.

By far the most prominent prophets in Kings are Elijah and Elisha, whose stories span twelve chapters. Readers might wonder why so much space is devoted to the exploits of these two northern prophets, neither of whom ever challenges the existence of shrines at Dan and Bethel. Perhaps it is because their theological agenda—exclusive and uncompromising Yahweh worship—corresponds in part to the agenda of our historians. By including these stories, our historians also demonstrate that the northern kingdom had been warned of its impending doom by Yahweh's prophets.

The **Elijah cycle** (1 Kgs. 17–2 Kgs. 2) is set during the reign of Ahab, who through his marriage to Jezebel formed an alliance with Israel's northern neighbor Phoenicia. Like the wives of Solomon, Jezebel appears to have imported her deities (**Baal** and **Asherah**) into Israel. It is also possible that Ahab permitted these religious practices as part of his domestic policy to appease the local Canaanite population. The king's actions might make sense politically, but they do not please Elijah. The prophet proclaims a drought to prove that rains are sent by Yahweh, not by the storm god Baal or the fertility goddess Asherah. Meanwhile, Elijah takes refuge in the house of a widow from Zarephath, located in Phoenician territory. Yahweh provides for the needs of Elijah and the widow's family right in the middle of Baal's turf.

The contest between Yahweh and Baal climaxes in a staged match on Mount Carmel. A sardonic Elijah mocks four hundred Baal prophets as they try in vain to persuade their god to light a sacrifice with fire from heaven. When Yahweh does consume Elijah's sacrifice, despite the significant handicap of it being drenched in water, there is a clear victor. The prophet's uncompromising zeal for Yahweh then drives him to massacre the Baal prophets. As in the conquest tradition, violence is approved by Deuteronomistic Historians when used against those who compromise the devotion of Israel to Yahweh. Although many modern readers are repelled by this violent impulse, it is not alien to contemporary religions.

Having incurred Jezebel's wrath, Elijah embarks on a wilderness journey that leads him to Mount Horeb (Sinai). The prophet becomes a Moses-figure by paralleling many of Moses' experiences (CD Chart IVC.4). Perhaps Elijah hopes that by revisiting the source of Israel's religious traditions he will receive a new revelation from Yahweh. The deity does indeed speak to the prophet, and he experiences wondrous natural phenomena usually associated with theophanies. However, Yahweh is not in the wind, the earthquake, or the fire; nor does the deity give Elijah any revelation beyond what had already been vouchsafed to Moses. Rather, Yahweh is found in "sheer silence" (translated in the King James Version as a "still small voice"). Assuring Elijah that he is not alone in his faith, the deity instructs him to anoint two new kings (Hazael over Aram/Syria and Jehu over Israel) and an assistant (Elisha). Elijah himself only anoints his assistant, leaving Elisha to complete the other tasks later.

After anointing his successor, Elijah next appears in an account that contains strong echoes of the David and Bathsheba story (1 Kgs. 21). This time, however, the king covets a neighboring vineyard rather than a neighboring wife. When the small landholder Naboth honorably refuses to sell his ancestral land (Lev. 25:23-24), Jezebel stages his execution on false charges, allowing Ahab to claim the property of the deceased. Like the David and Bathsheba story, this account juxtaposes two very different conceptions of monarchy. Phoenician royalty can command their own way by any means necessary, but Israelite monarchs stand under the judgment of the covenant. Elijah abruptly appears at the end of the narrative to pronounce that judgment. Ahab's dynasty will end, and both he and Jezebel will, in essence, become dog food!

In the biblical tradition, Elijah's career ends not with death but with a miraculous ascension into heaven (2 Kgs. 2). The account in which Elijah is whisked away by a whirlwind in a fiery chariot is intended to establish the legitimacy of his successor, Elisha. Their master-disciple relationship, especially in this story, in some ways resembles that of Moses and Joshua (CD Chart IVC.5). This spectacular account also forms a fitting introduction to the cycle of the prophet who took up Elijah's mantle and inherited a double share of his spirit. Much more so than the Elijah traditions, the **Elisha cycle** (2 Kgs. 3–10) illustrates prophetic authority through the performance of miracles. Many readers will be struck by the similarity of several of Elisha's miracles to the earlier mighty deeds of Elijah as well as to those later attributed to Jesus in Christian scripture (CD Chart IVC.6). Readers may also be startled by stories such as the one in which Elisha causes she-bears to maul several taunting boys (2 Kgs. 2:23-25)!

Elisha is also more closely involved in political affairs than his predecessor. Most significantly, he instigates a political coup in Israel by anointing Jehu (by proxy) to overthrow Ahab's house (2 Kgs. 9). Jehu systematically executes every member of Ahab's family, including the Judean king Ahaziah (CD Special Topic IVC.3). After seizing the throne for himself, Jehu purges the northern kingdom of apostasy by massacring all of the prophets, priests, and worshipers of Baal. Jehu's bloody insurrection earns a grudging nod from our historians, who fault him only for failing to destroy the northern shrines at Dan and Bethel. However, the prophet Hosea later condemns Jehu's violent tactics (Hos. 1:4).

After reporting this purge in great detail, our historians rush through the remaining northern kings to arrive at Israel's fall to Assyria (2 Kgs. 17). In 722 B.C.E., Sennacherib deported much of the northern population to other Assyrian provinces and moved in other conquered peoples to take their place. For all practical purposes, the northern kingdom ceased to exist. Our historians interpret Israel's demise in theological terms, claiming that God had caused Israel's fall as a deserved punishment for her continued accommodation to surrounding cultures. Israel and her kings had sinned by worshiping other gods and continuing in the sin of Jeroboam. Because they had ignored repeated prophetic warnings, their fate was deserved. Most of 2 Kings 17 likely dates from the Josianic edition of the Deuteronomistic History. But verses 19-20, which extend Israel's punishment to Judah as well, might belong to the later exilic edition.

Once Israel falls, Judah becomes the sole focus of our historians' attention. The account of Judah's history follows a different course from that of her sister kingdom. Our historians have no kind words for northern monarchs with the possible exception of Jehu. In contrast, eight southern kings receive qualified approval (Solomon, Asa, Jehoshaphat, Joash, Amaziah, Azariah, Jotham, and Hezekiah) and one receives total approval (Josiah). For this reason, Judah's history vacillates between really bad kings and not-so-bad kings. As the storyline progresses toward Josiah, the not-so-bad kings get better and the really bad kings become dreadful. This seesaw effect is most evident in the way our historians present the reigns of Hezekiah, Manasseh, and Josiah.

Hezekiah's nationalistic religious reforms are depicted positively, as is his pious response to a military crisis (2 Kgs. 18–19). Yet our historians also subtly criticize Hezekiah for stripping the temple (2 Kgs. 18:15-16) and for allowing Babylonian ambassadors free access to Judah (2 Kgs. 20:12-19, an account probably added by exilic historians). When Isaiah declares that the Babylonians will one day return to cart away the treasures they have seen, the complacent Hezekiah does not seem disturbed so long as this defeat is not to occur in his own lifetime.

While our historians give Hezekiah mixed reviews, they clearly loathe Manasseh, who is depicted as the worst of the Judean kings (2 Kgs. 21:1-18). He is condemned for rebuilding the high places that Hezekiah had destroyed and committing virtually every form of apostasy imaginable. His reign represents such a low point in Kings that the exilic edition of the Deuteronomistic History blames him for the ultimate destruction of Jerusalem (2 Kgs. 21:10-15).

Our historians next focus on King Josiah, who alone is given their wholehearted approval. As we noted earlier in this chapter, Josiah reasserted Judean independence from Assyria through political and religious reforms. It is likely that an early version of the Deuteronomistic History was composed in order to legitimate his activities. As reported in Kings, Josiah's Reform is motivated by the discovery of a Mosaic law book in the temple that was almost certainly some form of Deuteronomy (CD Chart IVC.7). Inspired by this document, Josiah purges the temple precinct, eradicates Judean high places, and even extends his efforts into Assyrian-held territory that was once the northern kingdom. In the process, he fulfills the prophecy with which our historians began their account of the divided monarchy by destroying and defiling the altar at Bethel (1 Kgs. 13:1-3; 2 Kgs. 23:15-20). Our historians heap upon Josiah praise elsewhere associated only with Moses and depict him holding the first national Passover celebration since the days of Joshua (2 Kgs. 23:21-23; cf. Josh. 5:10-12). The first edition of the Deuteronomistic History likely ended with Josiah's covenant reaffirmation, which bookends Joshua's earlier ratification of the covenant at Shechem.

What is now the ending of Kings (23:26–25:30) was added by exilic historians who updated and revised Josiah's Deuteronomistic History (CD Chart IVC.8). These chapters quickly relate the demise of Judah without the theological reflection typical of earlier chapters (cf. 2 Kgs. 17). Exilic historians also inserted warnings into the earlier Josianic edition that make Judah's ultimate downfall seem inevitable from the very beginning.

Preliminary Exercise IVC.1: The Divided Monarchy
Preliminary Exercise IVC.2: Jezebel's Story
Map IVC.1: The Kingdoms of Israel and Judah
Chart IVC.1: A Chronology of the Northern Kings
Chart IVC.2: A Chronology of the Southern Kings
Chart IVC.3: Regnal Formulas in Kings

STUDYING THE OLD TESTAMENT

The Journey Continues

Overall, the Deuteronomistic History is shaped by two competing theological traditions—one Mosaic and the other Davidic. Mosaic theology emphasizes God's continued fidelity to Israel and her obligation to mirror that fidelity by upholding covenant requirements. It presupposes that everyone, including a king, can experience the positive consequences of obedience and suffer the negative consequences of disobedience. Davidic theology, on the other hand, emphasizes God's unassailable devotion to David and his descendants, who are "ordained" as Israel's divinely appointed rulers. It presupposes that, while God might punish Davidic kings, they will always reign over Israel.

Josiah temporarily embodied both of these two covenant traditions as a Davidic king who shrewdly embraced the book of Deuteronomy as his religious charter. But larger political events led to an untimely death for the young king and transformed what might have been a triumphant story into a tragic one. In its final form, the Deuteronomistic History is a theological account of Israel's journey from conquest to exile. Because exilic historians understood God as the driving force behind that journey, they interpreted national catastrophes in both kingdoms as a deserved punishment for the cumulative sins of the people and their kings.

Did these historians believe that Israel's historical journey would end with exile? The Former Prophets do repeatedly illustrate the efficacy of repentance (1 Kgs. 8:46-53), just as the prophets featured within these books offer both judgment and promise. Although sin will have its consequences, perhaps the promise itself had not been voided. This hope

Former Prophets: A Nation's Journey   *165*

could account for one peculiar detail in the detail-sparse final chapters of Kings: a scion of the Davidic line still lived and ate at the royal table in Babylon (2 Kgs. 25:27-30). Perhaps this modest hope at the end of the Deuteronomistic History signals the possibility of a new beginning. Yahweh might yet enable a return from exile.

CHAPTER FOUR

LATTER PROPHETS: ISRAEL'S MORAL COMPASS

In the last chapter we traced the Deuteronomistic account of Israel's national journey from conquest to exile. Important landmarks along this journey included the conditional gift of a promised land, the emergence of a monarchy and its accompanying royal ideology, the division of Israel into two separate nations (Israel and Judah), and the fall of both kingdoms in the crush of larger international events. In its final form, this history suggested that the tragic course of Israel's journey was determined by her covenant disobedience. Despite the promise of the Davidic covenant and the abortive reform efforts of two late Judean monarchs, the history ended with only the barest hint of hope that Judah might have a future beyond exile.

Prophets like Samuel, Nathan, Elijah, Elisha, and Isaiah were prominent characters in the narratives of the Deuteronomistic History. Readers will observe a sudden shift as we now turn to books that are attributed to individual prophets. These books consist primarily of poetic speeches and sayings, while stories about prophets appear only rarely. Partly for this reason, we are entering a more difficult phase of our journey through the Hebrew Bible. Although the imagery employed by biblical prophets is powerful and haunting, Hebrew poetry is unlike anything most modern readers have previously encountered. We will therefore need to familiarize ourselves with basic characteristics of this literary form (see CD Special Topic IB.2).

We will also need to contend with the perplexing internal arrangement of prophetic books. Each is an anthology of material that is traditionally associated with the prophet for whom the book is named. However, these anthologies do not seem to be organized according to any consistent principle. Readers instead encounter amid occasional narratives a confusing jumble of sayings that leap from topic to topic. Most prophetic sayings appear to address particular audiences and historical settings, but these are rarely identified explicitly. The reader's dilemma is analogous to someone who overhears snippets of a telephone conversation from another room. To understand even in part, we must figure out the context of the conversation and who is on the other end of the line.

The placement of these books within the Jewish canon also suggests the importance of historical context. These books constitute the second half of the Prophets (Hebrew *nevi'im*), which is the second of three canonical divisions represented by the consonants of the acronym Tanakh (*torah, nevi'im, ketuvim*). This arrangement invites readers to familiarize themselves with the narrative of Israel's historical journey found in the first half of the *nevi'im* (Joshua through Kings) before reading the words of the prophets. Not until the Middle Ages did a formal distinction arise between Former Prophets (narrative historical books) and Latter Prophets (poetic anthologies). Such a distinction is misleading for several reasons, not the least of which is that it suggests the anthologies are later than the history. In actuality, most of the Latter Prophets fit within the events described in 2 Kings, and many begin with headings that date the prophets' careers in relation to Israelite and Judean kings. Such headings encourage readers to interpret the anthologies in tandem with the historical books in which accounts of these kings appear.

Another distinction is sometimes made between **Major Prophets** (Isaiah, Jeremiah, and Ezekiel) and **Minor Prophets** (Hosea, Amos, Micah, Joel, Obadiah, Jonah, Nahum, Habakkuk, Zephaniah, Haggai,

Zechariah, and Malachi). This terminology is also potentially misleading if it is taken to mean that the so-called Major Prophets are more important. In reality, these labels indicate nothing more than the relative length of the anthologies. Isaiah, Jeremiah, and Ezekiel are much longer than the books attributed to other prophets. Because scrolls in antiquity were fairly standard in length, each of the Major Prophets required a separate scroll whereas the other twelve appeared together on a fourth. For this reason, the Minor Prophets are often referred to collectively in Jewish circles as the **Book of the Twelve**.

Whereas the Latter Prophets occupy the middle of the Jewish canon, Christian canons place them at the end of the Old Testament as an introduction to the New Testament Gospels. Early Christians found within the Latter Prophets a vision for the future that they felt had come to fruition in the life and mission of Jesus. Unfortunately, the sequence adopted by Christian canons divorces prophetic anthologies from the narrative of Israel's history and potentially reduces all of the rich and varied themes within prophetic literature to "predictions of Jesus."

To appreciate the Latter Prophets fully, we must first read them within their own historical contexts. Clearly, the prophets did not speak in a vacuum but were closely attuned to the international developments of their day. The headings and other historical clues within these books place most of them into three distinct chronological periods during the latter halves of the eighth, seventh, and sixth centuries B.C.E. Each of these periods corresponds to the dominance of a different political superpower that effected sweeping changes across the ancient Near East: the Assyrians, the Babylonians, and the Persians. On the course of Israel's national journey, these turbulent centuries represented particularly rugged terrain. Like a moral compass, the biblical prophets helped interpret the ever-changing map of the ancient Near East in terms of Israel's own covenant traditions.

THE ASSYRIAN PERIOD
(745–612 B.C.E.)

Because we cannot understand the Latter Prophets adequately apart from their historical contexts, our journey through this section of the Hebrew Bible will proceed more or less chronologically. This approach will require us to depart from the sequence in which these books appear in either the Jewish or Christian canons. A brief overview of Israel's history was provided in chapter 1. In this section, we will take a closer look at the Assyrian period and its effect upon the Bible's prophetic literature. We will use this first leg of our journey to search for clues to the social origins of prophecy and the literary origins of prophetic literature—topics that we will examine in the Interlude of this chapter.

A Closer Look at the Assyrian Period (CD Chart IA.1)

The beginning of the eighth century found both the northern and southern kingdoms enjoying unprecedented levels of prosperity. The Assyrian threat that was to shape their history for the next century had not yet materialized. Israel and Judah were experiencing territorial gains and economic success under the leadership of King Jeroboam II (787–746 B.C.E.) and King Uzziah (783–742 B.C.E.), respectively. Many in both kingdoms surely interpreted this prosperity as a sign of divine favor and blessing.

Admittedly, however, this affluence was mostly enjoyed by the elite inhabitants of large cities like Samaria and Jerusalem. The rise of a wealthy urban upper class coincided with the impoverishment of another segment of the population. A widening gulf between rich and poor was exacerbated by the need to sustain state bureaucracies in both kingdoms and a temple complex in the south. In addition to imposing a tax burden, the monarchy also eroded old tribal structures that at one time had provided an economic safety net for the poor (for example, Deut. 15). Now farmers who experienced crop failure were forced to seek loans that often resulted in inescapable debt and loss of land, while a wealthy minority accumulated large estates. As some Israelites celebrated God's blessing upon the land, others mourned the loss of traditional covenant values and decried the resulting social injustice.

New theological questions arose after the death of Jeroboam II when the northern kingdom was suddenly plunged into a period of political chaos. Over the next twenty-four years, four of the six kings who ruled Israel would be assassinated. In the midst of this domestic turmoil loomed a growing international threat. Tiglath-pileser III (who is called "Pul" in 2 Kings) ascended to the Assyrian throne in 745 B.C.E. and began a period of aggressive expansion (CD Map IA.1). Under his rule, Assyria's highly disciplined standing army began to systematically capture fortified towns using sustained **sieges**, massive earthen ramps, and battering rams. Conquered populations were kept under control with fear tactics such as the threat of atrocities against civilians and mass deportations. **Vassal** kings who exhibited signs of disloyalty were usually replaced with Assyrian sympathizers. If resistance continued, the vassal state would be annexed as an Assyrian province, its upper class deported, and a foreign population resettled in its place. This policy discouraged rebellion by depriving the local population of their most capable leaders and blurring its distinctive national identity.

The struggling northern kingdom must have wondered why its fortunes had changed so rapidly and what role Yahweh might play in these tumultuous circumstances. Northern kings had to decide whether to resist the looming Assyrian threat by mounting Israel's defenses or submit to the empire by paying **tribute**. Regardless, the resulting economic burden was passed on to the lower class. As Israel's economic resources were depleted, existing social inequities worsened.

Israel became a vassal state of the **Assyrian Empire** when King Menahem (745–738 B.C.E.) opted to pay tribute to Tiglath-pileser (2 Kgs. 15:19-20). But, in 737 B.C.E., the throne of Israel was seized by Pekah, who forged an anti-Assyrian alliance with King Rezin of Syria. These two kings appealed for support from their southern neighbor, King **Ahaz** of Judah (735–715 B.C.E.). When Ahaz refused to join their coalition, Pekah and Rezin decided to invade Judah and replace him with someone more sympathetic to their cause. This conflict, remembered as the **Syro-Ephraimite War**, drove the Judean monarch to seek aid from no other source than Assyria itself. To escape from the barracuda attacking him, Ahaz called upon a shark!

Tiglath-pileser willingly accepted Judah's hasty petition to become a vassal state of his empire and then turned to crush his disloyal vassals as he doubtless would have done anyway. The Syro-Ephraimite coalition quickly fell before the might of the imperial army. All of Syria and large portions of Israel were annexed as Assyrian provinces. Much of the native population was deported and foreigners were resettled there from other parts of the empire. What remained of Israel was entrusted to a new vassal king named Hoshea (732–724 B.C.E.). Foolishly, Hoshea also rebelled, leading to the final defeat of the northern kingdom in 722 B.C.E., around the time Sargon II ascended to the Assyrian throne. Even more of Israel's population was deported, and its remaining territory became the Assyrian province of Samaria. Some Israelites likely fled south to Judah at this time. The population that remained mixed with the foreign groups whom Assyria continued to settle in Samaria (CD Special Topic IA.1). For all practical purposes, the ten northern tribes were lost forever.

The population of Judah had witnessed up close what might happen to nations who resisted Assyrian authority. Some Judeans likely interpreted Israel's fall as a deserved punishment for their rebellion against the Davidic house and congratulated themselves for their moral superi-

STUDYING THE OLD TESTAMENT

ority. Others took the fate of the northern kingdom to heart as a warning of what theological judgment might await them as well. The lesson was repeated early in the reign of the Judean king Hezekiah (715–687 B.C.E.) when Assyria crushed another coalition sponsored by Egypt at the Philistine city of Ashdod.

Nevertheless, like many other vassal kings, Hezekiah saw the unrest accompanying the death of Sargon II in 705 B.C.E. as an opportune moment to reassert his nation's independence. Hezekiah's religious reform (which we discussed in chapter 3) should be understood in part as a nationalistic declaration aimed at ridding his kingdom of so-called foreign elements. Centralization of worship in the Davidic capital would have strengthened his control of the Judean countryside as a prelude to rebellion. Hezekiah also pursued an alliance with Egypt, fortified many Judean cities, and even constructed a tunnel that would provide water for Jerusalem in the event of a siege. Unfortunately, the king's building projects and the pilgrimages instituted by his reforms placed additional burdens upon the poorest of Judean society.

Moreover, these subversive activities brought the predictable response. Once Sennacherib gained possession of the Assyrian throne, he set about securing his hold over the empire. In 701 B.C.E., he mounted a devastating campaign against Judah. Jerusalem, however, did not fall, despite Sennacherib's claim to have shut up the Judean king "like a bird in a cage." Although Assyrian and biblical accounts of the Jerusalem siege diverge, both report that Hezekiah paid a large ransom before Sennacherib's army withdrew. For many Judeans this close call proved that God would protect Jerusalem and the Davidic king. Nevertheless, Judah had barely survived the rebellion and would continue to live under Assyrian rule for nearly another century.

Map IA.1: The Assyrian Empire
Chart IA.1: Timeline of the Assyrian Period (745–612 B.C.E.)
Special Topic IA.1: Who Were/Are the Samaritans?

Latter Prophets: Israel's Moral Compass

Assyrian Period Prophets
(CD Preliminary Exercises IB.1 and IB.2)

Assyrian expansion and the loss of political independence raised profound theological questions for Israel and Judah. Primarily, the inhabitants of both kingdoms must have wondered why Yahweh did not protect them from this foreign oppressor. In response, many prophets of the eighth century insisted that Yahweh still firmly grasped the reins of history and was using Assyria as an instrument of divine judgment for covenant infidelity. Whereas to an objective observer Israel and Judah would appear merely as "bit players" in the midst of sweeping political changes, the prophets saw them as the center of ancient Near Eastern events.

Assyrian Period Prophets at a Glance	
Amos (ca. 760–750 B.C.E.): a Judean who preaches in Israel that God will soon destroy the prosperous kingdom for the social injustices of its elite.	**First Isaiah/Isaiah 1–39** (ca. 742–701 B.C.E.): a prophet from Jerusalem who advises Judean kings to accept Yahweh's judgment at the hands of Assyria and trust that the deity will ultimately protect Zion and its king.
Hosea (ca. 750–722 B.C.E.): a northerner who draws a comparison between his marriage to an unfaithful woman and Yahweh's covenant with unfaithful Israel.	**Micah** (ca. 730–701 B.C.E.): a rural southerner who warns that Jerusalem will soon fall to Assyria because its wealthy residents have exploited the poor.

Amos (Am. 1–2; 5:18-24; 7–9)

The book of Amos begins with a **superscription**, or heading, that relates this prophet's activity to the reigns of Jeroboam II and Uzziah (Am. 1:1-2). Because it refers to the prophet in the third person and mentions an earthquake that occurred two years after his career had ended, it was probably added by a later editor. This is an important clue to the literary origins of prophetic books, which we will revisit in the Interlude of this chapter. Such a memorable earthquake may well have been taken as a confirmation of the prophet's message (cf. Zech. 14:3-5). Because traces of it are still visible in excavations at Hazor, we can date Amos's prophetic career within the decade between 760–750 B.C.E.

The superscription also tells us that Amos's activity involved *speaking* and *seeing* ("The words of Amos . . . which he saw . . ."). Observant readers will notice that the first six chapters of the book are dominated by **oracles**, or sayings that are attributed directly to Yahweh but presumably spoken by the prophet. These chapters are punctuated periodically with the refrain "Thus says [Yahweh] . . . ." Without the aid of telephones or email, rulers in the ancient world often employed messengers to communicate with people at a distance. Such messengers would speak to their audience as if they actually were the person they represented (for example, 2 Kgs. 18:28-29). Amos and most of the other prophets make liberal use of this **messenger formula**. The last three chapters of the book are dominated by first-person reports of **visions** experienced and interpreted by the prophet (CD Chart IB.1).

Finally, the superscription gives us a tantalizing bit of biographical information. Amos was "among the shepherds of Tekoa," a small town little more than ten miles south of Jerusalem. In other words, although he prophesied in Israel, he was a native of Judah. Amos's "outsider" status is later reiterated in a biographical report of his confrontation at Bethel with a northern priest named Amaziah (Am. 7:10-17). The priest accuses Amos of political conspiracy and demands that he return to Judah and prophesy there instead. Surprisingly, Amos disparagingly replies that he is not a prophet or a member of a **prophetic guild** ("sons of prophets"), but a herdsman and tender of sycamore-fig trees (CD Special Topic IB.1). His words suggest contempt for professional prophets, whose income might depend upon delivering pleasing oracles.

Amos's Judean background likely contributed to his poor reception in Israel (Am. 5:10), but the content of his message certainly did not help matters either. Ironically, in the context of the peaceful and prosperous reign of Jeroboam II, Amos warns of divine judgment in the form of an imminent national catastrophe. What crimes had Israel committed to deserve such a fate? For many, the nation's current prosperity demonstrated God's approval and blessing. For Amos, however, the nation's so-called success was part of the problem because the wealthy lived on the backs of the poor.

This prophet's passionate critique of an unjust society has inspired many later social and religious activists. For example, Martin Luther King, Jr. echoed Amos's call to "let justice roll down like waters, and righteousness like an ever-flowing stream" (Am. 5:24). Amos vividly depicts his audience trampling upon the poor, pushing aside the afflicted, and selling the needy for a pair of shoes. In this total absence of social compassion, the desperately poor shivered through the night because their garments had been taken as collateral on loans that they could never hope to repay. Their creditors apparently ignored laws that forbade interest-accruing loans and that demanded the return of cloaks taken in pledge before nightfall (Exod. 22:25-27; Deut. 24:10-13, 17).

Clearly, the prophet's audience is not the poor whose plight he so movingly represents. Rather, Amos addresses the social elite who were benefiting from this unjust system (Am. 3:15; 4:1; 6:4). He also directs his message toward the political and religious leaders whose responsibility it was to ensure justice (Hebrew *mishpat*) and righteousness (Hebrew *tsedakah*). These twin ethical categories, which appear together frequently throughout the book, are similar but not synonymous. The first indicates acts of charitable generosity, whereas the second refers to the attitude that produces such acts. Hebrew poetry often pairs such words to add rich layers of nuance and meaning (CD Special Topic IB.2).

Where justice and righteousness are absent, worship is unpleasing to God. Amos's criticism of Israelite sanctuaries and sacrifices must be read within the context of his social critique. The prophet is not claiming that organized worship and animal sacrifice are wrong in and of themselves. In fact, it would be unthinkable for a person of his era to conceive of religion apart from such forms. What Amos does passionately condemn is worship that is divorced from social justice (Am. 5:21-24).

We may assume that the wealthy of Israel considered themselves very religious and viewed their affluence as a sign of divine favor. After all, the prophet depicts a non-stop barrage of festivals, songs, and offerings at northern sanctuaries! These Israelites were patriotically certain that Yahweh was their patron deity. To jar them out of this optimistic complacency, Amos reverses traditional beliefs and expectations. For instance, it was commonly expected that a **Day of Yahweh** was imminent when the deity would elevate Israel before the world and destroy their enemies (CD Special Topic IB.3). The prophet, however, ominously warns that when it arrives this will be a day of darkness, not light (Am. 4:12; 5:18-20; 8:9-10).

The formulaic series of oracles that begins the book is another example of expectations reversed (Am. 1:3–2:16). These "oracles against foreign nations" would delight Amos's listeners by declaring God's judgment against their neighbors for atrocities and war crimes. The seventh and presumably last nation condemned is Judah, Israel's sister-state and the prophet's own homeland. Just as his audience is ready to applaud, Amos reaches his unexpected punch line—Israel stands under judgment as well! This series of oracles presupposes the deity's international sovereignty. Yet the charges leveled at Judah and Israel are different from those made against other nations. Because they have been chosen by God and received special divine revelation, Israel and Judah are expected to meet higher standards. Amos interprets election as a call for greater moral responsibility rather than national arrogance.

The indictments of Israel in the early chapters of the book are matched in intensity by the visions of judgment in its final chapters. In the first two visions the deity shows Amos locusts (Am. 7:1-3) and fire (Am. 7:4-6), both of which the prophet understands spell doom for Israel. In each case, Amos intercedes on behalf of the threatened people and God relents. The third vision of a plumb line (Am. 7:7-9) reveals the reason for imminent judgment. A plumb line is a weight attached to a string that provides a standard of verticality that allows builders to determine whether walls are straight. When Yahweh uses such an instrument on Israel, they turn out to be hopelessly crooked. Significantly, the prophet no longer intercedes, and God no longer relents. Amaziah's rebuke of Amos appears before the fourth vision, perhaps to illustrate that the prophet's warning has been rejected by Israel. The fourth vision (Am. 8:1-3) rests upon a Hebrew pun that is, unfortunately, lost in translation. Showing Amos a basket of fruit (Hebrew *qayits*), the deity declares that the end (Hebrew *qets*) has come upon Israel. Sure enough, in the final vision (Am. 9:1-4) the prophet sees Yahweh call for destruction.

The mounting intensity of these vision reports suggests that Israel's punishment is unavoidable. Readers cannot help but notice an almost unrelenting spirit of doom in this book. We might doubt whether Amos believed that even sincere repentance could avert the coming disaster. In an abrupt change of tone at the very end of the book, readers do find one hopeful oracle of consolation (Am. 9:11-15). But strangely, this epilogue refers to Judah whereas Amos's warning had been directed toward Israel. This oracle presupposes that the southern kingdom had already fallen and anticipates its restoration. Moreover, it is steeped in Davidic royal ideology, which is rarely found elsewhere in the book (cf. Am. 1:2). Although a southerner, Amos seems much more interested in Mosaic-exodus traditions than in Jerusalem or the Davidic house. In all likelihood, this hopeful epilogue is a much later addition to Amos (another important clue regarding the literary origins of prophetic books). Apparently, Amos himself could only hope that mauled pieces of Israel's body might be retrieved from the lion's mouth (Am. 3:12)!

Hosea (Hos. 1–3; 11)

Whereas Amos was a Judean interloper in Israel, Hosea appears to have been a native of the northern kingdom. His prophetic career began during that of Amos but lasted much longer. It is usually dated based on historical references within the book from the latter days of Jeroboam II (ca. 750 B.C.E.) to shortly before the fall of Israel in 722 B.C.E. Strangely, however, the book's superscription completely ignores the last six Israelite kings while listing all of the Judean monarchs who ruled during this period (Hos. 1:1). This suggests that the heading was added later, probably by a southern editor who was not particularly interested in the details of northern history.

Hosea witnessed the fall of Jehu's dynasty, the rise of Assyria under Tiglath-pileser III, and the political chaos occasioned in Israel by both of these developments. Unlike Amos, who warned of an unspecified danger in a time of security, Hosea's warnings concerned an Assyrian threat that stood upon Israel's very doorstep. Although several passages echo Amos's accusations of social injustice (Hos. 8:10; 10:6; 12:7-8), that is not Hosea's primary concern. Instead, this prophet attributes Israel's domestic and foreign crises to its infidelity to Yahweh. Hosea places the blame for this situation on inept kings and a corrupt priesthood.

Chapters 1–3, perhaps the best-known part of the book, present Hosea's domestic life as a parable of God's relationship to unfaithful Israel. God gives Hosea the rather strange command to initiate a relationship with a wanton woman, but a quick comparison of English translation reveals some confusion regarding exactly how wanton this woman was to be! She is variously described as a promiscuous woman, an adulteress, a cult prostitute, and a professional whore. Observant readers will note that the first two chapters of Hosea are biographical whereas the third is autobiographical. It is unclear if these two accounts refer to two different marriages or if the unnamed woman in the second account is also Gomer. Although prophets did occasionally perform outrageous symbolic acts (cf. Isa. 20:1-6), it is uncertain whether Hosea's marriage(s) actually occurred or served as a literary metaphor personifying disloyal Israel as an unfaithful wife.

If a marriage did occur, we might pity Hosea's children on account of their unenviable symbolic names. Jezreel (Hebrew *yizreel*), meaning "God sows," sounds suspiciously like Israel (Hebrew *yisrael*) and is the name of the valley where Jehu had conducted his bloody purge of the preceding dynasty (2 Kgs. 9). Thus, this name presages doom for both the nation and its current ruling house. The name Lo-ruhamah, meaning "not pitied," symbolizes the lack of compassion Israel deserved from Yahweh. The name Lo-ammi, meaning "not my people," indicates a break in the covenant relationship (cf. Exod. 6:7).

These children are implored to help Hosea stop their mother's promiscuous behavior. Chapter 2 describes measures taken by the prophet to punish and discipline his wife. Here the book's chosen metaphor becomes uncomfortable for many modern readers. The physical and psychological abuse inflicted upon both Gomer and her children must be understood in terms of ancient Israelite marriage customs (CD Special Topic IB.4). Many readers are also disturbed by the analogy that the book draws between God and an abusive husband (however much provoked). Hosea's actions toward his wife are intended to symbolize God's imminent judgment upon unfaithful Israel. The ultimate reconciliation of husband and wife suggests that Israel's punishment will serve a disciplinary function and not permanently eradicate the nation. However, this metaphor works only in a context where it is assumed that women are totally dependent upon men and violence is justified when wives and daughters behave "dishonorably." Modern readers might also object to this text's confident association of a masculine role with God and a feminine role with the sinful people (CD Special Topic IB.5). Hosea later employs a parent-child metaphor that avoids this difficulty (Hos. 11:1-9).

Hosea is the first prophet to use the metaphor of marriage to describe the covenant between God and Israel. Such erotic language is actually drawn from the mythology associated with the Canaanite fertility god Baal, whose worship Hosea condemns. Baal mythology connects the annual death and resurrection of this deity with the transition from the dry season to the rainy season. More specifically, intercourse between Baal and the goddess Anath, who enables his resurrection, was thought to bestow fertility upon the land. In the northern prophetic tradition of Elijah, Hosea declares that it is Yahweh rather than Baal who actually controls fertility and provides for Israel. Thus, there is no need to turn for assistance either to another deity or to political superpowers like Assyria and Egypt (Hos. 5:13; 7:8-15; 8:9-10; 12:1). Moreover, Hosea claims that Yahweh is married to Israel herself rather than a goddess. Israel's worship of Baal (ba'al means "master/husband") is tantamount to adultery, and Yahweh longs for his people like a jealous husband (Hos. 2:16).

Hosea, who draws heavily from exodus traditions, especially romanticizes the wilderness period as a "honeymoon" between God and Israel. He calls for a return to the wilderness where the vows of the covenant relationship can be renewed (Hos. 2:14-15; 9:10; 13:4-6). In this spirit, the prophet renames his two younger children; Lo-ruhamah becomes Ruhamah, meaning "pitied," and Lo-ammi becomes Ammi, meaning "my people" (Hos. 2:23). Such optimism appears not just in isolated oracles; each section of the book moves systematically from images of doom to hope (CD Chart IB.2).

Unfortunately, Hosea was wrong. The prophet describes a period of discipline followed by restoration, but the northern kingdom never recovered from its fall to Assyria. The words of the prophet lived on, however, in the memory of some who survived the destruction of 722

B.C.E. These words were reapplied to later generations in Judah by southern editors who supplemented the northern prophet's message with their own theological traditions (Hos. 1:7; 3:4-5; 11:12b).

First Isaiah (Isa. 1–12; 28–33)

The anthology associated with the Jerusalemite prophet Isaiah presents many ideas already familiar to us from northern prophets of the Assyrian period. Like Amos, Isaiah is concerned with social compassion and frequently indicts his audience for their neglect of justice and righteousness. Like Hosea, Isaiah sometimes depicts Yahweh as a parent and his audience as a rebellious child. He often criticizes national leaders and the wealthy social elite. Most important, like his counterparts in the northern kingdom, Isaiah proclaims divine judgment in the form of an imminent catastrophe upon his nation.

Yet careful readers will discover much that is new in the book of Isaiah. Alongside declarations that all the cities of Judah will be laid waste (Isa. 6:11-13), we find oracles promising that Yahweh will protect Jerusalem from harm (Isa. 31:5). In addition to judgment, we also find sketches of a glorious age when Jerusalem will rule over other nations in an era of peace—swords shall be made into plowshares and spears into pruning hooks (Isa. 2:2-4). In some passages, this spirit of disarmament extends even into the animal kingdom where we find the wolf coexisting peacefully with the lamb (Isa. 11:6-9). Such jarring contrasts can make the book of Isaiah rather difficult to interpret.

Another difficulty is the very length and complexity of this book, which is the first of the so-called Major Prophets. It should come as no surprise at this stage of our journey to find that the words of Isaiah have been shaped and supplemented by later editors. We have already seen evidence of such editing in Amos and Hosea. We will return to the question of how prophetic books were formed in the Interlude of this chapter. For now, let it suffice to say that later generations contributed much to Isaiah. Only material within chapters 1–39 is usually associated with the eighth-century prophet, so for the sake of convenience we will call these chapters **First Isaiah** (CD Chart IB.3). Because even here we find signs of later editing, we will confine our discussion to chapters 1–12 and 28–33, which clearly reflect the concerns of the Assyrian period.

According to the book's superscription, Isaiah was active during the reigns of Uzziah, Jotham, Ahaz, and Hezekiah (Isa. 1:1). If he indeed began his prophetic career in the year that King Uzziah died (Isa. 6:1), we can date his activity between 742–701 B.C.E. His first-person **call narrative** depicts a vision of Yahweh enthroned within the temple and surrounded by six fiery angelic beings called **seraphim** (Isa. 6). A comparison of Isaiah's call narrative with those of other prophets reveals that these stories tended to have certain standard features: upon receiving a divine commission, the prophet typically expresses reservations and must be persuaded and equipped for the task ahead (CD Chart IB.4). Everything about Isaiah's call draws attention to divine holiness. The vision takes place in the temple, the seraphim modestly cover their faces and genitals (for which "feet" is a common biblical euphemism), and Isaiah protests that he is too unclean to even be there. Before he can receive a prophetic call, his lips must be purified with a burning coal. The vision also reinforces Yahweh's sovereignty. Uzziah might be dead, but Israel's deity still sits upon the heavenly throne. Strangely, the prophet is commissioned to obfuscate rather than enlighten (Isa. 6:9-10). This could suggest that Isaiah's call narrative was shaped after his message of judgment had fallen on deaf ears.

This happens in the next chapter when the prophet advises King Ahaz on the eve of the Syro-Ephraimite War (Isa. 7). Readers might recall that Ahaz was *not* Uzziah's immediate successor. In fact, there is an eight-year gap between the time of Isaiah's call in chapter 6 and the events related in chapter 7. Because it is highly unlikely that the prophet remained silent for eight years, we might wonder how the book came to be arranged this way. Again we have located an important clue about the literary origins of prophetic books, which we will revisit in the Interlude.

Isaiah seems to have had much easier access to the royal court than did Amos or Hosea. He also is depicted as a trusted advisor to the king in 2 Kings 18–20 (cf. Isa. 36–39). Yet he does not always say what kings would have wanted to hear. With Judah under invasion by the armies of Israel and Syria, Isaiah advises King Ahaz against taking rash action or, in fact, any action at all! His message is simply to trust Yahweh, whose plans for Judah are inevitable. Because part of that plan is the continued advance of Assyria, the Syro-Ephraimite coalition will fail.

The prophet offers a **sign** to verify his message. Prophetic signs were generally not miraculous events but natural occurrences that were given significance by their interpretation. Isaiah had already named his own son Shear-jashub ("a remnant shall return"), indicating hope beyond Judah's judgment. He now points to the birth of a child named Immanuel ("God is with us") as a sign of deliverance from Judah's present crisis (Isa. 7:10-17). This passage has taken on great significance in Christian tradition because it is quoted by Matthew's Gospel, where it is associated with Jesus (CD Special Topic IB.6). Isaiah, however, is clearly referring to a more immediate birth. He could hardly expect King Ahaz to be comforted by the assurance that his attackers would be gone in a little over seven hundred years!

It is likely that the young woman (the Hebrew text does not call her a "virgin") is Ahaz's own wife and her unborn child is Hezekiah, Israel's next king. The birth of a royal heir to continue the Davidic line would be interpreted as a sign of hope and divine blessing. Moreover, Hezekiah was born around the time of the Syro-Ephraimite conflict and, incidentally, came of age around the time Israel fell to Assyria. As a second sign Isaiah himself has another son, whom he names Maher-shalal-hash-baz ("the spoil speeds, the prey hastens"), indicating that Syria and Israel will soon become prey and spoil for Assyria. When Ahaz disregarded Isaiah by unnecessarily volunteering to become an Assyrian vassal, the prophet

STUDYING THE OLD TESTAMENT

seems to have retired temporarily from public activity. It may have been at that time that he taught his message to a group of disciples (Isa. 8:16-17)—yet another clue to the literary origins of the Latter Prophets.

The prophet's career resumes during the reign of Hezekiah, and the hymn in Isaiah 9:2-7 likely celebrates that king's birth or ascension. Unlike Amos and Hosea, who drew upon Mosaic-exodus traditions, Isaiah presupposes the Davidic covenant and Zion theology. Although he had been disappointed in Ahaz, the prophet hopes that the next Davidic king will prove more faithful. Isaiah also views the Davidic capital as Yahweh's invincible residence. Surely Jerusalem would weather the coming judgment and be the base from which a surviving **remnant** would usher in a glorious new age.

The prophet's advice to Hezekiah is consistent with his earlier counsel to Ahaz: take no action to resist God's plans. Because Isaiah considers Assyria to be God's chosen instrument, he discourages Hezekiah from participating in any anti-Assyrian alliance. In an outrageous symbolic act, the prophet walks around Jerusalem barefoot and naked like a prisoner of war for three years to illustrate the consequences of resisting Assyria (Isa. 20). Isaiah urges the king to rely on Yahweh for protection rather than putting his trust in military might (Isa. 31:4-9). Despite Isaiah's advice, Hezekiah did eventually form an alliance with Egypt (Isa. 30:1-7; 31:1-3).

Yet, as First Isaiah currently stands, it ends with a narrative that was copied from 2 Kings. This narrative, which depicts a pious Hezekiah relying heavily upon the advice of the prophet during the Assyrian invasion, presents a more favorable picture of this king than do the oracles in Isaiah 28–33. It also forms a counterpoint to the book's earlier account of the Syro-Ephraimite War in chapters 7–8. The placement of these narratives at either end of First Isaiah contrasts the foolishness of King Ahaz with the piety of his son. To later generations, King Hezekiah becomes a model of how to respond to crisis situations. In the dark days to come, Judah would need such a model.

Micah (Mic. 1–3; 6:1-8)

The prophet Micah also offered a theological interpretation of Judah's situation during the Assyrian period. Although responding to some of the same historical events as Isaiah, Micah often saw matters differently. The preservation of both prophets' messages within the biblical canon greatly enriches our appreciation for the diversity of religious thought in ancient Judah.

The book's superscription (Mic. 1:1) says that this prophet's career coincided with the reigns of Jotham, Ahaz, and Hezekiah. However, nothing within this prophetic anthology presupposes a context prior to 730 B.C.E. If Micah was active during the reign of Jotham, his message from that time was not preserved. The book does reflect upon the fall of the northern kingdom in 722 B.C.E., which it takes as a harbinger of things to come in Judah (Mic. 1:2-16). Even more attention is given to events surrounding the Assyrian invasion of 701 B.C.E. In fact, the book is shaped by the prophet's conviction that Jerusalem was about to be "plowed as a field" by the Assyrian army (Mic. 3:12). Micah's career can, thus, be dated rather securely between 730–701 B.C.E.

Micah relies heavily upon exodus traditions (Mic. 6:1-5) and scorns the prophets of his day who proclaimed peace and security based upon Zion theology (Mic. 3:5-12). Readers might wonder whether he would have gotten along very well with Isaiah, who insisted that God would spare Jerusalem from the coming destruction (Isa. 31:4-5). The different perspectives of these prophets might be explained in part by their different social backgrounds. Whereas Isaiah was likely a member of the Jerusalem aristocracy who frequently rubbed elbows with kings, Micah was from the village of Moresheth (Mic. 1:1). Micah's hometown was located near Lachish, a city Sennacherib captured and used as a base of operations during his siege of Jerusalem. It is likely that Micah and his neighbors felt the effects of the devastation the Assyrians inflicted on the Judean countryside (Mic. 1:10-16).

This rural prophet decries the corruption of the Jerusalem establishment (Mic. 3) and the economic injustices inflicted on small farmers (Mic. 2:1-5; 6:9-16). Like Amos, he addresses the wealthy elite that oppressed the poor for their own advantage. Micah graphically portrays those who pervert justice as cannibals feasting on the flesh of his people (Mic. 3:1-3). The prophet also criticizes the sacrificial system that placed such a drain on agrarian resources and declares that Yahweh only requires worshipers "to do justice, and to love kindness, and to walk humbly with your God" (Mic. 6:8).

Micah's call for social compassion is timeless, but his prediction that Jerusalem would fall before Sennacherib's army failed. The southern capital narrowly escaped disaster and even outlasted the Assyrian Empire. Nevertheless, his words were preserved by later generations who updated them to address their own circumstances. Some later editors envisioned a glorious future for Jerusalem that clashes with the prophet's own disdain for Zion theology (Mic. 2:12-13; 4:1–5:1). One such passage has been lifted almost verbatim from Isaiah (Mic. 4:1-3; cf. Isa. 2:2-4). Those who witnessed Jerusalem's fall to Babylon in 587 B.C.E. likely believed that Micah's message of judgment had found a belated fulfillment (Mic. 4:9-10). Likewise, the final verses of the book hold out hope that God's anger will soon subside so that the Davidic kingdom can be restored (Mic. 7:8-20). The final shape of this book is the work of many hands and, perhaps intentionally, alternates between words of judgment and hope (CD Chart IB.5).

In summary, Assyrian period prophecy contains several common themes. First, these prophets were all protesters against the establishment. Although the precise content of their message varied, they all denounced nationalistic piety that would reduce Yahweh to a patron deity who offers protection and blessings but does not sit in judgment against idolatry and social injustice. They would not allow the religious and political establishments of their day to domesticate the deity for their own gain. Second, they all insisted that despite appearances

Yahweh was still in control of historical events and determined to punish covenant violations. Assyria was merely an instrument in Yahweh's hands for this purpose. Finally, as they now stand, each of these prophetic books concludes with hope for a future beyond judgment.

INTERLUDE:
THE SOCIAL ORIGINS
OF PROPHECY AND THE
LITERARY ORIGINS OF
THE LATTER PROPHETS

Moving beyond Naïve Assumptions
(CD Preliminary Exercise IIA.1)

By this point in our journey through the Latter Prophets, we have seen enough to begin forming a preliminary understanding of prophecy and prophetic literature. Many readers of the Hebrew Bible assume the prophets were solitary figures that functioned more or less as God's secretaries—receiving inspired words and visions pertaining to the future that they faithfully proclaimed and copied into the books that bear their names. Our observations thus far force us to reject such romantic notions. This is not necessarily a rejection of the belief that prophets were inspired individuals. Yet the way in which prophets functioned and the way in which prophetic literature was produced were clearly much more complicated than this naïve image suggests.

First of all, we must question the common assumption that prophets were solitary persons. Clearly, a prophet's message would not have survived unless some people considered it meaningful and authoritative. There are many hints that the prophets were surrounded by disciples or were parts of social groups that had a role in transmitting their words. A group of disciples memorizes the teachings of Isaiah (Isa. 8:16). A group of elders quotes Micah a century after his career has ended (Jer. 26:1-19). Jeremiah is assisted by the scribe Baruch (Jer. 36:4-6) and supported by the family of Shaphan (Jer. 26:24; 39:14; 40:5-6). We might wonder to what extent a prophet's behavior and message were shaped by the expectations of such supporters.

Because prophets did not operate within a vacuum, we must also consider the role of prophecy within Israelite and Judean society. Prophecy is closely linked to kingship from the beginning of that political institution (1 Sam. 8). Amos, Hosea, Micah, and Isaiah criticize prophets who serve as "yes-men" for the ruling establishment or the cult (Am. 7:14-15; Hos. 4:5-6; Mic. 3:5-12; Isa. 9:13-16; 28:7; cf. 1 Kgs. 22). Jeremiah and Ezekiel will also conflict with blindly patriotic prophets during the final years of Judean monarchy (Jer. 28; Ezek. 13). Yet most canonical prophets hold the king accountable for perceived abuses of power. Similarly, many prophets critique the priesthood (Hos. 4:4-10; Mic. 3:11), while others are closely associated with the cult (Hag. 1:7-15; Zech. 3). Clearly, prophecy was a multifaceted phenomenon in the biblical world.

We have also observed that a prophetic message might be shaped by one of two competing theological perspectives—**Mosaic-exodus theology** or **Davidic-Zion theology.** As we repeatedly saw in the previous chapter, the Mosaic and Davidic covenants provided two very different lenses for viewing the world. The former emphasizes Yahweh's past fidelity to Israel and Israel's resulting covenant obligations. The latter emphasizes Yahweh's special connection to Jerusalem and the Davidic house. Amos, Hosea, and Micah (all northern or rural prophets) view the world through the lens of Mosaic-exodus traditions. Isaiah (an urban southerner) relies upon Davidic-Zion traditions. This critical difference leads Isaiah and Micah to anticipate different outcomes when Sennacherib's army besieged Jerusalem (Mic. 3:12; Isa. 31:4-5, 8-9).

We must also rethink the naïve assumption that the main job of a prophet was to predict the future. Many readers are likely surprised to find that the Assyrian period prophets were often mistaken in their prognoses. Amos incorrectly predicted a violent death for King Jeroboam II (Am. 7:11). Hosea's optimistic belief that Israel would be restored following a period of judgment proved to be unfounded. Jerusalem was not laid waste by Sennacherib's army as Micah predicted. Yet Isaiah's assurance that God would defend Jerusalem did not prevent its destruction a century later by the Babylonians.

A first-hand look at these prophets reveals that they were not fortune-tellers. Despite popular notions about prophecy in the modern world, predicting the future was not the primary concern of biblical prophecy. Rather, the biblical prophets analyzed circumstances of their own day in light of the values that they believed defined the covenant community. Because they assumed that God was active in history, international threats were interpreted as a result of the nation's relationship to the deity. The prophets might extrapolate about the immediate future based on their understanding of the covenant relationship and their assessment of the nation's faithfulness. Thankfully, however, the words of Amos, Hosea, Micah, and Isaiah were judged worthy of preservation despite the occasional inaccuracy of their forecasts.

Finally, our observations demand we rethink the common assumption that prophetic books were authored by the prophets whose names they bear. These books contain a mixture of autobiographical (first-person) and biographical (third-person) material. The current arrangement of prophetic books often seems to have been imposed by later editors who were unfamiliar or unconcerned with the original context of individual oracles. Passages regularly appear that presuppose later historical developments or reinterpret the prophet's original message for the benefit of a later generation. We also find passages that appear to have been copied directly from Kings or other prophetic books (Isa. 36–39; Jer. 52; Mic. 4:1-3).

To summarize, our journey thus far through the Latter Prophets has revealed the importance of examining afresh the social phenomenon of prophecy and the literary origins of prophetic literature. In the next two sections we will consider ways in which biblical scholars have attempted to make sense of observations like ours as they wrestle with two related questions: What are prophets? And what is prophetic literature?

Preliminary Exercise IIA.1: Getting to Know the Prophets

What Are Prophets?

Had the prophets lived today, they would probably find themselves institutionalized for their eccentric behavior and theological interpretations of political events. Yet prophets were recognized as potentially authoritative figures throughout the ancient Near East, where it was commonly presupposed that divine forces shaped human lives and larger historical events. Therefore, it was imperative to discover as much about these forces as possible. Prophets served as one kind of valuable **intermediary** between the human and divine spheres.

Prophetic activity was certainly not confined to ancient Israel or peculiar to worshipers of Yahweh. Hebrew scripture often refers to non-Israelite and non-Yahwistic prophecy (Num. 22–24; 1 Kgs. 18; Jer. 27:1-15). Such activity is also attested in extrabiblical documents, the most notable of which are royal archives from Mari dating to the eighteenth century B.C.E. Here we find numerous letters to the Amorite king containing messages that intermediaries had received from various deities through dreams, visions, and self-induced trances. Like biblical prophecy, these communications are often introduced by the messenger formula ("Thus says X . . ."). Yet most prophetic messages in the Mari archives are supportive of the king's political and military policies. Of course, unsupportive messages may not have been preserved by the king (cf. Jer. 36:20-26)! The Mari texts also assume that a prophet's words should be authenticated by consulting omens, whereas biblical texts generally prefer prophecy to other forms of divination (Deut. 13:1-3; 18:10-11).

In biblical and extra-biblical texts, the variety of titles attributed to intermediaries attests to a diversity of prophetic roles. In Israel several titles (like visionary, seer, and man of God) were eventually grouped under the umbrella term **nabi**. The Septuagint translates this Hebrew term into Greek as **prophētēs**, meaning "one who calls/proclaims," from which we get the English word **prophet**. It is more likely, however, that the word *nabi* meant "one who is called," indicating a sense of vocation. The importance of a prophet's divine commission is also seen in the frequent occurrence of call narratives and the messenger formula. Hence, the Hebrew prophets understood themselves as emissaries called by God to deliver a message.

We can surmise that the prophetic role was patterned after the role of a messenger in the ancient world. Because royal emissaries usually delivered messages orally, we can assume that the Hebrew prophets typically spoke face to face with their audiences. Only rarely do the prophets commit their words or visions to writing. We may also assume that Hebrew prophets exercised the same autonomy and creative license that royal messengers had in the ancient world. Messengers were not simply ventriloquist's dummies, as we can see in 2 Kings' account of the Jerusalem siege. In this story, a messenger of the Assyrian king has been sent to Jerusalem to persuade the Judean leaders to surrender. Using the messenger formula, the Assyrian emissary speaks in the first person as though his voice was that of his king (2 Kgs. 18:19-25). Yet, when he is entreated not to frighten the Judeans who are listening on the city wall, this wise emissary not only repeats his message but intensifies it to scare them even more (2 Kgs. 18:28-35). Clearly, he is improvising to press the advantage of his master.

We may conclude that prophets, like messengers, used their own reason and personal experience to communicate more effectively. In addition to speaking *for* God through the messenger formula, biblical prophets often speak *about* God in their own voice (Jer. 8:18-19; Hab. 1). They also frequently borrow established **forms** of speech that they and their audiences would have regularly encountered at the temple, city gate, or other sectors of daily life (CD Special Topic IIB.1). Their messages are richly illustrated with images drawn from their own experiences. Prophets used every means at their disposal to convey their messages through colorful speech and dramatic symbolic action.

To some extent, a prophet's speech and behavior were likely shaped by expectations of the people who provided him or her with encouragement, support, and protection and later helped preserve the prophet's message. Research on the roles of intermediaries in many cultures indicates the importance of such **support groups** and their location within society. Some biblical scholars, such as Robert Wilson, distinguish between northern and southern prophetic traditions. Others, such as David Petersen, distinguish between **central prophets**, who are supported by influential members of society, and **peripheral prophets**, who are supported by marginal members of society. Using this language, Isaiah would be considered a central prophet although he did not always conform to the expectations of the Jerusalem elite who supported him. At the other end of the spectrum, prophets who belonged to **ecstatic bands** likely occupied the margins of society.

Much work concerning the social dimensions of Hebrew prophecy has focused on the relation of prophecy to the priesthood and the monarchy. The distinction between prophets and priests was far from absolute in ancient Israel except that the priestly office could only be inherited by males of the appropriate lineage and priestly duties required higher standards of purity. Like prophets, priests provided another form of intermediation between the human and divine spheres. Prophets frequently borrowed the hymns and ritual language that priests would have used (for example, Joel 1:8-20). Jeremiah, Ezekiel, and Zechariah even belonged to priestly families. Within the biblical canon, prophets of the Persian period tend to be more supportive of the temple and Israel's cultic practices than those of the Assyrian or Babylonian periods. However, modern readers must keep in mind that even the prophets who critiqued Israel's sacrificial system were not antiritual. Their criticism was leveled specifically at priests who allowed sacrifices to be offered to other deities or without concern for social justice.

Biblical prophets also frequently criticized kings who pursued foreign and domestic policies without regard for Yahweh's intentions. Yet court prophecy also existed from the earliest stages of the monarchy. Prophets also played major roles in the formation of the Israelite state, in the schism between the northern and southern kingdoms, in the endorsement of the Davidic house in Judah, and in the rise and fall of several dynasties in Israel.

The prominence of prophets during the late monarchic period, the exile, and the restoration suggests that prophecy played a crucial role in helping Israel and Judah navigate the most critical transitions of their history. In the midst of social and political stress, they breathed new life into inherited religious traditions. Some prophets associated with the royal court or cult presented Yahweh as a patron deity who simply promises national affluence and security. Other prophets challenged such self-serving theology and held the ruling establishment accountable to covenant ideals.

Special Topic IIB.1: Forms of Prophetic Speech

What Is Prophetic Literature?

We have seen that Hebrew prophets considered themselves divinely commissioned emissaries who delivered oral messages that they sometimes illustrated with symbolic actions. They rarely committed their words and visions to writing, and when they did so, it was always in the service of their roles as messengers to their contemporaries (Isa. 8:1-4; Jer. 29; 36; Hab. 2:2). If the prophets were not authors, then how were books that bear their names assembled and preserved?

We have already observed several clues within these books suggesting that their literary formation was a long process to which many hands contributed. We have noticed several passages that do not seem to derive from the prophet in question. Superscriptions, headings, and some narratives refer to the prophet in the third person. Other passages contrast with the overriding message and tone of the book or presuppose later historical circumstances. For example, much of the material in Isaiah 1–39 addresses the final generations of the Judean monarchy, while chapters 40–55 address an exilic audience, and chapters 56–66 presuppose the restoration. In this case we can clearly observe how later generations updated the prophet's message by appending supplements to an earlier collection. In other cases, prophecy was updated and reinterpreted in less obvious ways.

The first stage in the growth of a prophetic book begins with the oral messages proclaimed and the symbolic actions performed by a prophet for particular audiences in particular times and places. Thus, the prophets' messages were directed first and foremost to their own contemporaries. It is possible that the prophets themselves began the process of recording their words and actions. They occasionally recorded some part of their message as part of a symbolic action or when a direct audience was impossible (Isa. 8:1-4; 30:8-11; Jer. 29; 36; Ezek. 43:11; Hab. 2:2).

More commonly a prophet's words circulated orally among those who had come to recognize them as authoritative. The prophet's death may have triggered a second stage in the literary growth of a prophetic book by prompting disciples to compile, interpret, and arrange whatever utterances they could remember. Often the original context of an oracle was forgotten and sayings were grouped together according to catchwords or similar themes (Jer. 21:11–23:8; 23:9-40). This explains why the contents of a prophetic book usually are not arranged chronologically. As disciples began to record remembered sayings, they also added biographical anecdotes about the prophet (Am. 7:10-17; Hos. 1:2-9; Isa. 2:1; 7:1-25).

As years passed, the scrolls on which disciples had recorded prophetic words and legends had to be copied and recopied if they were not to be lost. Each such occasion provided an opportunity for scribes to update, correct, clarify, and supplement the prophet's message in order to enhance its value to the community for which it was being preserved. This process of editorial transmission constituted an important third stage in the literary formation of a prophetic book. We can thus begin to understand a **prophetic book** as a collection of a prophet's words and deeds that was updated and amplified by editors for the benefit of later generations.

Understanding the complex editorial process behind the formation of a prophetic book should increase our appreciation of this literature in two ways. First, it allows us to distinguish a prophet's own words from those of later editors so that we can place all of these words in their appropriate historical contexts. Second, it allows us to appreciate the ingenuity of biblical editors who recognized the continuing relevance of the prophetic message and adapted it so skillfully to meet the needs of later generations as the biblical journey continued into exile and beyond.

THE BABYLONIAN PERIOD
(612–539 B.C.E.)

Having uncovered much about the nature of biblical prophecy and prophetic literature, we are now prepared to continue our journey through this section of Hebrew scripture. We have already experienced four prophetic anthologies rooted in the Assyrian period, which spanned from the opulent decades preceding the rise of Tiglath-pileser's empire to Sennacherib's siege of Jerusalem in 701 B.C.E. The next flurry of prophetic activity for which we have evidence occurred more than fifty years later. To fully appreciate the anthologies associated with these prophets, we must take a closer look at historical events of the Babylonian period, which formed the backdrop for their careers.

A Closer Look at the Babylonian Period (CD Chart IIIA.1)

By the beginning of the seventh century, Israel no longer existed and Judah had been reduced to a vassal state within the Assyrian Empire. Hezekiah's failed rebellion had resulted in heavier tribute and territorial losses for the southern kingdom, leaving his successor, Manasseh (687–642 B.C.E.), little choice but to comply with Assyrian rule.

The Deuteronomistic Historians condemn Manasseh for undoing Hezekiah's reforms and promoting the worship of other gods (2 Kgs. 21:1-18). Clearly this king was more cosmopolitan than his predecessor, although many of these "foreign" practices might be explained by a resurgence of Judean popular religion after the failed reform. As Assyria reasserted its dominance over Judah, Manasseh would also have been required to replace statues of Assyrian gods in the Jerusalem temple as a sign of his political subservience. Some of Judah's ruling elite even emulated the customs and dress of the presumably superior culture of their overlords (Zeph. 1:8). This pro-Assyrian party around Manasseh perhaps believed that further resistance was futile and that Judah's survival depended on appeasing the empire.

Indeed, during Manasseh's reign, Assyria reached the height of its power with the conquest of Egypt in 671 B.C.E. Yet the tide was soon to turn against this mighty empire, whose military resources were now stretched very thin. Assyria's hold upon Egypt was soon broken. Meanwhile, Babylon spearheaded a revolt at the other end of the empire, which encouraged anti-Assyrian sentiment in other vassal states. In 640 B.C.E., conspirators assassinated Manasseh's successor, who had continued his father's policy of collaborating with the empire. Perhaps fearing Assyrian reprisal, a group of wealthy Judean landowners eliminated the conspirators and restored to the throne Manasseh's minor grandson, Josiah (640–609 B.C.E.). But the anti-Assyrian party rapidly gained influence in the royal court. Josiah himself would soon instigate a nationalistic reform and attempt to claim the Assyrian province that had once constituted the northern kingdom (see chapter 3).

Josiah's Reform was made possible by a temporary power vacuum created by Assyrian decline. The empire suffered a series of ineffective rulers and a renewed assault by an alliance of Babylonians and Medes. These forces made deeper and deeper incursions into Assyria until they captured the capital city, Nineveh, in 612 B.C.E. Vassal states throughout the Assyrian Empire obviously rejoiced in this turn of events. Certainly most Judeans resented the foreign rulers who had for so long drained their economic resources. They greeted the news of Nineveh's fall with grim satisfaction, which lent fuel to the fires of patriotic reform. It must have seemed as though Yahweh was at last restoring their fortunes and punishing their enemies.

However, Judah's rejoicing proved to be shortsighted, and Josiah's Reform was prematurely terminated by an unexpected tragedy. The Egyptian pharaoh Necho, who nursed his own imperial ambitions, had grown alarmed by the sudden rise of Babylon. Hoping to maintain a weakened Assyrian state between himself and this rising power, he led his army north through Palestine. Josiah rode out to meet Necho probably intending to intercept Assyria's reinforcements, but the Judean king was killed. This devastating blow dashed Judah's hopes for a national revival and ended its short-lived political independence. Necho, appointed one of Josiah's sons, Eliakim (who was renamed Jehoiakim), as a puppet king and charged him with collecting tribute for Egypt.

However, a few years later the map of the ancient Near East was once again redrawn (CD Map IIIA.1). Egypt and Assyria fell before Babylonian forces at the **Battle of Carchemish** in 605 B.C.E., and Judah found itself passed into the hands of yet another foreign master. Jehoiakim now swore allegiance to Nebuchadnezzar, ruler of the

Babylonian Empire. Once again Judah's policy toward her foreign rulers began to vacillate between compliance and resistance. A foolhardy rebellion soon caused Nebuchadnezzar's forces to descend upon Jerusalem. Jehoiakim died in the early days of the siege, leaving his son, Jehoiachin, to surrender. In 597 B.C.E. he and other members of the Jerusalem elite were deported to Babylon. This exilic community maintained close ties with their homeland (Jer. 24; 29:24-28), and many Judeans continued to view Jehoiachin and his descendants as their legitimate kings. The notice of his parole at the end of 2 Kings could be read as a hopeful signal for a future restoration of the Davidic monarchy (2 Kgs. 25:27-30).

After squashing this rebellion, Nebuchadnezzar placed Jehoiachin's uncle Mattaniah upon the throne of Judah and rechristened him Zedekiah (597–587 B.C.E.). By this time Judah's most capable leaders had already been deported, and the indecisive Zedekiah found himself pulled between pro- and anti-Babylonian parties within the royal court. He was eventually persuaded to rebel by assurances of Egyptian support, and Babylonian forces again descended on the Judean capital. In 587 B.C.E. Nebuchadnezzar breached the walls of Jerusalem and burned the city and its temple. Zedekiah was forced to watch the execution of his children before he was blinded and led into exile with more of Judah's population.

Growing impatient with Judean rebellions, Nebuchadnezzar this time bypassed the Davidic ruling house and appointed a government official named Gedaliah as governor of Judah. This governor advocated submission to Babylon, probably reasoning that it was better to serve the empire than be destroyed by it. However, others still advocated resistance, and Gedaliah was soon assassinated by a member of the Davidic house. Fearing more reprisals and deportations, many of the people remaining in Judah fled to Egypt at that time.

The tremendous theological crisis that the **Babylonian exile** precipitated for Judeans cannot be overstated. Judah's inherited religious traditions emphasized the promise of land and the reign of a Davidic monarch as God's agent of blessing upon the nation. Recent religious reforms sponsored by Hezekiah and Josiah had attempted to restrict Yahweh-worship to the Jerusalem temple. Now the exilic community had been stripped of its land, its king, and its temple. To all objective observers it would appear that Yahweh had either abandoned Judah or had been defeated by the Babylonian gods.

The northern kingdom had ceased to exist because of the Assyrian exile, and it now seemed likely that a similar fate awaited the southern kingdom. That the Babylonian exile did not extinguish Judah and its religion is rather remarkable. In part, the exiles owed their survival to the fact that they were allowed to settle in separate communities. These enclaves of the old country enabled Judean immigrants to preserve vestiges of their national identity. New prominence was bestowed on rituals that could be observed anywhere—such as circumcision, Sabbath-keeping, and dietary restrictions. Links with the past were also maintained through correspondence with Judeans who had remained in the homeland. Key to their survival as a distinctive people, however, were the efforts of Judean scribes who began to compile and edit national traditions. These texts would form the core of the Hebrew canon and shape emerging postexilic Judaism.

Map IIIA.1: The Babylonian Empire
Chart IIIA.1: Timeline of the Babylonian Period (612–539 B.C.E.)

Babylonian Period Prophets
(CD Preliminary Exercises IIIB.1 and IIIB.2)

During this period of its history, Judah experienced a series of drastic changes as one foreign oppressor fell only to be replaced by another. Momentary hopes of restored independence gave way to national humiliation and despair. Enormous challenges were presented by the end of monarchy, national defeat, and the grim realities of exile. In the

STUDYING THE OLD TESTAMENT

midst of these challenges, prophets continued to reinterpret inherited religious traditions as they sought answers to the theological questions raised by national catastrophe.

Babylonian Period Prophets at a Glance	
Zephaniah (ca. 640–622 B.C.E.): prior to Josiah's Reform he announces judgment against Judah's corrupt leaders but expects a righteous remnant to survive.	**Obadiah** (ca. 587 B.C.E.): announces God's judgment against Edom for allying themselves with the Babylonians when Jerusalem fell.
Nahum (ca. 612 B.C.E.): a nationalistic prophet who celebrates God's destruction of the Assyrian capital.	**Jeremiah** (ca. 627–587 B.C.E.): before the temple was destroyed, announced God's intention to bring an enemy from the north to destroy Jerusalem and afterwards urged submission to Babylon and rededication to covenant ideals.
Habakkuk (ca. 608–598 B.C.E.): views the rising Babylonian Empire as the rod of God's anger against Judah but wonders about the justice of God's plans.	**Ezekiel** (ca. 593–571 B.C.E.): a priest among the first deportees to Babylon who announced God's intent to destroy Jerusalem. After the fall of Jerusalem he announced restoration.

Zephaniah (Zeph. 1:1-9; 3)

The superscription of this short book sets the prophetic career of **Zephaniah** in the days of King Josiah (640–609 B.C.E.). We might safely assume that his career preceded Josiah's Reform (622 B.C.E.), which eliminated many of the practices that this prophet condemns (2 Kgs. 23:1-24). It is possible that Zephaniah's words either inspired or gave legitimacy to the reform. The book's superscription also preserves an unusually long genealogy for Zephaniah (four generations), which traces his ancestry to a "Hezekiah," possibly the same Hezekiah who was Judah's last reforming king and Josiah's own great-grandfather. Whether or not the prophet is a member of the Davidic house, he is certainly a member of the anti-Assyrian group that became Judah's inner circle during Josiah's reign. The prophet clearly hopes to see Judah purged of foreign influences and restored to a position of independence and prominence.

Like many prophetic books, Zephaniah contains oracles against foreign nations, including a mocking condemnation of the once proud Assyria (Zeph. 2:13-15). But the book devotes more attention to criticizing Judah for corrupt practices and religious perversions that lingered after the reign of Manasseh (CD Chart IIIB.1). He contrasts the proud, who participate in syncretistic cults and dress in foreign attire, with the humble of the land, who keep Yahweh's commandments. Like Amos, Zephaniah proclaims an imminent Day of Yahweh when Judah will be punished for her unfaithfulness (Zeph. 1:2–2:3). Although he initially describes this day hyperbolically as the end of all life on earth, he later announces that a faithful remnant will survive to plunder Judah's historic enemies (Zeph. 2:7-10).

The book ends with a sudden shift from nationalistic judgment to international optimism (Zeph. 3:8-20). A concluding hymn envisions a time when Zion would be exalted and the nations would gather there to worship Yahweh, whom all peoples would call upon in one language (cf. Gen. 11:1-9). This hopeful passage could reflect the beginning of Josiah's Reform, but at least part of the hymn is a later addition to the book. The promise of a gathered return community clearly addresses an exilic audience. Nevertheless, the book's present conclusion reinforces for later generations the prophet's hope that purifying judgment would give way to a rededicated covenant community.

Nahum (Nah. 1; 3:1-7, 18-19)

The book of Nahum anticipates the imminent destruction of Nineveh, Assyria's capital, which occurred in 612 B.C.E. Although some commentators date Nahum's career as early as 650 B.C.E., he likely prophesied somewhat later, at a time when Assyrian decline had begun to loosen the empire's grip on its provinces. The prospect that the yoke of oppression would soon be lifted causes the prophet to release pent-up resentment that many Judeans doubtless felt after a century of foreign rule.

Nahum confidently describes Nineveh's downfall as an act of Yahweh intended to punish Assyria for its cruelty toward Yahweh's people. Many Hebrew prophets uttered oracles of judgment against foreign nations (Am. 1–2; Isa. 13–23; Jer. 46–51; Ezek. 25–32), but most of their words were addressed to their own people. If the prophet Nahum offered any criticism or advice to Judah, it is not preserved in this book. Its single topic is the prophet's gloating over the misfortunes of Judah's enemy (CD Chart IIIB.2). Readers may be disturbed by the evident pleasure that the prophet takes in describing vivid details of Nineveh's capture and humiliation. No compassion is spared for the innocent, who would likely be included among the "heaps of corpses" (Nah. 3:3).

Likewise, readers may be disturbed by the prophet's assumption that the enemies of Judah are ultimately the enemies of God as well. That kind of patriotic theology, combated by prophets like Amos and Micah, classifies Nahum as a central prophet and might suggest that he was an employee of the cult or the ruling establishment. Other central prophets, like Zephaniah and Isaiah, critiqued the ruling establishment from the perspective of an insider. Nahum apparently did not. It is perhaps an expression of the humanity and richness of the Hebrew canon that the book of Nahum appears alongside books like Jonah that express very different ideas about God's concern even for the people of Nineveh, Israel's most hated enemies.

Habakkuk (Hab. 1:1–2:5; 3)

The short book of Habakkuk provides neither personal information about the prophet nor a historical context for his career in its superscription. The book's one clear historical indicator anticipates an invasion by **Chaldeans** (another name for Babylonians, Hab. 1:6), which likely dates this prophet to the reign of Jehoiakim (608–598 B.C.E.). Thus, when Habakkuk addressed Judah, the national revival inspired by Josiah's Reform had already ended in tragedy, and the heady liberation occasioned by Assyria's downfall was fading in the dawning realization that a new empire was on the rise (CD Chart IIIB.3).

The book opens with a dialogue between the prophet and Yahweh (Hab. 1:2–2:5). First, Habakkuk accuses the deity of failing to correct injustice. Like many of his predecessors, the prophet is disturbed by corruption within his society, but Habakkuk poses a question that they had not. How could God allow this to continue? The deity responds by proclaiming an invasion of Chaldeans to topple Judah's corrupt government and punish iniquity. Yet this answer does not satisfy the prophet! Habakkuk points out violence perpetrated by the haughty Chaldeans, Yahweh's chosen instrument of justice.

Readers should immediately recognize that we are in new territory. Unlike most prophets, who deliver God's messages to the people, Habakkuk often addresses, implores, and questions the deity. Like Abraham's dialogue with God about the fate of Sodom and Gomorrah (Gen. 18), this book explores the issue of **theodicy**. How can we affirm the rule of a just deity despite the reality of an unjust world? This conundrum will later be addressed in Israel's wisdom literature (see chapter 5). That Habakkuk raised this question in the late seventh century suggests the first stirrings of a crisis in Hebrew theology, particularly in the prophetic assumption that God's judgment was evident in historical events.

Yahweh's response may sound familiar to Christian readers because part of it is quoted (out of context) by the apostle Paul in the New Testament (CD Chart IIIB.4). The deity assures Habakkuk that divine justice would come in due time and advises him to wait patiently for it (Hab. 2:2-5). Meanwhile the righteous must "live by their faith" (or better, "live faithfully"). In other words, this theodicy suggests that at times when God's justice is not readily apparent in the world, the appropriate human response is unwavering, disinterested fidelity.

A slightly different theodicy is offered by the prayer in chapter 3, which is regarded by some as a later addition to the book. Yet the common themes of theodicy, patience, and faithfulness unite the hymn with the book's earlier chapters. In form, chapter 3 resembles a liturgical psalm and even employs technical musical terms often used by the Psalter (see chapter 5). If this prayer was composed by the prophet himself, Habakkuk may have been a central intermediary associated with the Jerusalem cult. If so, that might explain why he is twice labeled a *nabi* ("prophet") while Amos and others eschew that title (Hab. 1:1; 3:1; cf. Am. 7:14).

Regardless of its origin, the prayer that concludes the book entreats Yahweh to deliver Judah from her enemies. The poet extols the deity's power in allusions to mythic battles with the sea and cosmic forces. Yahweh is called upon to control the realm of history in the same way that the forces of chaos were subdued in ordering the cosmos. The prayer ends with an eloquent affirmation of faith in Yahweh in the face of human adversity (Hab. 3:17-19).

Obadiah (Obad. 1-14)

Obadiah is the shortest book in the Hebrew canon (CD Chart IIIB.5). Its single chapter denounces the neighboring country of Edom for its involvement in Judah's demise and proclaims a coming Day of Yahweh on which the deity will punish Edom along with the rest of Judah's enemies. The details and emotional intensity of this oracle suggest that it was composed shortly after the destruction of Jerusalem and **second**

deportation in 587 B.C.E., although we know virtually nothing about the prophet Obadiah himself.

This book's anti-Edom theme is found in many other biblical passages, but nowhere dominates as it does in Obadiah (cf. Ps. 137:7; Lam. 4:21-22; Ezek. 25:12-14; 35:1-15). Here the Edomites stand accused of gloating over Jerusalem's destruction, hunting down and handing over Judean refugees, looting, and otherwise exploiting Judah's day of national distress for their own advantage. The seriousness of these crimes is heightened by allusions to the ancestral tradition claiming a common lineage for Israel and Edom. Because Esau is the traditional ancestor of the Edomites and Jacob the traditional ancestor of the Israelites (Gen. 25:22-34), this is a betrayal between brothers. The book ends by proclaiming that what goes around comes around. Therefore, Judah will one day be restored to retaliate against Edom and other enemies. Like the book of Nahum, Obadiah unapologetically assumes that the enemies of his nation are also the enemies of Yahweh.

Jeremiah (Jer. 1; 7; 18:1-12; 20:7-18; 24; 26:1–29:23; 31:15-34; 32:6-41; 36–38)

The book of Jeremiah can be very daunting for students due to its length and complexity. It is the second largest book in the Hebrew canon, partly because it presents the legacy of a prophet who had an exceptionally long career. Jeremiah's activity encompassed almost the entire Babylonian period, from the middle of Josiah's reign (ca. 627 B.C.E.) until after the fall of Jerusalem in 587 B.C.E. Perhaps because he addressed Judah during such pivotal historical events, his words remained meaningful to later generations who reworked his message to address the circumstances of an exilic audience.

The book as we have it is plainly the product of a long interpretive process (CD Chart IIIB.6), but a clue to its composition may be preserved within its own pages. Chapter 36 reports that, about two decades into his career, Jeremiah dictated his oracles from memory to the scribe

Baruch. This scroll was destroyed by the unreceptive King Jehoiakim, but it was later reconstructed and expanded by the prophet and scribe. Such a written collection could have formed the nucleus of the present book. Doubtless, oracles from Jeremiah's later career would have been added to that original collection. At a later stage, his supporters (including Baruch) likely added biographical narratives before exilic scribes supplemented and edited the whole.

Although it is difficult to separate the "historical Jeremiah" from the legendary figure he becomes in the book, the superscription claims that he belongs to a priestly family in Anathoth (Jer. 1:1). This is an important detail because these priests descended from Abiathar, the priest whom King Solomon had "fired" and banished to Anathoth for supporting his rival for the throne (1 Kgs. 2:26-27). The memory of this indignity inflicted on his ancestor may have contributed to Jeremiah's antipathy for Solomon's temple. It also identifies this prophet as an "outsider" to the Jerusalem establishment.

Jeremiah's call narrative, which is placed at the beginning of the book (Jer. 1:4-19), follows the typical pattern: divine call, human protest, divine reassurance, and confirming signs. Yet more than most call narratives, it echoes Moses' conversation with Yahweh before the burning bush (Exod. 3–6). Like Moses, Jeremiah expresses reluctance to assume the prophetic role due to ineloquence and receives the promise that Yahweh will provide words for him to speak. This parallel may be intended to cast Jeremiah as a "prophet like Moses" (Deut. 18:15).

Jeremiah's career begins during the reign of Josiah. Although the prophet contrasts this king favorably with his successors (Jer. 22:11-17), the book contains no direct reference to Josiah's Reform (CD Special Topic IIIB.1). Rather, Jeremiah's earliest oracles reflect his conviction that Yahweh will soon punish Judah for her immorality and apostasy by bringing upon her an unnamed invader from the north. This message is reinforced by several symbolic acts and prophetic signs such as likening Judah to a smashed earthen vessel or a ruined waistcloth. National catastrophe is described as unavoidable (Jer. 13:23), and Jeremiah is even forbidden to intercede on behalf of his people (Jer. 7:16; 15:1). Either these oracles preceded Josiah's Reform, or the prophet considered the reform ineffective.

The book focuses more attention on the prophet's uneasy relationship with two of Josiah's successors, Jehoiakim and Zedekiah. In fact, Jeremiah is depicted delivering his controversial temple sermon shortly after Jehoiakim assumed the throne of Judah (Jer. 7). Standing in the temple doorway, the prophet issues a scathing repudiation of Zion theology. He scoffs at the belief held by many Judeans that Yahweh resides in the temple and would, therefore, protect Jerusalem. He reminds them that the sanctuary at Shiloh had been destroyed even though it had housed the ark of the covenant (1 Sam. 4). So too, Yahweh would destroy Jerusalem if its inhabitants did not amend their ways.

This Mosaic prophet clearly presupposes a conditional understanding of the covenant, which he sets in opposition to Davidic-Zion theology. To do so in Jerusalem within feet of the temple was to invite hostility! The reaction of the Jerusalem establishment to Jeremiah's temple sermon appears several chapters later (Jer. 26). Jeremiah is placed on trial and nearly executed for treason. He is saved only because a group of elders recall the precedent the prophet Micah had set for proclaiming judgment against Jerusalem.

Nevertheless, this sermon may have resulted in Jeremiah's ban from the temple, which, in turn, necessitates his relationship with the scribe Baruch (Jer. 36). The prophet dictated his oracles to Baruch around the same time as the Babylonian army won their victory at the Battle of Carchemish (605 B.C.E.). This scroll found a receptive audience among some court officials but failed to move the king to repentance. Attentive readers may recognize in this account echoes of 2 Kings 22:8-20, where another scroll (the Book of the Law) was brought to the attention of another king (Josiah). In contrast to Josiah's pious reaction upon hearing the Book of the Law, Jehoiakim slowly mutilates and burns Jeremiah's scroll.

Jeremiah hardly fares better in his relationship with Zedekiah, who becomes king after the **first Babylonian deportation** (597 B.C.E.). The book of Jeremiah presents this king as a weak figure controlled by members of the royal court (Jer. 38:24-28). His authority certainly is not enhanced by the popular view that his exiled nephew Jehoiachin was the legitimate king of Judah! While many royal advisors call for rebellion, Jeremiah urges Zedekiah to submit to Babylonian rule. The prophet embodies his message by fashioning a wooden yoke, which he wears upon his own neck (Jer. 27). Again Jeremiah is perceived as a traitor by many within the Jerusalem establishment.

His message also brings him into conflict with central prophets who are delivering more optimistic oracles. Jeremiah's clash with a prophet named Hananiah illustrates two very different ways of interpreting God's role in Judah's political situation at the beginning of the sixth century (Jer. 28). Operating out of the Mosaic-exodus tradition, Jeremiah views defeat and captivity as Judah's deserved punishment for covenant violations. Operating out of Davidic-Zion theology, Hananiah predicts that Yahweh will soon restore the captured temple vessels and the exiled Davidic king. To illustrate his conviction, Hananiah removes the wooden yoke from Jeremiah's neck and smashes it into pieces. Not to be outdone, Jeremiah returns later wearing an iron yoke and predicts the imminent death of his rival for uttering false prophecy.

The Judeans who witnessed this confrontation must have wondered which prophet to believe (CD Special Topic IIIB.2). Both claimed to speak in the name of Yahweh, and the Deuteronomic dictum of following the prophet whose words eventually prove true was hardly helpful in the moment (Deut. 18:20-22). Perhaps recognizing this dilemma, Jeremiah advises his listeners to be suspicious of the prophet who tells you what you want to hear! Later editors of the book settle the dispute once and for all by noting that Hananiah did in fact die later that year.

Jeremiah also encourages the exilic community to accept the reality of Babylonian rule for the foreseeable future. In a letter to the exiles, he advises them to build houses, plant gardens, and get married rather than place their lives on hold waiting for a speedy return. He even suggests that they pray for the welfare of the empire! According to the prophet, their own well-being will be inextricably linked with the fortunes of Babylon for seventy years (the average Israelite lifespan, cf. Ps. 90:10). In other words, the exiles can expect a lifetime to pass before Yahweh will restore them to their homeland.

The prophet's pessimism is legitimated when Jerusalem is sacked and the temple destroyed in 587 B.C.E. Yet, during the siege, Jeremiah is condemned by many Judeans as a Babylonian sympathizer. Attempting to leave the city on personal business, he is arrested as a deserter and imprisoned (Jer. 37:11-16). Later, court officials attempt to kill Jeremiah by casting him into a cistern (Jer. 38:4-6). Fortunately for the prophet, the cistern is nearly dry and a friend at court intercedes on his behalf.

Jeremiah's unpopular views made him the subject of public scorn and mistreatment throughout his career. Moreover, he apparently felt called to remain unmarried and live a life of social isolation as a prophetic sign of the impending disaster (Jer. 16:1-9). His personal frustration is expressed in a series of autobiographical **complaints** sometimes called "Jeremiah's **confessions**" (Jer. 11:18–12:6; 15:10-21; 17:14-18; 18:18-23; 20:7-18). Like individual laments found in the Psalter (see chapter 5), these speeches sometimes voice feelings of anger both at his opponents and at the deity who has forced him into his present position.

After the second deportation in 587 B.C.E., the Babylonians released Jeremiah from prison and allowed him to remain in Jerusalem under the protection of Gedaliah, the newly appointed Judean governor (Jer. 39:11–40:6). After that governor's assassination, Jeremiah was forcibly taken to Egypt by a group of Judean refugees where he presumably remained until his death (Jer. 42–44). The group that preserved

Jeremiah's message after his death likely included the family of Baruch (Jer. 32:12; 51:59) and the family of a court official named Shaphan (Gedaliah's grandfather; Jer. 26:24; 36:9-19; 39:14). These supporters apparently agreed that Judah should submit for the time being to Babylonian rule and rededicate herself to covenant ideals.

It is difficult to tell which parts of the book derive from the prophet himself and which parts derive from his supporters and later editors. It is possible that the hope for a future restoration originated with Jeremiah himself, but this idea is clearly expanded by later editors for the benefit of an exilic audience. During the darkest days of the Jerusalem siege, the book depicts Jeremiah investing in Judah's future by purchasing a field in Anathoth (Jer. 32). This financial outlay by the prophet signified that defeat and deportation would not be the final word for Yahweh's people. That hope is particularly vested in the group of Judeans who were deported in 597 B.C.E. by Jeremiah's vision involving two baskets of figs (Jer. 24). This important passage locates Judah's future with the exilic community (the good figs) rather than with the people who had remained in the land or fled to Egypt (the bad figs).

Many of the book's hopeful oracles appear in chapters 30–31, which are sometimes labeled the "Book of Comfort." Here readers find the image of Mother Rachel weeping for her children but consoled by the promise that they will one day return from exile. Here the prophet envisions a day when the law will be written upon the hearts of God's people. Here Jeremiah promises a new covenant that will reestablish the relationship between Yahweh and the restored community (CD Special Topic IIIB.3).

Ezekiel (Ezek. 1–5; 8–11; 13; 16; 18; 23; 33–34; 37:1-14; 43:1-12; 48:35)

Readers quickly discover that the book of Ezekiel is unlike other prophetic anthologies. Whereas most are loose compilations, it is neatly organized by subject matter into three sections (CD Chart IIIB.7). Fourteen dated passages, which appear more or less in chronological order throughout Ezekiel, also create the impression that this is a well-planned book. Moreover, while most prophetic anthologies are dominated by poetic oracles, this book is mostly prose, including elaborate allegories, parables, arguments, and vision reports. These features make Ezekiel seem less like an edited collection of remembered sayings and more like an intentional literary creation either by the prophet himself or by his disciples.

Yet none of the book's unusual literary features grabs the attention of readers in the same way as does the seemingly deranged man who dominates its pages. The prophet Ezekiel performs bizarre street theater that involves extended periods of muteness, lying bound on his side for days on end, digging holes through the walls of his house, shaving off his hair with a sword, and cooking his food over dung. He also reports ecstatic visions involving many-faced creatures and reanimated human bones. Although we have encountered symbolic actions and visions from other prophets, nowhere else are they as fantastic as here. The peculiar personality of this prophet has even provoked speculation that he may have suffered from some form of psychosis! Yet it is equally possible that both the eccentricity of the prophet and unusual form of the book reflect the traumatic events experienced by this prophet and his audience.

As a member of an elite priestly family, Ezekiel was among the first Judeans forcibly deported from their homeland by the Babylonian Empire in 597 B.C.E. This early exilic community was the prophet's primary audience (2 Kgs. 24:14-16). They had been Jerusalem's educated upper class but had now lost nearly everything. After enduring a devastating siege, they had been marched over seven hundred miles to Babylonia as captives of war. Undoubtedly, along the way lives were disrupted, possessions were lost, loved ones died, and faith was shaken.

Within the alien environment of exile, Ezekiel's community posed theological questions about their experiences. Had their sins or the sins of their ancestors really merited such a severe punishment? Or was Yahweh powerless before the gods of Babylon? Or had their God simply abandoned them to their plight? If possible, the survival of Jerusalem and its temple made the future even more uncertain. Zion theology claimed that Yahweh resided in the temple and would forever protect the holy city in which it stood. Did Jerusalem's survival mean that this promise was still in effect? If so, with whom did the future lie? Were those who had remained in the land the righteous remnant or might those in exile expect a speedy restoration?

Ezekiel's prophetic career was profoundly shaped by the tremendous crisis of exile and the questions it raised. Although deportation had taken him far from the temple cult, he continued to view the world as a priest. That grounding in priestly traditions is evident from the moment of his prophetic call in the fifth year of exile. Ezekiel's call narrative, which is much longer and more complex than we have come to expect (Ezek. 1–3), is dominated by an elaborate theophany described in minute detail. Yet this description is too evasive for readers to develop a clear mental image of Ezekiel's vision. The prophet appears to be struggling for words to describe an enigmatic experience. Within what first appears to be a storm arising in the north he discerns four hybrid creatures, each with four faces and four wings. Upon closer inspection, he perceives that these creatures are part of a chariot bearing a throne upon which is seated the **glory** (Hebrew *kavod*) of Yahweh. Rather than claiming to see the deity directly, Ezekiel uses priestly language to indicate the aura of God's presence.

As a priest, Ezekiel would normally assume that Yahweh's glory dwelt in the Jerusalem temple, but in his inaugural vision that presence has apparently departed the temple and traveled to Babylonia upon a chariot-throne. This vision offers a remarkable critique of Zion theology by affirming divine freedom and mobility. Yahweh cannot be bound by

Jerusalem or by the temple but can choose to join the exilic community in a foreign land in order to commission a prophet. Rather than resist this call, Ezekiel willingly takes and eats the scroll offered to him by the deity. He even notes that it tastes "sweet as honey" in his mouth despite the fact that it is covered with words of warning, lamentation, and woe.

Like the message of Jeremiah, Ezekiel's early prophetic career is dominated by his conviction of Judah's sinfulness and impending doom (Ezek. 1–24). Both of these prophets believed that the defeat and deportation suffered in 597 B.C.E. had been brought about by Yahweh and that the deity's anger had not yet abated. The greatness of Judah's sin demanded that Jerusalem and the temple itself must fall. While this message is not particularly surprising from an outsider to the Jerusalem cult like Jeremiah, it is startling from Ezekiel.

His methods of expressing these convictions are equally arresting. In a series of symbolic actions (Ezek. 4), Ezekiel dramatizes his message by making a clay model of Jerusalem under siege, binding himself to symbolize captivity, and consuming limited rations—although the priest balks at the idea of defiling himself by preparing his food over human dung! He then shaves his head with a sword and disposes of his hair in ways that symbolize the fates awaiting the remaining residents of Jerusalem (Ezek. 5). Later, the prophet pretends to flee from a coming catastrophe by hastily packing a bag and digging through a wall (Ezek. 12).

The reasons for Yahweh's unabated rage become clear in a vision of the Jerusalem temple (Ezek. 8–11). Here the prophet describes an experience in which he is forcibly transported by the deity back to his homeland in order to observe rampant corruption within the temple and its precincts. The prophet is shown men bowing toward the sun and women weeping over a foreign god. He even discovers the city's leaders secretly worshiping other gods within a hidden room. Finally, Ezekiel watches helplessly while Yahweh's glory abandons the profaned temple and leaves the city on the chariot-throne that the prophet had seen in his earlier call vision. In other words, Judah's ritual abominations had voided the promises of Zion theology and driven God away from the temple.

Ezekiel's early preaching reinforces his dramatic visions and symbolic actions. Like Jeremiah, he condemns "false prophets" who offer a comforting message to an audience that is willingly deluded (Ezek. 13). In contrast to prophets who "smear whitewash" with their words, Ezekiel boldly proclaims that destruction is unavoidable because of the weight of Judah's sins. In one historical recital (Ezek. 20) and two marriage allegories reminiscent of Hosea (Ezek. 16; 23), the prophet reviews the nation's long-standing habit of repaying Yahweh's generosity with covenant infidelity. Clearly these word pictures are intended to demonstrate that Jerusalem's punishment is deserved. However, modern readers might object to the somewhat disturbing allegories graphically depicting both the perversity of Yahweh's unfaithful wives and the violence that the deity-husband plans to inflict in retaliation.

These three portraits of a vengeful deity are tempered—or perhaps contradicted—by another passage that raises questions of moral responsibility and theodicy (Ezek. 18). Here Ezekiel addresses members of the exilic community who blame their present crisis on the sins of previous generations, citing the proverb "the parents have eaten sour grapes, and the children's teeth are set on edge" (cf. Jer. 31:27-30). The prophet responds with a parable about a three-generation family (consisting of a grandfather, a father, and a son) in which each member is held responsible only for his own actions. It is possible that Ezekiel is arguing for an individual rather than collective morality. It is equally possible that he is affirming the fresh start available to each collective generation. Either way, the prophet defends the justice of God and raises the possibility of a hopeful future.

The destruction of Jerusalem in 587 B.C.E. is a pivotal event for Ezekiel. It coincides with the death of his beloved wife, whom he is forbidden to mourn as a symbol of Yahweh's resolve to destroy the beloved temple. It also marks an important transition in his prophetic career from a message of doom (Ezek. 1–24) to one of hope (Ezek. 33–48). In between these two sections of the book appear oracles against foreign nations, which many interpreters view as a later addition (Ezek. 25–32). Likewise, a later passage concerning Yahweh's cosmic defeat of Gog (possibly a composite caricature of Judah's enemies) is often considered a later insertion (CD Special Topic IIIB.4). As the book stands, the promise that these nations will be destroyed clears the way for a restoration of Judah and ensures their future security. Like Jeremiah, Ezekiel places his hope for the future with the exilic community in Babylon (Ezek. 33:23-29).

Following the defeat of Jerusalem, the exilic community surely found the idea of a future restoration almost ludicrous. With Zion and the temple gone, upon what could such a hope be based? The prophet captures the prevailing mood of despair by quoting the words of his fellow deportees (Ezek. 33:10): "Our transgressions and our sins weigh upon us, and we waste away because of them; how then can we live?" An answer to this question is provided in Ezekiel's vision of a valley filled with dry bones (Ezek. 37). Like these bones, the exilic community seems to have no prospect of living again. Yet in his vision, Ezekiel is commanded to prophesy words of hope that cause the bones to reassemble, grow flesh, and be resuscitated in a dramatic image of restoration.

The prophet articulates a future in which Judah will no longer be ruled by irresponsible shepherds who place their own desires before the welfare of their sheep (Ezek. 34; cf. 1 Sam. 8:10-18). Instead Yahweh will become the "good shepherd"—another image later borrowed and adapted by New Testament writers. Although Ezekiel does not directly criticize any Judean ruler other than Zedekiah (Ezek. 17:1-21), he appears to avoid the word *king* and ascribes a very limited role to the Davidic house in his image of the restoration. Unsurprisingly, as a priest he gives much more attention to the restored temple, which is presented in excruciating detail (Ezek. 40–48). Yahweh's glory will return to the temple, and it will become the heart of a pure community ordered by right worship.

Especially in this description of the restored temple, readers might recognize Ezekiel's affinities to priestly traditions. Like the Priestly source of the Torah, Ezekiel attempts to reassure an exilic audience that Yahweh is still in control of history. Perhaps for that reason, he places enormous stress on the transcendent power and majesty of the deity, in contrast to the prophet's status as a mere mortal, or **"son of man"** (*ben 'ādām*). Repeatedly, this priest/prophet claims that both judgment and restoration are effected so that "they shall know I am Yahweh"—echoing a refrain from the Holiness Code (Lev. 17–26). Ultimately, Ezekiel bases Judah's future not upon the repentance of the exilic community but upon the initiative of Yahweh, who is determined to fulfill the covenant promises for the sake of the deity's own holy name (Ezek. 36:31-36).

 Preliminary Exercise IIIB.1: Babylonian Period Prophecy
Preliminary Exercise IIIB.2: Being a Prophet
Chart IIIB.1: The Structure of Zephaniah
Chart IIIB.2: The Structure of Nahum
Chart IIIB.3: The Structure of Habakkuk
Chart IIIB.4: Habakkuk 2:4 and the New Testament
Chart IIIB.5: The Structure of Obadiah
Chart IIIB.6: The Structure of Jeremiah
Chart IIIB.7: The Structure of Ezekiel
Special Topic IIIB.1: Was Jeremiah the Deuteronomistic Historian?
Special Topic IIIB.2: The Dilemma of "False Prophecy"
Special Topic IIIB.3: Supersessionist Claims and Christian Anti-Semitism
Special Topic IIIB.4: Gog of Magog (Ezek. 38–39)

In summary, prophecy of the Babylonian period was shaped by what were perhaps the most tumultuous years of Judah's history. The end of Assyrian rule and the optimistic patriotism of Josiah's Reform left clear imprints upon this literature. Yet here we also find the indelible mark of Judah's tragic demise before the Babylonian Empire. These prophets and their later editors dealt with difficult theological issues arising from the crises of the late monarchic and early exilic periods. They struggled to discern God's hand in confusing historical circumstances and affirm the deity's control of their national destiny despite outward appearances that often suggested the contrary. They also strove to reconcile their belief in a just and powerful God with their observations of a desperately unjust world. Remarkably, in the context of defeat and exile, they managed to envision a hopeful continuation of their national journey beyond captivity.

THE PERSIAN PERIOD
(539–330 B.C.E.)

After the career of Ezekiel, we have no evidence of Hebrew prophecy until shortly before Babylon's fall to Persia in 539 B.C.E. The next prophetic voice that we encounter anticipates the disintegration of the Babylonian Empire and the restoration of the exilic community. That voice inaugurates the Bible's last cluster of prophetic activity, which includes leaders in the postexilic reconstruction of Judah's social and religious life under Persian rule. To prepare for the final leg of our journey through the Latter Prophets, we must take a closer look at the events of the Persian period that provide the context for these prophets' careers.

A Closer Look at the Persian Period (CD Chart IVA.1)

The destruction of Jerusalem and its temple in 587 B.C.E. was a watershed moment in biblical history that brought to an end the Davidic monarchy along with all other vestiges of Judah's national sovereignty. That this moment did not also spell the end of the Judean people and their religious traditions is quite remarkable. Instead, this tragedy became the crucible in which inherited religious traditions were tested

STUDYING THE OLD TESTAMENT

and refined as exilic scribes gave shape to the Torah and prophetic literature.

Because the Hebrew canon and other formative elements of **Judaism** began to emerge in this period, we can now legitimately refer to the Judean people as **Jews**. This term, derived from the Hebrew word *yehudi* (meaning "Judean"), was first applied to the exiled Judeans and later extended to those who descended from this ethnic group or worshiped Yahweh (CD Special Topic IVA.1). As a consequence of Judah's demise, the Jewish people had been widely scattered across the ancient Near East. Whereas many had been forcibly deported to Babylonia, others had remained in the land under foreign rule and at least some had found their way to Egypt as refugees. This dispersion of the Jewish people outside of their ancestral homeland, which is still an abiding feature of Judaism, is sometimes called the **Diaspora**.

Throughout the Babylonian Empire, small Jewish communities were eclipsed by a very different prevailing culture. Especially in the shadow of great Babylonian cities dominated by towering stepped temples called ziggurats, exiled Jews must have wondered why they should cling to the religion of their faraway homeland. Near the beginning of exile, Jeremiah and Ezekiel had insisted loudly that Yahweh was neither impotent before the gods of Babylon nor apathetic to the plight of the exilic community. Both of these prophets had painted hopeful pictures of a future beyond the present captivity. Yet, as half a century passed in exile, many surely wondered whether their God had forgotten them. While some held tenaciously to their distinctive Jewish identity, doubtless many assimilated into the surrounding culture.

It became the task of an anonymous late exilic prophet (Second Isaiah) to inspire hope in the midst of such despair and cynicism. He did so in part by pointing his contemporaries to a significant new political development—the emergence of the **Persian Empire** under Cyrus the Great (CD Map IVA.1). The once mighty Babylonian Empire had gradually declined under a series of weak kings after the death of

Nebuchadnezzar. The last of these kings was replaced by a widely unpopular usurper who neglected the temples of Babylon's patron deity, Marduk. In 539 B.C.E., the city of Babylon was taken without a fight by the Persian army, whom many Babylonians welcomed as liberators rather than conquerors! Capitalizing on that perception, Cyrus presented himself as a worshiper of Marduk and claimed that he had been chosen by that deity to restore his cult. In fact, Cyrus did devote funds to renovating several Babylonian shrines—an investment that allowed the Persians to solidify their hold over their empire more effectively than they might have through threat or force.

Doubtless many Jews believed that Yahweh was at work in Cyrus the Persian as he displaced the rulers of Babylon. This conviction must have been reinforced when Cyrus issued an **edict** allowing Jewish deportees to return to their homeland and rebuild Yahweh's temple in Jerusalem (Ezra 1:2-4; 2 Chr. 36:23). This edict was in keeping with Cyrus's policy toward other conquered subjects and in his own best interest. Not only would a restored Jewish community owe Cyrus loyalty, but their presence would extend Persian control to the borders of Egypt. Nevertheless, to many within the exilic community, it seemed as though Yahweh had sent Cyrus to be their own personal deliverer. Surely, now that they had paid for their sins, Yahweh would soon inaugurate the glorious future envisioned by Second Isaiah and earlier prophets.

Clearly, not all of the exilic community shared these sentiments since many Jews elected to remain in Babylon or to settle in other parts of the Persian Empire. The first group of those who chose to return to Yehud (as Judah was now called) did so in 538 B.C.E. under the leadership of an appointed Jewish governor named Sheshbazzar. This group laid the foundations for a new temple but encountered many obstacles. In particular, returning families discovered that property they had held before exile had been claimed during their long absence by Jews who had remained in the land. The returnees—who had been or were descended from Jerusalem's former elite and had suffered the purification of exile—believed that they constituted the "true Israel." Such conflicts, apathy, and a general lack of resources stalled rebuilding until another wave of returnees arrived. This second group, led by a new governor named Zerubbabel and a high priest named Joshua, finally managed to complete the temple by 515 B.C.E. during the reign of Darius I, who had succeeded Cyrus's son on the Persian throne.

The **Second Temple**, as it is often called, paled in comparison to the grandeur of Solomon's original temple. Likewise, the hardships suffered by the returnees contrasted starkly with the glorious future they had been promised. Jerusalem and its economy were still recovering from the devastation of 587 B.C.E. The tiny postexilic community still lived under the jurisdiction of a foreign empire, they had not been blessed with peace and prosperity, and the whole world had not come to acknowledge the God of Israel. Jews of the Persian period must have wondered why they continued to meet with so many frustrations in the aftermath of exile.

Map IVA.1: The Persian Empire
Chart IVA.1: Timeline of the Persian Period (539–330 B.C.E.)
Special Topic IVA.1: Who Is a Jew?

Persian Period Prophets
(CD Preliminary Exercises IVB.1 and IVB.2)

The final cluster of biblical prophecy attempts to articulate a brighter future for audiences situated in the final days of Babylonian exile and during the postexilic readjustment. Although the threat of judgment is not absent from these prophetic books, their primary message is one of hopeful encouragement. The exiles had been punished for their sins and redemption was at hand. However, persistent difficulties faced by the return community led to a crisis in biblical prophecy. Their sins had been punished—why was renewed obedience not rewarded? The incongruence between the community's expectations and their lived reality forced the prophetic movement in new directions.

Persian Period Prophets at a Glance	
Second Isaiah/Isaiah 40–55 (ca. 546–539 B.C.E.): an exilic prophet who announces Yahweh's intention to liberate the exiles through Cyrus the Persian and envisions a glorious return.	**Zechariah** (ca. 520–518 B.C.E.): a postexilic prophet who reports eschatological visions of a renewed Judah.
Third Isaiah/Isaiah 56–66 (ca. 539–520 B.C.E.): a postexilic prophet who preserves Second Isaiah's hopeful vision and calls for social justice.	**Malachi** (ca. 500–450 B.C.E.): a postexilic prophet who encourages cultic and marital fidelity and announces an eschatological Day of Yahweh that will reveal God's justice.
Haggai (520 B.C.E.): a postexilic prophet who encourages temple construction so that conditions might improve in the return community.	**Joel** (ca. 400–350 B.C.E.): calls for a cultic response to a locust plague and announces an eschatological Day of Yahweh that will reveal God's justice.
Jonah (probably written in the Persian period but set in the time of Jeroboam II): a story about a reluctant prophet called to announce judgment against the Assyrian capital. The prophet is angered that God shows mercy when the city repents.	

Second Isaiah (Isa. 40:1–41:4; 42:5-9; 44:1–45:7; 52:13–53:12)

In the middle of the sixth century, there lived a prophet who was one of the Hebrew Bible's greatest poets and most daring theologians. We do not know his name, but he was likely a third-or fourth-generation disciple of the eighth-century prophet Isaiah. Because his words survive only as a supplement to Isaiah's oracles, he is often called **Second Isaiah** (Isa. 40–55). Attentive readers can easily discern that different historical circumstances lie behind these chapters. Whereas First Isaiah addressed Judean kings in the heyday of the Assyrian Empire, Second Isaiah addresses the exilic community in Babylon. He proclaims to the exiles that Yahweh is about to topple the Babylonian Empire and return them to their homeland in a second exodus. Because this anonymous prophet specifically identifies Cyrus as the agent of Yahweh's imminent redemption (Isa. 44:28; 45:1), we can confidently locate his career in the years just before Cyrus's conquest of Babylon in 539 B.C.E.

The opening verses of chapter 40 are often read as Second Isaiah's call narrative (CD Chart IVB.1). Here the prophet is commissioned to comfort God's people and to reassure them that exile is nearly over because their sins have now been atoned for twice over. A voice commands that a smooth highway be stretched across the wilderness in preparation for the exiles' return to Jerusalem. Yet the prophet hesitates because of the uncertainty and finitude of human life—we are, after all, nothing more than grass that quickly withers (Isa. 40:6-7). The voice agrees with this assessment of human beings but proclaims that Yahweh's word is enduring nonetheless. Second Isaiah's protest likely reflects the mood of the beleaguered and insignificant exilic community. Many surely believed that Yahweh had forsaken them in a foreign land (Isa. 40:27), but the prophet's task was to convince them that they were still the chosen people. The God who gives power to the faint and bears them up on eagles' wings (Isa. 40:28-31) was finally ready to intervene on their behalf.

The prophet also recognizes the temptation among exiles to assimilate into the dominant culture around them by worshiping Babylonian gods. Even though recent historical events might suggest that Babylonian deities were stronger, the prophet insists that all power actually belongs to the God of Judah. According to Second Isaiah, Yahweh does not merely determine the fate of the Jewish people but controls the entire scope of human history. The gods of other nations are powerless and, in fact, nothing but dumb idols (Isa. 44:9-20). In the Bible's first explicit affirmation of **monotheism**, Second Isaiah proclaims that Yahweh is not only the God of Israel but the only true God, who directs the fates of all nations. That a member of a small group of displaced persons from a defeated nation should make such a claim for his deity is incredibly audacious!

For Second Isaiah, universal sovereignty guaranteed Yahweh's ability to direct political events on behalf of the Jews. The military success of Cyrus was not simply an accident of history but proof that Yahweh had indeed chosen him as an agent. Even though this Persian ruler did not recognize Yahweh, Second Isaiah does not hesitate to bestow upon him royal titles like the "anointed" (sometimes translated "messiah," Isa. 45:1). The restoration of Judah, accomplished through Cyrus, would become a sign of Yahweh's sovereignty to other nations. Although the covenant community remains at the center of Yahweh's plans in Second Isaiah, the prophet suggests that in the future a restored Judah would serve as a "light to the nations" (Isa. 42:6; 49:6).

Servanthood is the unifying theme of several distinctive passages in Second Isaiah that are sometimes called **Servant Songs** (Isa. 42:1-6; 49:1-6; 50:4-9; 52:13–53:12). In these passages, an unidentified figure designated as Yahweh's "servant" is called before birth to execute justice and serve as a light to the nations. In two of the songs, this servant willingly suffers abuse, trusting that God will vindicate him in the end. He is beaten, classed with sinners, and possibly killed. Remarkably, the servant's suffering is interpreted by witnesses as redemptive for the sins of others—much like a human scapegoat (cf. Lev. 16).

Although Christian audiences traditionally identify this mysterious figure with Jesus, the sixth-century prophet likely had in mind someone more immediately relevant to his own historical situation (CD Chart IVB.2). Perhaps the most likely candidate is collective Israel (Isa. 49:3), who had suffered doubly for her sins in exile and whom Second Isaiah frequently dubs Yahweh's servant outside of the Servant Songs. Another possibility is the prophet himself, whose message regarding Cyrus's imminent victory may have raised the ire of Babylonian authorities or of fellow exiles who regarded his views as too dangerous and revolutionary.

The message of this audacious theologian was indeed revolutionary. Second Isaiah drew from inherited religious traditions to construct a clear theological interpretation of current events running entirely counter to the logic of his day. While any objective observer of the time would have judged the Jews and their religion to be of no special significance, he places both squarely in the center of the world stage. Cyrus was on the march not because of military superiority or the might of Persian gods, but because it suited Yahweh's purpose for the exilic community. In incredibly unlikely circumstances, Second Isaiah is the first biblical writer to declare the universal sovereignty of the Jewish God. In another bold move, the prophet concludes his message by extending the promises that were formerly associated with the Davidic house to the covenant community as a whole (Isa. 55:3).

Third Isaiah (56:1-8; 58:1–59:2; 61:1-7; 66:1-5)

The exuberant prophecy of Second Isaiah could not have prepared the return community for the difficulties that rebuilding a life in the land would entail. At the end of what was supposed to be a triumphant return from exile, they were confronted with the ruins of Jerusalem. In this context arose the prophet(s) responsible for Isaiah 56–66, which is often termed **Third Isaiah**. Whereas Second Isaiah (Isa. 40–55) addressed an audience situated in Babylon in the final years of exile, Third Isaiah addresses a frustrated return community in postexilic Judah. Although we do not have sufficient information to date these oracles precisely, most scholars place them early in the restoration period (539–520 B.C.E.).

The prophet(s) behind these chapters attempts to sustain the vision of Second Isaiah and explain why God's promised salvation has apparently been delayed (CD Chart IVB.3). Third Isaiah insists that soon Yahweh will create a new heaven and new earth that will wipe the present suffering from their minds. Zion will be glorified, weeping will be replaced by joy, the land will be fertile, and all will live to a ripe old age (Isa. 65:17-25). Third Isaiah also revives the earlier prophetic concern for social justice, claiming that the neglect of such matters has thus far prevented a complete restoration (Isa. 58; 59:1-2). Like Micah, Third Isaiah insists that Yahweh cares more about kindness and mercy than ritual observances. Restoring the temple cult does not assume tremendous importance in these oracles (Isa. 66:1-5), although they do call for the avoidance of idolatry and observance of the Sabbath (a practice that had increased in significance during the exile).

Unlike preexilic prophets, Third Isaiah does not announce judgment against the community as a whole. Rather the prophet(s) insists that Yahweh's judgment will fall only on those who do not turn from transgression (Isa. 59:18-20). The unfaithful will be eradicated, whereas the faithful will be comforted. If covenant membership in the restoration era is to be determined by faithfulness rather than ancestry, then even foreigners might be included. Occasionally, Third Isaiah does embrace a universal vision in which Yahweh's temple becomes "a house of prayer for all peoples" (Isa. 56:3-8; 66:18-21). Yet in other oracles, the nations merely serve and enrich Israel in the coming world order (Isa. 60:3-16; 61:5-11).

Haggai (Hag. 1; 2:20-23)

Conditions did not soon improve for the return community. According to the prophet **Haggai**, restoration efforts were impeded by poor harvests, deprivation, and a general lack of enthusiasm (Hag. 1:5-6; 2:15-16). This prophet's career took place in the second year of Darius, the third ruler of the Persian Empire (520 B.C.E.). Haggai's oracles are addressed to the return community and its local leaders, the Persian-appointed governor, Zerubbabel, and the high priest Joshua (CD Chart IVB.4). Apart from his message, we know almost nothing about this prophet other than his apparent influence within the postexilic community around Jerusalem.

Prior to his appearance, the project of rebuilding Yahweh's temple had dragged on for almost twenty years. Within five years after his short career, the Second Temple was dedicated.

This prophet's evident concern for the temple contrasts with the sharp criticism that preexilic prophets often leveled against the established cult. Temple advocacy, combined with the absence of social critique, might lead readers to class Haggai with the cult prophets that Jeremiah and others had condemned. Clearly, several of the postexilic prophets are more closely associated with the cult than were their preexilic counterparts. However, it would be a mistake to dismiss Persian period prophets on that account. The preexilic temple had encouraged self-satisfied piety expressed through simplistic Zion theology, but few would suggest after 587 B.C.E. that a reconstructed temple would guarantee Jerusalem's future security. Nevertheless, the rebuilding project did provide a means for unifying the postexilic community around a common goal, and in the coming years the Second Temple would provide a religious center for Diaspora Judaism, without which the Yahwistic faith may not have survived.

For Haggai, temple rebuilding was a necessary prerequisite to the glorious future that earlier prophets had described. He attributes the repeated setbacks experienced by the community to their neglect of Yahweh's temple. Although they had already constructed dwellings for themselves, Yahweh's house still lay in ruins! Haggai announces that the only way to improve their circumstances is by resuming work on the temple immediately.

According to the text, the prophet successfully mobilizes the community around this project in little more than three weeks (Hag. 1:12-15). As work progressed, comparisons with the temple of Solomon that had once stood on this site were inevitable. Some members of the community recalled the grandeur of the original structure and expressed disappointment with the poorer Second Temple (Hag. 2:3). Haggai assures his audience the new temple would soon outstrip the old one in splendor because Yahweh intended to bring to Jerusalem the wealth of nations by shaking heavens and earth (Hag. 2:6-9).

The theme of "shaking" recurs at the end of the book in a private oracle addressed to Zerubbabel (Hag. 2:20-23). Here Yahweh intends to shake heavens and earth to overthrow the present world order and establish a new one. Haggai announces that a special role will be played in the new order by Zerubbabel, whom the deity has chosen as a "signet ring" (cf. Jer. 22:24). Such a ring made a distinctive impression in clay or soft wax and carried the force of a validating signature in the ancient world. To entrust a person with your signet ring was to give them full authority to act on your behalf. Zerubbabel, who descended from the line of David, was the focus of postexilic hopes for restored Judean political independence under a Davidic king. This cautiously worded endorsement of Zerubbabel may suggest that Haggai shared such a hope.

Zechariah (Zech. 1:1–6:8; 8:1-23)

Haggai's was not the only prophetic voice that encouraged the project of temple building. He was assisted in the task by a slightly younger contemporary named Zechariah, whose career was a bit longer (520–518 B.C.E.). Like Haggai, Zechariah felt that a new temple was essential to the restoration, but his paramount concern was the morale and purity of the postexilic community (CD Chart IVB.5). Much of his message is presented in the form of symbolic visions interpreted for the prophet by an angelic guide. This feature brings the book of Zechariah a step closer to the later apocalyptic movement (see chapter 5). An apocalyptic tone is even more evident in the latter half of the book (Zech. 9–14), which appears to be a later addition and is often labeled **Second Zechariah** (CD Special Topic IVB.1).

The audience addressed by the sixth-century prophet Zechariah was likely voicing the question found in his first vision (Zech. 1:12b): "O [Yahweh] of hosts, how long will you withhold mercy from Jerusalem and the cities of Judah, with which you have been angry these seventy years?" Cyrus's edict had ended the exile and enabled a return to the Jewish homeland, but conditions faced by the restored community were still difficult. Zechariah comforts his audience with the assurance that Yahweh has already returned to Jerusalem and was about to restore this city to its former greatness. In fact, Yahweh intends to make Jerusalem the center of a new world order where all the nations will gather to worship (Zech. 2:11; 8:20-23). The prophet also encourages Diaspora Jews to return to the holy city (Zech. 2:6-10).

This message is reinforced by a series of eight related visions intended to inspire hope in his audience. The first two visions anticipate Yahweh's imminent punishment of nations that have oppressed Judah. The third vision promises that Jerusalem will soon be too big for walls to contain and that Yahweh will personally protect the city. The next two visions concern the leaders of the restored community. In the fourth vision, the high priest Joshua is on trial before the heavenly council, about to be accused by an adversary (often translated "Satan," CD Special Topic IVB.2). But Yahweh acquits Joshua of sin and has him symbolically purified with a change of clothes so that he can perform his priestly duties. This vision attempts to justify the enhanced authority assumed by the high priest in the postexilic period. The fifth vision features both Joshua and Zerubbabel as olive trees that provide oil for a golden lamp stand that illuminates the whole earth. The sixth and seventh visions deal with the problem of sin in the restored community. A flying scroll devours those who steal or bear false witness while a flying basket carries a woman called "Wickedness" to Babylon, where she is worshiped as an idol. The series concludes by returning to the imagery of the initial vision.

Overall, Zechariah's visions provide encouragement that the fortunes of the return community would soon change for the better (Zech. 8). Once the temple was rebuilt and a purified community followed God's commandments, fasting would be transformed to rejoicing. Scattered

Jews would return to Jerusalem and grow old there amidst their grand-children. Finally, people from other nations would stream into Zion to worship Yahweh.

Malachi (Mal. 1; 3–4)

A few generations after the Jews' return from exile, conditions were not greatly improved for the restoration community. Ironically, cautious prophetic affirmations of Zerubbabel may have led Persian authorities to revoke his appointment as the local governor of Judah. Shortly after the dedication of the Second Temple, all local authority was concentrated in the hands of the priesthood. Hope for restored political independence under a Davidic king began to fade. As economic hardships and internal discord continued to plague the Second Temple community, the zeal momentarily inspired by Haggai and Zechariah quickly waned.

The book of **Malachi** originates in this context sometime between 500–450 B.C.E. We know virtually nothing about the prophet behind this book, who probably was not even named Malachi. The book's title literally means "my messenger" (Mal. 3:1). The prophet (whom for convenience's sake we will continue to call Malachi) addressed a discouraged and increasingly cynical postexilic community that questioned divine justice and the value of worshiping Yahweh. Malachi uses a question-answer technique to cajole, inspire, and shame his audience toward true religious devotion (CD Chart IVB.6).

He complains primarily about abuses in the temple cult. Although biblical law demanded unblemished animals be placed on the altar (Lev. 22:17-25; Deut. 15:21), Malachi claims that blind and sickly animals were being sacrificed instead. Perhaps the economically suffering community did not want to "waste" their best livestock, or perhaps the priests were keeping the better animals for themselves. The prophet enjoins the priests to execute their sacrificial and teaching duties faithfully and encourages the people to pay faithfully their tithes to support the temple.

Malachi's concerns also extend beyond the temple cult into the realm of personal righteousness and community ethics (Mal. 3:5). He devotes considerable space to criticizing marriage to foreigners, marital infidelity, and divorce (Mal. 2:10-16). Similar concerns appear in the postexilic books of Ezra and Nehemiah (see chapter 5). However, this passage may also be interpreted metaphorically as condemnation of apostasy and covenant infidelity (cf. Hos. 1:2–3:5).

Ultimately, Malachi encourages his audience by contrasting the rather pathetic present with an **eschatological** future when Yahweh would act directly to vindicate the faithful and punish the wicked. The image of a coming judgment day (a variation of the "Day of Yahweh" motif) anticipates later developments in apocalyptic thought (see chapter 5). Malachi invokes this idea as a theodicy to assure his audience that, despite perceived injustice in the present, faithfulness will one day be rewarded and iniquity punished (Mal. 3:14-15). A messenger will purify the priesthood as a harbinger of that day, before Yahweh suddenly appears in the temple (Mal. 3:1-4). The final verses of the book, usually regarded as later additions, identify this messenger as Elijah—a claim that has become significant in later Judaism and Christianity (CD Special Topic IVB.3). These verses also draw attention to the emerging canon in postexilic Judaism, which included the Torah (associated with Moses) and the Prophets (epitomized by Elijah).

Joel (Joel 1–3)

The book of **Joel** reveals no personal information about this prophet other than his father's name and a few hints that likely place him in the Persian period (CD Chart IVB.7). Although the book is occasionally dated to the preexilic era, its promise of restored fortunes for God's people and vengeance against those who have scattered them among the nations better fits a postexilic context (Joel 3:1-3). Joel also shows a level of respectful concern for the priesthood and cult that is more characteristic of Persian-period prophecy. Moreover, the book frequently quotes and alludes to the words of earlier prophetic anthologies and other biblical books. Because he presupposes a functioning temple and mentions walls around Jerusalem, we should probably date Joel between 400–350 B.C.E.

The book begins with a terrifying description of a locust plague that is at some points depicted metaphorically as an invading army (Joel 1:2–2:27). The resulting agricultural devastation is so complete that sacrifices have ceased. Interpreting this disaster as a divine act, Joel calls upon priests to lament, proclaim a fast, and assemble all the people. Although the prophet does not specify particular sins within the community, he calls for repentance and renewed dependence on God in this time of crisis (Joel 2:12-14). Joel quotes an old confession that describes Yahweh as "gracious and merciful, slow to anger, and abounding in steadfast love" (cf. Exod. 34:6-7; Num. 14:17-19). Following this cultic activity, the prophet announces Yahweh's promise to remove the plague and restore fertility.

An averted locust plague then becomes an occasion for eschatological prophecy concerning the Day of Yahweh. Joel envisions this as a day heralded by cosmic signs and the democratic distribution of God's spirit to all of the Jewish people—providing young and old, male and female with unmediated access to the deity. Then Yahweh will intervene in history to judge and to redeem. Whereas the eighth-century prophet Amos had warned that the Day of Yahweh would be dark for Israel (Am. 5:18-20), Joel announces divine judgment only upon other nations. This prophet anticipates a day when Judah will be blessed, while other nations are gathered in the Valley of "Jehoshaphat" (literally, "Yahweh judges") and laid waste by the deity. Reversing an earlier prophetic slogan, he mockingly advises the nations to "beat your plowshares into swords, and your pruning hooks into spears" (Joel 3:10; cf. Isa. 2:4; Mic. 4:3). Here Joel's intense nationalism allows no compassion for anyone outside of his own people!

Jonah (Jonah 1–4)

We conclude our journey through the Latter Prophets with the book of
Jonah. Although conclusive evidence for dating this book is lacking, it
is often placed in the postexilic period based upon its language, its theology, and its tendency to quote or allude to other biblical books. We
have saved Jonah for last because it departs so drastically from other
prophetic anthologies. It is not a collection of oracles uttered during a
time of moral or political crisis. Rather, it is a story about a prophet that
subtly reflects on the entire prophetic tradition. As such it is a fitting
conclusion for this chapter.

Sophisticated readers will quickly recognize that the book is not historical literature. Although the character of Jonah is apparently based
on a real prophet (an eighth-century contemporary of Amos, 2 Kgs.
14:25), this book is not a historical account of his career. Rather, its use
of intentional exaggeration and ironic humor suggests that it should be
read as a parable or a teaching story. Readers who insist upon a literal
interpretation for such a story miss its point!

This well-told tale delights in frustrating the expectations of its readers (CD Chart IVB.8). By now, we easily recognize the formulaic beginning of a prophetic call narrative that opens the book. God commissions
a prophet to deliver a message of judgment against a sinful city, but surprisingly the city in question is not found in Israel. Readers may recall
that Nineveh was the capital of the brutal and hated Assyrian Empire,
the first of three eastern superpowers that dominated Israel's history for
over four centuries. Prophets did occasionally utter oracles of judgment
against Assyria and other foreign nations, and the entire book of Nahum
celebrated the imminent fall of Nineveh. But Nahum's venomous words
were addressed to an appreciative Hebrew audience. Why would God
call a prophet to *go* to Nineveh?

Our familiarity with prophetic call narratives conditions us to expect
initial resistance from the prophet that will be overcome by divine
reassurance. Here Jonah wildly exceeds our expectations! The prophet

Latter Prophets: Israel's Moral Compass   233 does not simply demur but runs in the opposite direction, attempting to escape the presence of Yahweh by leaving Israel in a ship. Of course, such an attempt is futile since Jonah himself later admits that Yahweh made both the sea and the land (Jonah 1:9). Yahweh's sovereignty over nature (even outside of Israel) is affirmed by a storm that almost sinks Jonah's ship—so much for divine reassurance!

Ironically, the Israelite prophet is at first oblivious to the deity's actions and must be roused and urged to pray for mercy by the Phoenician mariners. Moreover, once Jonah is identified as the cause of their plight, the mariners hesitate to toss him overboard and offer acts of devotion to Yahweh. Whereas the prophet is disobedient, these foreigners fear God. Even Jonah's insistence that he be thrown overboard could be viewed as another attempt to escape his call rather than as a selfless sacrifice.

Yahweh mercifully saves the rebellious prophet by appointing a large fish to swallow him. Readers who recognize the story as a parable need not be troubled with explaining how Jonah could survive in this situation. From the belly of this creature, Jonah utters a psalm of thanksgiving rather than the expected plea for help. Nevertheless, God makes the fish vomit him out on dry land and repeats the earlier commission. This time the chastened prophet obeys but shows little enthusiasm for the task. Although the narrator claims that it takes three days to walk across Nineveh, Jonah prophesies for one day and appears to utter one sentence: "Forty days more, and Nineveh shall be overthrown" (Jonah 3:4b). Given the poor reception most biblical prophets experienced from Israelite and Judean audiences, readers surely expect Jonah's lackluster message to go unheeded by the Ninevites. Yet once again our expectations are thwarted. The king of Nineveh and all of his subjects (from the nobles to the sheep!) fast, mourn, and repent in hopes that Yahweh will spare them.

In contrast to the book of Nahum, where God's unrelenting hatred for Nineveh is taken for granted, here God extends mercy toward the

Ninevites—much to Jonah's dismay. The irate prophet now reveals the reason behind his earlier reluctance—he was afraid that God would prove merciful! He angrily paraphrases an old Israelite creed describing Yahweh as "a gracious God and merciful, slow to anger, and abounding in steadfast love" (4:2; cf. Exod. 34:6-7; Num. 14:17-19). Is Jonah upset because God has made a fool of him? If Nineveh survives, then Jonah becomes a "false prophet" whose words are not vindicated by history (Deut. 18:21-22). Or is Jonah jealous that God's compassion is not limited to Israel but extends to other nations?

The book ends with an object lesson for the prophet, who has withdrawn from the city and is hopefully watching for its destruction. Jonah appreciates a shade plant that God causes to grow over him, but he is angry when God appoints a worm to kill the plant. The deity questions how Jonah can care for the plant but cannot understand divine concern for the large human and animal population of Nineveh. The book closes abruptly with that rhetorical question.

What are readers to make of this odd story included among the Latter Prophets? Many different interpretations of this book have been offered, and they are not mutually exclusive. It is often seen as a critique of narrow nationalism based upon the notion of Israel's divine election. Although hints of universalism are present in other prophetic books (Am. 9:7; Isa. 2:2-4; 42:4-6; 45:1-6; 56:3-8; 66:18-21; Zeph. 3:9-10; Zech. 2:11; 8:20-24), nowhere is it more blatant than in Jonah. The foreigners in this story are portrayed much more positively than the Israelite prophet, who resents the idea that divine compassion might be extended to "outsiders." Readers could also find here a subtle criticism of the covenant community, which rarely responds so well to prophetic calls for repentance! Or perhaps the book offers a satirical critique of prophecy itself, especially prophets who insincerely preached repentance without really wanting to see it. By depicting God as more inclined toward mercy than judgment, the book overturns the prophet Jeremiah's pessimistic claim that oracles of doom are more reliable than hopeful prophecy (Jer. 28:6-9). Perhaps most important, the story of Jonah declares that God may not be bound by the words of prophets or by a rigid doctrine of retribution. God is free to extend mercy to both insubordinate prophets and sinful Assyrians.

In summary, Persian period prophecy begins with Second Isaiah's anticipation of a glorious restoration that would vindicate the demoralized exilic community. Yet the harsh circumstances faced by returnees did not measure up to their idealistic expectations. In the face of repeated disappointments, postexilic prophets were forced to go in new directions. The Second Temple became a rallying point championed by many prophets as a religious center for the return community and Diaspora Judaism. Eschatological language and visions also provided a means to inspire hope in otherwise discouraging circumstances. Prophetic forerunners of the apocalyptic movement looked to the distant future for the consummation of Yahweh's redeeming activity. Meanwhile, preserving the identity of the community under foreign rule remained a persistent concern. Although Second Isaiah had described the restored community as a "light to the nations," much postexilic prophecy sounds narrowly nationalistic and sectarian. Yet, alongside prophets who call for the annihilation of their enemies, we find other prophetic voices that affirm Yahweh's concern for all people.

The Journey Continues

As this leg of our journey through Hebrew scripture draws to a close, we might pause to reflect on what we have learned about biblical prophets and prophetic literature. Amos, Jeremiah, Haggai, and the rest did not speak in a vacuum but were responding to real moral and political crises in their communities. They did not offer predictions about the remote future, but they did offer guidance for their immediate audiences, who were experiencing drastic changes and difficult challenges. Their words were remembered, recorded, and shaped by disciples and editors who reinterpreted the prophets' messages for the benefit of later generations.

As one empire after another exerted control over the ancient Near East, the biblical prophets refused to see Israel and Judah as bit players in this international drama. Rather, they cast these tiny kingdoms in starring roles and cast the mighty empires as tools of judgment or salvation in the hands of Yahweh. Along the way, most of the biblical prophets drew attention to ways in which Israel and Judah were failing to meet their covenant obligations. These prophetic protestors offered a challenging call for social justice and sincere worship in place of self-interest and national arrogance. Yet even while prophetic literature depicts a righteous God who punishes covenant violations, it also recognizes that Yahweh's character prevents judgment from having the last word.

The prophetic movement provided a moral compass that helped Israel traverse the rough terrain represented by these turbulent centuries. Yet questions arose as early as the late seventh century about the prophetic assumption that God's justice was evident in historical events. The theological crisis experienced by the return community brought these questions to a crescendo and forced prophecy in new directions that anticipate many of the developments we will encounter in the Writings.

CHAPTER FIVE

WRITINGS:
THE HOMEWARD JOURNEY

We are approaching the end of our long and enriching journey through Hebrew scripture. A backward glance reveals how far we have traveled through daunting textual terrain. In chapter 2, we toured Israel's foundational narratives (the Torah) and, in chapter 3, traced the tragic history of her national failure (the Former Prophets). In chapter 4, we encountered the words of Israel's prophets as they were preserved and shaped by later generations (the Latter Prophets). Now we undertake the final stage of our journey into another section of the Hebrew Bible, the **Writings** (Hebrew *ketuvim*).

These books form the last of three canonical divisions within the Jewish canon that are represented by the three consonants of the acronym Tanakh (*torah, nevi'im, ketuvim*). Although the title "Writings" is not attested until the rabbinic period (70–500 C.E.), the existence of this collection was noted as early as the second century B.C.E. in the prologue to the Greek translation of Sirach. The translator who added that prologue refers three times to the Law, the Prophets, and "the other books." Such casual mention of this third collection suggests that it retained a degree of fluidity long after the two earlier collections had been more or less canonized. It is generally agreed that the Writings assumed a more formal shape by the late first century C.E., although we do not know exactly when or how this section of the canon was closed.

239

In the Jewish Bible, the books that comprise the Writings appear in the following order: Psalms, Proverbs, Job, Song of Songs, Ruth, Lamentations, Ecclesiastes, Esther, Daniel, Ezra, Nehemiah, and 1–2 Chronicles. This arrangement reflects the tradition of linking five short books—the Song through Esther—that have developed associations with major Jewish festivals and fast days. These five books are collectively called the **Megilloth** (meaning "scrolls"). The Jewish canon concludes with the triumphant edict of Cyrus calling upon faithful Jews to return to Jerusalem and rebuild the holy temple (2 Chr. 36:22-23).

Whereas the Writings are grouped together at the end of Jewish scripture, Christian Bibles scatter them among the Former and Latter Prophets based on perceptions (or misperceptions) about chronology, authorship, and genre. For example, Ruth is placed after the book of Judges because this story is set during the Judges period (although it was written much later). First and Second Chronicles are placed with other historical literature and followed by Ezra and Nehemiah, which appear to pick up the storyline where Chronicles ends. Proverbs, Ecclesiastes, and the Song of Songs are grouped together because of the erroneous assumption that all three were authored by Solomon. Daniel was mistaken for a prophetic book and grouped with the Major Prophets. As a result of this arrangement, the Christian Old Testament ends with the Minor Prophets. More specifically, the Old Testament closes by looking forward to Elijah's return (Mal. 4:5-6), a reference that Christians have traditionally considered fulfilled by the ministry of John the Baptist in the New Testament.

The temptation to divide the Writings up as in Christian Bibles is understandable, because it is certainly difficult to conceive of these books as a unified collection. To many readers, the third section of the Tanakh appears to be a catchall category lacking real coherence. These books exhibit a wide range of genres and perspectives. What could the soaring love poetry of the Song of Songs have to do with the somber reflections of Ecclesiastes? How could the winsome narrative of Ruth be related to the pedantic rulings of Ezra? Because of this variety, we will adapt the customary route of our journey in this chapter. Instead of seeking a single explanation for the literary origins of this diverse literature, we will be exploring several interpretive trajectories, or "paths," through the Writings.

Yet it would be a mistake to ignore certain features that characterize the Writings as a whole. Perhaps most important, we must remember that all of these books took shape after the exile. Some may contain earlier material (especially Proverbs and Psalms), but in their final form they all reflect circumstances of the postexilic era. As we discussed in the last chapter, those who returned from exile under the edict of Cyrus experienced at best a partial restoration in which they retained provincial status within the Persian Empire. Their monarchic state and political autonomy were no more, and their homeland was reduced to a small area in the immediate vicinity of Jerusalem. Priests replaced kings as the dominant authority within the return community.

Nonetheless, conflicts persisted among competing groups. Samaritans, who were descended from the old northern kingdom and also professed to worship Yahweh, were rebuffed by the restored community. Judeans who had remained in the land and not experienced the exile clashed with those who had returned from Babylon. Many other Jews remained dispersed across the ancient Near East, choosing not to return to their ancestral homeland. Yahweh worship now occurred in many places under many circumstances. The diversity of the Writings clearly reflects the new pluralism of the postexilic period and a lack of consensus among these groups over what should be central to Judaism.

Membership within the covenant community had once been determined by nationality and territorial boundaries. But in these radically changed circumstances it was difficult to determine who the "true Israelites" were. This concern runs like a thread through many of the Writings. How should Jewish identity be construed? Lacking political autonomy and often living as minorities, how could Jews avoid the threat of cultural and religious assimilation? How far should Jews accommodate themselves to the dominant culture? Which group of Jews should define normative Judaism? The Writings provide multiple answers to such questions.

While these books engage in dialogue with the contemporary concerns and diversity of the postexilic era, they also converse with older traditions of the covenant community. Readers can easily perceive a desire to connect with Israel's past in the historical enterprise of the Chronicler or in the quaint story of Ruth. Many of the Writings draw upon, reinterpret, and sometimes even challenge inherited traditions. For example, the Song of Songs can be read as a reprise of the garden of Eden story, while Job takes issue with the basic premise of Deuteronomic theology. The end result is many new expressions of faith that attest to the adaptive flexibility of Second Temple Judaism.

In this chapter, we will explore three possible "paths" through the Writings: the path of worship, the path of wisdom, and the path of apocalyptic. For many Jews, the postexilic journey reflected in this section of the canon was literally a homeward one. But when these people left behind an exilic existence and returned to their ancestral homeland, they did not find there what they expected. For them and for the many other Jews of this diverse period, these three paths represented ways of reconfiguring inherited traditions to sustain the Yahwistic faith in radically changed circumstances.

THE PATH OF WORSHIP

On our first circuit through the Writings we will encounter texts representing a wide range of genres and theological perspectives. Chronicles retells the Bible's primary history found in Genesis through Kings, whereas Ezra and Nehemiah present an account of the Persian period. Alongside this historical literature, we will also encounter a large compilation of prayers and songs that is sometimes called the hymnbook of the Second Temple. Finally, we will browse through the collection of texts called the Megilloth, which contains songs, wisdom literature, and short stories. Despite the great diversity of these writings, they share at least one important characteristic—they all relate to the worship life of Second Temple Judaism.

Yahweh worship clearly continued after the destruction of Solomon's temple and the dispersion of 587 B.C.E., but it was forced to assume new forms in the absence of a central sanctuary and cult. For some, the destruction of the temple was not so traumatic. Despite King Josiah's earlier attempt to displace popular religion and impose a centralized cult, Yahweh continued to be venerated (sometimes alongside a goddess) in cultic centers outside of Jerusalem. For Samaritans, worship centered on Mount Gerizim rather than Mount Zion. For others, the Jerusalem temple was essential to the Yahwistic cult and its loss was devastating. The prophet/priest Ezekiel, for example, could envision Yahweh leaving the defiled temple to join the exilic community in Babylon—but only as a temporary measure until the Jerusalem cult could be purified and reestablished (Ezek. 1; 10; 40–48).

We know little about the worship practices of Jews in the exilic period, but it is likely here that we should seek the origins of the **synagogue**—at least if the early synagogue is understood as a gathering of people for study, prayer, and worship rather than as a building or an institution. Perhaps this would explain why so many who maintained a Jewish identity nonetheless opted not to return to their ancestral homeland under the edict of Cyrus in 539 B.C.E. Their religious needs were obviously being met in ways that did not require a temple. Others, like Ezekiel before them, continued to view the temple and its cult as foundational to Yahwistic worship. For these Jews, rebuilding the central sanctuary in Jerusalem was imperative.

The diverse literature that follows reflects the many communities that constituted Second Temple Judaism. While the temple plays a role in some of these texts, its significance in the absence of the Davidic nation-state is variously interpreted. We will also find new forms of piety advocated that could as easily be practiced by Diaspora Jews. The Psalter provides us with another window into the personal and communal piety of this period, while the Megilloth attest to the diverse voices that eventually became associated with the Jewish liturgical cycle.

The Historical Books (1 Chr. 10:1–11:3; 15–16; 22; 2 Chr. 29–30; 33; Ezra 4–7; 9–10; Neh. 1–2; 4; 8–9; 13; CD Preliminary Exercises IA.1 and IA.2)

Many first-time readers of the Hebrew Bible are surprised to discover that the "Adam-to-exile" storyline found in the Torah and Former Prophets appears again within the Writings. Genesis through 2 Kings is sometimes called the Bible's **Primary History**, whereas 1–2 Chronicles, Ezra, and Nehemiah are called its **Secondary History**. There is a great deal of overlap between these two accounts, although the second extends the story of Israel into the Persian period. Nevertheless, Chronicles has often been accused of presenting a less interesting and less reliable account of Israel's past than that found in Samuel and Kings. This judgment ignores the fact that both histories are interpretive and both were produced to meet the needs of their respective audiences rather than to preserve an "objective" account of the past.

The Secondary History is an important part of the biblical canon because it provides a window—or possibly two windows—into the world of Second Temple Judaism. It was once common to assume that Chronicles was penned by the same hand that penned Ezra and Nehemiah, but that assumption is now being challenged. These books do have certain linguistic similarities and share a priestly perspective evinced by their common interest in the temple, cultic personnel, lists, and genealogies. They are further linked by the edict of Cyrus, which appears at the conclusion of 2 Chronicles and again at the beginning of

Ezra. But there are also interesting differences between 1–2 Chronicles and Ezra–Nehemiah that suggest separate authorship. We will explore those differences in the following discussion and consider what visions of Israel as a worshiping community are advocated by these writings.

The Chronicler

Like 1–2 Samuel and 1–2 Kings, 1–2 Chronicles was originally a single book. The **Chronicler** (as its author is called) clearly wrote during the postexilic period since the book's storyline encompasses the rise of the Persian Empire and the return under Cyrus. Other historical references (1 Chr. 29:7), the extent of its Davidic genealogy (1 Chr. 3), and allusions to other postexilic texts (2 Chr. 16:9) place Chronicles in the late fifth or early fourth century B.C.E. But if these passages are viewed as later additions to the text, a somewhat earlier date is feasible.

The book of Chronicles divides easily into four sections, the first of which uses a long genealogy to quickly summarize the storyline of Genesis through 1 Samuel (1 Chr. 1–9). Beginning this genealogy with Adam establishes a universal context for the narrative that follows. The Chronicler shapes these chapters to emphasize Judah (the eponymous ancestor of the returning Judeans) over the other sons born to Jacob/ Israel. Digressions trace David's house and the families of other prominent returnees into the Persian period (1 Chr. 3; 9). Special attention is also given here and elsewhere in the book to Levites (1 Chr. 6; 15:1-24; 23–26; 2 Chr. 29:3-34). In the Second Temple period only Levites who descended from Aaron through Zadok were called "priests" and allowed to offer sacrifices, while other members of this tribe performed subsidiary roles. The Chronicler, however, supports these second-class Levites whenever possible, which has led to speculation that he may have belonged to this group.

Narrative dominates the rest of Chronicles, beginning in the book's second major section, the reign of David (1 Chr. 10–29). Here it becomes obvious that the Chronicler is using the Primary History as a source, since parts of 2 Samuel are copied verbatim (CD Primary Text IA.1). By comparing the **Chronicler's History** to its main sources (2 Samuel and 1–2 Kings), we can better appreciate how the Chronicler has reshaped the earlier story to communicate his own theological point of view (biblical scholarship that examines this process is called **redaction criticism**). Most readers notice that the Chronicler omits most of the spicy stories found in 2 Samuel and adds other information that results in a very different portrait of David. Gone are the questionable details of this young rogue's rise to power over the house of Saul. Gone is David's scandalous encounter with Bathsheba and its murderous cover-up. Gone are the dynastic struggles within the royal house. Instead, readers encounter a David who is entirely preoccupied with plans for the Jerusalem temple and its cult. Astute readers will quickly realize that this history replaces sex and politics with priestly concerns. David becomes a priest-king and the legitimacy of the temple is enhanced through its closer connection with him.

Solomon also receives a facelift in the third section of the book through a similar process of editorial shaping, omissions, and additions (2 Chr. 1–9). Gone is the rivalry for succession among the sons of David. Gone are Solomon's despotic and idolatrous tendencies. Gone are the seven hundred wives and three hundred concubines. What remains is the wealthy and wise temple builder. Because the Chronicler credits David with making preparations for temple building, all that Solomon must do is to oversee the implementation of his father's plans and the dedication of the completed structure.

The final section of Chronicles traces David's dynasty from the end of the united monarchy to the destruction of Jerusalem (2 Chr. 10–36). Along the way, each Judean monarch is evaluated based upon his or her disposition toward the Jerusalem temple, with David and Solomon providing the model of royal piety. Much of this material seems to be drawn from 1–2 Kings, but northern monarchs are largely ignored by the Chronicler unless they interact with the Davidic house. Neither are the

STUDYING THE OLD TESTAMENT

northern prophets Elijah and Elisha featured prominently in Chronicles, and the fall of the northern kingdom to Assyria is not even mentioned!

Throughout this southern-focused account, the Chronicler again retouches the portraits that the Deuteronomistic Historian(s) had painted of several monarchs. For example, readers of Chronicles encounter a less-perfect version of the Deuteronomistic hero Josiah (2 Chr. 35:20-24; cf. 2 Kgs. 23:25). Readers also find a fuller account of Hezekiah's Reform, which had been downplayed in Kings to enhance Josiah's importance (2 Chr. 29–31). Only in the Chronicler's History does Hezekiah preside over a Passover festival in Jerusalem that included "all Israel"—north and south. Here and elsewhere, the Chronicler appears open toward those in the northern kingdom who are willing to acknowledge the Jerusalem sanctuary's preeminence (2 Chr. 11:13-17; 15:9; 30:7-8; 35:17-18). This may well suggest that the Chronicler advocated a more inclusive view of "Israel" in his own postexilic context—possibly encompassing the Samaritan descendants of the long-defunct northern kingdom.

The most drastic difference between Chronicles and Kings may be their contrasting depictions of Manasseh. Whereas Kings uses this monarch as the scapegoat for Judah's downfall (2 Kgs. 21; 23:26), Chronicles transforms him into a model of repentance and renewal (2 Chr. 33). Prefiguring Judah's experience of exile and return, Manasseh is taken by the Assyrians as a prisoner to Babylon (in an anachronistic twist), where humble repentance leads to his restoration. In the latter years of his reign, this former reprobate enacts a religious reform and restores Yahweh's altar in the Jerusalem temple. Chronicles later blames Judah's defeat and exile upon the people as a whole (2 Chr. 36:14). Yet the Chronicler's postexilic audience also has the opportunity to follow Manasseh's example by humbling themselves, returning to their ancestral homeland, and restoring the temple cult (2 Chr. 36:22-23).

While the Chronicler's History retains the idea of divine retribution characteristic of Deuteronomic theology, it also emphasizes that disaster can be averted or reversed through sincere repentance. This creates a more optimistic account of the nation's past than is provided by the earlier Deuteronomistic Historian(s). Key to Judah's success or failure in Chronicles is the level of commitment demonstrated by the people and their leaders toward the Jerusalem temple. Since the Chronicler connects the temple so closely to David, he may have viewed the construction of the Second Temple as a step toward a future restoration of the Davidic monarchy. Yet readers could also argue that the Chronicler transforms David and his line into the forerunners of a postexilic priestly aristocracy.

Ezra–Nehemiah

Originally a single book bearing the title Ezra, the books of Ezra and Nehemiah piece together a variety of sources to provide a selective and interpretive account of the Persian period through the late fifth century B.C.E. This account focuses on the community of returned exiles in Jerusalem and their Persian-appointed leaders. It may be divided into three sections centering in turn on the early restoration (Ezra 1–6), the leadership of a priest-scribe named Ezra (Ezra 7–10; Neh. 8–9), and the leadership of a governor named Nehemiah (Neh. 1–7; 10–13).

Ezra's brief cameo in the middle of Nehemiah's career raises questions about the chronological relationship of these two leaders. The latter was clearly appointed governor of Judea by Artaxerxes I in 445 B.C.E., but the former might have been commissioned either by Artaxerxes I in 458 B.C.E. or by Artaxerxes II in 398 B.C.E. Uncertainty over whether Ezra preceded or followed Nehemiah complicates assigning a date to these books. The account clearly could not have been composed prior to Nehemiah's second trip to Jerusalem sometime after 433 B.C.E.

From the perspective of this anonymous late fifth- or fourth-century writer (whom we will call Ezra–Nehemiah), the construction of the

Second Temple was merely a prologue for the Persian period. Ezra–Nehemiah's account of the initial restoration begins with the edict of Cyrus (Ezra 1:1-4) and relies heavily on Haggai (Ezra 5:1). However, it blames delays in rebuilding on external adversaries rather than on the flawed priorities of the returnees themselves. Opposition comes from several quarters, including local Persian officials and a group called the "people of the land" (possibly those Judeans who had not been exiled). Ezra–Nehemiah carefully distinguishes the return community (his "true Israel") from the people of the land and from the Samaritans who offer to help rebuild the temple (Ezra 4:1-6). Meddlesome local officials are finally put in their place when the emperor Darius issues a new edict forcing them not only to allow the rebuilding but to finance it (Ezra 6). Framing these chapters with the supportive edicts of Cyrus and Darius emphasizes Persian sanction for the return community.

At least fifty-seven years pass between the dedication of the completed Second Temple in chapter 6 and the appearance of Ezra in chapter 7. This Diaspora priest-scribe is authorized by a new Persian emperor to deliver tribute to Yahweh's temple and to teach Mosaic law to the restored Judeans. But when Ezra arrives in Jerusalem with his retinue, he is appalled to discover that many earlier returnees had married foreign women. Under threat of exclusion from the "congregation of the exiles," these men are forced to expel their foreign wives and children (Ezra 9–10; cf. Neh. 13:23-31).

Whereas Deuteronomic law forbade intermarriage on the grounds that it led to idolatry (Deut. 7:3), Ezra attempts to preserve Israel's "holy seed" from the threat of cultural assimilation. For this reason, Ezra–Nehemiah advocates a very restrictive definition of "Israel" that excludes both non-Jews and those judged to be "less-Jewish." The "real Jews" according to Ezra–Nehemiah are only those former exiles (and their descendants) who are marked by genealogical purity and Torah obedience. When Ezra resurfaces several chapters later at a covenant renewal ceremony, he reads publicly a Mosaic law book that he had brought from Babylon—likely an early edition of the Torah (Neh. 8–9). In the earliest record of biblical translation, this Hebrew book must be interpreted and explained for the benefit of the assembled crowd whose common tongue is now **Aramaic**.

Like Ezra, Nehemiah is also a successful Diaspora Jew who returns to Jerusalem under the authorization of the Persian emperor. He is appointed governor of Yehud and charged with rebuilding the ruined walls of Jerusalem. Again builders face opposition from neighboring groups, and Ezra–Nehemiah once more carefully distinguishes the "true Israelites" from the Samaritans led by Sanballat—although the narrative hints that this "us-versus-them" perspective is not universal (Neh. 6; 13). For Nehemiah, physical walls symbolically represent the cultural boundaries erected between the Torah-observant return community and everyone else. This becomes especially evident when the condition of Jerusalem's walls is described in terms of honor and shame. Ruined walls bring shame upon the covenant community, whereas rebuilt walls restore Israel's honor and inflict shame upon her neighbors (Neh. 1:3–2:17; 6:15-16). Significantly, Nehemiah uses the completed walls to seal off Jerusalem and enable pure Sabbath observance.

To summarize our discussion of the historical books, Chronicles and Ezra–Nehemiah share many concerns, most especially an interest in the Second Temple and its personnel. However, significant differences suggest that these books reflect the interests of two separate postexilic constituencies. Whereas Chronicles displays an interest in Davidic traditions, Ezra–Nehemiah is more concerned with Moses and the law. The Chronicler's History promotes a Jewish community centered on the temple cult, whereas Torah-piety is more central to the Judaism of Ezra–Nehemiah. In Chronicles the invitation to worship at the Jerusalem temple is universally extended to "all Israel." For Ezra–Nehemiah, only those descendants of exiles who maintain a separate cultural identity and strict obedience to the Torah belong to "Israel."

Hence, careful readers can discern behind these books two separate communities advocating competing visions for postexilic Judaism.

Preliminary Exercise IA.1: Redaction Criticism in the Chronicler's History
Preliminary Exercise IA.2: Ethnicity and Xenophobia
Primary Text IA.1: Parallels between Chronicles and Samuel/Kings

Psalms (Pss. 1–2; 19; 24; 72; 89; 100; 119; 150; CD Preliminary Exercises IB.1 and IB.2)

To continue along our first path through the Writings, we move from historical literature to the poetry of Psalms, also known as the **Psalter**. This collection provides an invaluable window into several centuries of personal and communal piety in ancient Israel. Although it is impossible to date individual **psalms** precisely, many clearly originated before exile—especially those that mention a king or celebrate royal theology (Pss. 2; 45; 72). Many others appear to have arisen later, out of the exile or Second Temple period (Pss. 37; 89; 137).

Because this book is evidently the work of many centuries, it could not have been written by David (or any other single person). The traditional association between David and the Psalter likely arose from his reputation as a musician and poet (1 Sam. 16:23) and the appearance of his name in many psalm titles or **superscriptions** (CD Chart IB.1). Although other individuals and groups are also named in these superscriptions, the most common title is *le-david*. Yet this expression is not a clear indication of authorship since it could be rendered in a number of ways, including "by," "for," "in the tradition of," or "in honor of" David (depending on how the ambiguous preposition *le-* is translated). Regardless of the translation issue, all superscriptions are late additions to the text that provide more information about how later editors read the psalms than they do about their actual origins.

Even though we cannot assign authorship to the psalms in any traditional sense, we can discern earlier stages in the collection and editing of the present Psalter (CD Chart IB.2). For example, Psalm 72 may once have concluded a collection of Davidic prayers (Ps. 72:20). Clusters of psalms associated with Asaph (Pss. 73–83) and Korah (Pss. 84; 85; 88) may reflect earlier collections used by guilds of Second Temple musicians (1 Chr. 6:31-43; 2 Chr. 20:19). Other clusters of psalms seem to have been assembled for particular liturgical uses, such as the "Songs of Ascent" (Pss. 120–134, sung while climbing the temple mount) and the "Hallelujah Psalms" (Pss. 106; 113; 146–150). Readers can tell that these various clusters once circulated independently because their combination has resulted in the duplication of entire psalms or psalm fragments (CD Primary Text IB.1).

Eventually, all of these diverse collections were incorporated into the present book of Psalms, which (like all of the Writings) is a product of the postexilic era. How then should readers approach this complex and diverse anthology? More to the point, what kind of window does the Psalter provide into the worship and piety of Second Temple Judaism? Readers must delve deeply into their bag of interpretive tools and employ a number of approaches in order to appreciate the Psalter fully. First, we must recall that each psalm is a distinctive literary creation even while noticing that many are strikingly similar in content and outline. Holding these ideas in tension allows us to identify and explore the significance of recurring patterns within the Psalter (**form criticism**) while also recognizing the psalmists' freedom to vary these patterns (**literary criticism**). Second, we must consider the ways in which postexilic editors may have intentionally arranged these psalms within the final collection (**canonical criticism**).

Literary criticism encourages us to read the psalms as poetry. Most readers recognize that the psalms are poetry because of the way that their lines are printed on the page. As poetry, the psalms pack a wealth of meaning into a few evocative words and images that must be unpacked by discerning readers. A variety of poetic devices might be employed to communicate a psalm's message more effectively. To enhance their encounter with the Psalter, readers should familiarize themselves with common features of Hebrew poetry (CD Special Topic IB.1). Many of these features will unfortunately be lost in translation, such as **acrostic** schemes in which successive units of a poem begin with successive letters of the Hebrew alphabet (for example, Pss. 9–10, 25, 34, 37, 111, 112, 119, 145). Other features, like the repetition of a key word or refrain, are more easily preserved by translators. The hallmark of Hebrew poetry is **parallelism,** the correspondence that commonly occurs between two or more lines. This can occur in a variety of ways, with the second line somehow repeating, advancing, or qualifying the sense of the first line. These features and others allowed the psalmists to create diverse and vibrantly expressive poetry.

Within the midst of this poetic diversity, astute readers may discern certain basic outlines that recur from psalm to psalm in a manner suggestive of conventional **forms** or genres. The psalmists did not follow such forms slavishly but felt free to depart from these outlines or even to mix genres. We can identify and describe recurring patterns, but most psalms will not conform precisely to any ideal form. Nevertheless, a form-critical approach allows readers to appreciate ways in which psalmists used and varied conventional genres. It also invites us to imagine the life situation in which recurring genres would have functioned.

The most common form within the Psalter is the **lament**, which communicates a plea for deliverance from a distressing situation (for example, Ps. 13). The speaker in these psalms is usually an individual, but occasionally psalms are voiced by the community as a whole (Ps. 44). Laments typically begin with an appeal to Yahweh, a description of the complaint, and a request for help. The exact nature of the complaint is difficult to determine because of the numerous images used to convey urgency. The psalmist might claim to be wasting away, facing nameless enemies, or sinking into the depths of **Sheol** (CD Special Topic IB.2). In fact, the more general the language of the lament, the more useful the psalm would be to many different worshipers in their own circumstances.

Most laments conclude by expressing confidence that Yahweh will respond to the psalmist's pleas. Form critics might explain this sudden change of mood as the moment when the petitioner(s) received a promissory oracle from a priest. Yet some laments never make this shift (Ps. 88), whereas others are wholly preoccupied with affirming the psalmist's trust in Yahweh despite adversity (Ps. 23).

Laments often end with vows to proclaim Yahweh's accomplished deliverance before the community, and many psalms appear to do just that (for example, Ps. 116). These psalms of **thanksgiving** describe a past experience of distress and celebrate the psalmist's restoration while affirming Yahweh's goodness and faithfulness. Like psalms of lament, thanksgivings also appear in both individual and communal forms. Occasionally, these psalms refer to sacrifices offered and vows paid in gratitude (Pss. 66:15; 116:17-18). Many form critics would suggest that such cultic occasions provided the typical life setting for psalms of thanksgiving.

Closely related to the thanksgiving psalm is the **hymn**. Whereas the former offer praise for a specific act of deliverance, the latter praise the deity in more general terms for a variety of reasons. A hymn might focus on the glories of creation (Ps. 19), divine kingship (Ps. 95), Yahweh's interaction with Israel (Ps. 106), or even Zion as the divine residence (Ps. 48). Several of these recurring themes echo ancient Near Eastern myths in which a deity orders the universe by defeating the powers of chaos and establishes his royal residence after being enthroned as high king. Based on this similarity, some form critics have speculated that these psalms originated in annual festivals celebrating Yahweh's enthronement.

Although these three genres dominate the Psalter, others have also been identified, including liturgies (Ps. 24), royal psalms (Ps. 45), torah psalms (Ps. 119), and so on. Doubtless the many forms within the Psalter arose in a variety of social and cultic settings. Form critics have tended to seek the origin of these genres within temple liturgies as part of rites accompanying petition, sacrifice, and festivals. Some psalms were clearly used within the temple, whereas others may have originated in less formal worship contexts. Although this entire collection is sometimes called the hymnbook of the Second Temple, its diversity attests to the many voices that it incorporates.

Whatever the origin of individual psalms, they eventually found their home within this larger collection. Readers must, therefore, ask whether the final arrangement of the Psalter was completely accidental or to some degree intentional. A canonical approach allows us to move beyond treating each psalm in isolation and view the book of Psalms as more than a random collection. In its present form, the Psalter is divided into five "books," each of which ends in a **doxology** (CD Chart IB.3). The final booming doxology actually consists of Psalms 146–150, all of which begin with the expression "hallelujah" (CD Primary Text IB.2). This five-book structure mirrors that of the Torah (God's decisive revelation to Israel), perhaps inviting readers to view the book of Psalms as Israel's decisive response to that revelation.

Readers may be prodded even further on the basis of Psalm 1, which is usually viewed as an intentional introduction to the Psalter as a whole. When this psalm advises the wise to meditate upon Yahweh's instruction (Hebrew *torah*), it may be suggesting how readers should approach what follows—not only as Israel's response to God, but as a source of divine instruction. Reinforced by later torah psalms (Pss. 19; 119), such an invitation would reflect the growing recognition of the Psalter itself as sacred literature.

If the placement of torah psalms provides a clue to the structure of the collection, so might the placement of royal psalms. It is a bit odd that psalms focusing on the king were preserved at all after the collapse of the monarchy in 587 B.C.E. Since kingship had long been defunct by the time the Psalter was taking shape, these psalms demanded reinterpretation. Observant readers might notice that royal psalms often appear at key junctures within Psalms' five-book structure (Pss. 2; 72; 89). Whereas early examples celebrate Davidic royal theology, Psalm 89 concludes Book III by demanding to know why God's covenant with

David has failed. Books IV and V then become the canonical response to that question. Seen in this light, the many hymns celebrating Yahweh's kingship in the latter part of the Psalter take on a fresh significance (Pss. 93; 95–99). Israel may no longer have a human king, but her deity still reigns over all the earth.

The prominence of both royal psalms (reflecting Davidic-Zion theology) and torah psalms (reflecting Mosaic-exodus theology) reflects the theological diversity of the postexilic era. No one perspective is allowed to dominate the Psalter. Neither is this collection dominated by any one mode of piety, but it instead encompasses almost the entire range of human experiences and emotions. Occasionally psalms even express sentiments that modern readers might find objectionable or impious (Pss. 44; 137:8-9). Israel's piety is characterized by unflinching candor. The psalmists do not shrink from expressing praise or blame, faith or doubt, trust or fear, joy or anger. Yet readers might notice a concentration of individual laments at the beginning of the Psalter and a preponderance of communal hymns at the end. In the book's final form, the voice of individuals raised in distress ultimately gives way to the voice of the community raised in praise.

Preliminary Exercise IB.1: Parallelism and Psalm Genres
Preliminary Exercise IB.2: Psalm 23 in Popular Music
Primary Text IB.1: Repetition and Duplications in the Psalter
Primary Text IB.2: Psalm 151
Chart IB.1: Superscriptions of the Psalter
Chart IB.2: Subcollections within the Psalter
Chart IB.3: The Psalter's Five Books
Special Topic IB.1: Basic Features of Hebrew Poetry
Special Topic IB.2: What Is Sheol?

The Megilloth (Song 1; 5; 7–8; Ruth 1–4; Lam. 1; 3:19-66; 5; Esth. 1–10; CD Preliminary Exercises IC.1 and IC.2)

To complete our first path through the Writings, we must explore one more group of texts that pertain to the worship life of Second Temple

STUDYING THE OLD TESTAMENT

Judaism. The Megilloth is a heterogeneous collection of books that seem to have little in common other than their liturgical function. Since the late Second Temple period, each of these "five scrolls" has been read aloud in its entirety during the observance of a different Jewish holy day (CD Chart IC.1). Yet only Lamentations seems to have originated in a cultic context, while the other four books were incorporated into the Jewish calendar secondarily. This propensity to absorb and repurpose various traditions attests to the adaptive flexibility of Second Temple Judaism. Ultimately many competing voices of the postexilic era were integrated into the liturgical cycle.

As we peruse each book in this diverse collection, we will first briefly examine its literary merits and any major interpretive problems. We will then try to read the text as a response to theological and social concerns of the postexilic era. Finally we will consider how the book has functioned canonically and liturgically within the life of later faith communities. However, because the "paths" of worship and wisdom intersect, consideration of Ecclesiastes will be postponed to our discussion of sapiential literature.

Song of Songs

Most readers are astonished to discover that a piece of literature like the Song of Songs exists within the Bible. This poem (or possibly collection of poems) unapologetically revels in the ecstasy and the anguish of sexual desire between a woman and a man. Although modern translations usually tone down its more explicit passages for the sake of decorum, this is a really erotic book (CD Chart IC.2). Nowhere does the Song explicitly place this eroticism within the context of marriage. In fact, a recurring motif is the frustration born from physical and social obstacles that bar the consummation of love.

The book is comprised of speeches by a man and a woman with the occasional appearance of a female chorus ("the daughters of Jerusalem") as the woman's conversation partner. Each lover rhapsodizes over the other's physical charms, employing a wide variety of images that may confuse or amuse modern readers. Metaphors ("your eyes are doves," 4:1) and similes ("your two breasts are like two fawns," 7:3) abound on these occasions. Alongside visual descriptions, the speakers also appeal to the other senses when communicating their lover's attractiveness and the delights of lovemaking (Song 1:2; 4:16; 7:8-9). As a poetic text it truly deserves to be called the "Song of Songs"—which is the idiom that Hebrew uses to express the superlative (for example, "king of kings").

Among the three voices within the Song, that of the female lover clearly dominates. In fact, hers is the only unmediated female voice in the biblical canon. This has led to (unprovable) speculation that the Song may have been authored by a woman. She speaks first, initiating contact with her beloved, and speaks more often throughout the book. Neither a reticent nor a passive character, the female protagonist candidly acknowledges her sexual desires and repeatedly seeks to satisfy them with her chosen lover.

Yet the many obstacles she confronts may suggest that their love somehow violates social expectations. If so, then the female character's repeated insistence that her lover belongs to her begins to sound defensive (Song 2:16; 6:3; 7:10), as does the repeated request that the daughters of Jerusalem not interfere with her romance (Song 2:7; 3:5; 8:4; CD Chart IC.3). Why this relationship might be forbidden is a matter of speculation. Perhaps the maiden's dark complexion indicates ethnic or class boundaries separating the would-be lovers (Song 1:5-6). Despite society's judgment, the Song celebrates the lovers' passion for one another and defends their right to be together.

When placed within a postexilic context, the Song could easily be cast as a foil to the postexilic reforms of Ezra and Nehemiah and to the postexilic legislation of the Torah's Priestly writer (P). Whereas Ezra and Nehemiah attempted to establish a clear Jewish identity by prohibiting intermarriage, the Song defends the right to love the person of your choice. Whereas some priestly laws sought to regulate and control a woman's sexuality, the Song celebrates the goodness of sex in general and female sexual expression in particular.

Later faith communities struggled with the Song's explicitly sexual themes. How could an erotic text that never once mentions God gain canonical status (CD Chart IC.4)? Its acceptance was probably facilitated by its connection with Solomon, who is occasionally mentioned in the book (Song 1:1, 5; 3:7, 9, 11; 8:11-12). In fact, most English translations title this text the "Song of Solomon." Since the book itself does not claim Solomonic authorship, this tradition probably arises from his reputation as a songwriter (1 Kgs. 4:32) and ladies' man (1 Kgs. 11:3). Yet linguistic evidence within the Song itself points toward a postexilic date of composition.

The Song's acceptance was also facilitated by the tendency of faith communities to interpret it allegorically. Within Judaism it has long been read as a song about the love of God for Israel. This interpretation allowed the rabbi Akiba to describe this text as the "holy of holies" among scripture and to proclaim that the whole world was not worth the day on which the Song of Songs was given to Israel (m. Yad. 3.5). When this text is read liturgically on the eighth day of **Passover**, Jewish communities are invited to reflect on God's commitment to Israel as enacted within the exodus story. Similarly, Christians have traditionally read the Song as an allegory about Christ's love for the church.

The Song's canonization places what once was likely a secular poem alongside the Bible's other sacred literature and invites readers to place these texts in conversation with one another. Canonically, the Song's depiction of a love affair between a man and a woman in a utopian garden setting echoes the garden of Eden story (Gen. 1–3). However, that story ended in discord and hierarchy, whereas the Song reflects a mutual and harmonious relationship. Its presence within the biblical canon provides a helpful corrective to the many texts that depict women and female sexuality in negative ways.

Ruth

Like the Song of Songs, the short story of Ruth is dominated by active female characters. But the Song's protagonist celebrates erotic love, whereas the title character in Ruth provides a model of loving-kindness or loyalty (Hebrew *chesed*), embodied in her actions on behalf of her late husband and her mother-in-law. Together Ruth and Naomi act boldly to survive and create a future in a society where childless widows were often impoverished and unprotected.

Although most modern readers admire these characters for their resourcefulness, we should also recognize that this is not a revolutionary story. After setting events in motion, the women recede into the background of the book's final scene as men decide their fate. Ruth is praised for acting selflessly, as a "good woman" should, to provide a male heir for her dead husband, but she disappears entirely from the narrative after giving birth to a son. Ultimately, these women can survive only by incorporating themselves into the household of a wealthy man.

Nevertheless, the book of Ruth is a very well-told story. Its rather simple plot consists of four carefully crafted scenes rich in symbolism, wordplay, and other literary motifs. Human and agricultural fertility intertwine as famine presages widowhood and romance blooms during the harvest. Indeed, the story capitalizes on the tension between food and famine, child and childlessness, life and death. These polarities are made explicit when Naomi ("pleasant") attempts to change her name to Mara ("bitter") after losing her husband and sons. Similarly, Ruth ("friend"), who stays with her mother-in-law, is contrasted with Orpah ("back of the neck"), who leaves.

Readers might expect a similar contrast between Bethlehem and Moab. Moabites were generally hated by the Israelites and, elsewhere in scripture, are usually associated with either hostility or sexual perversity (cf. Gen. 19:30-38; Num. 22–24; Deut. 23:3-6; Judg. 3:12-30). In the book of Ruth, however, famine rages in Bethlehem (which ironically means "house of bread") while refuge and legitimate wives are found in

Moab. No condemnation appears even when half of the book's initial characters die in this foreign land—a fate not entirely unexpected for Mahlon ("sickly one") and Chilion ("extinction"). Their deaths simply function as a plot device leading to the relationship between Ruth and Boaz.

At the heart of this story are two encounters between Ruth and Boaz, both set against the rustic backdrop of a barley harvest. The first occurs by chance at the beginning of the harvest when Ruth happens upon Boaz's fields as a **gleaner** (Lev. 19:9-10; Deut. 24:19-22). This scene, which takes place in the light of day and under the watchful eyes of laborers, echoes several other biblical betrothal stories (Ruth 2; cf. Gen. 24; 29:1-30; Exod. 2:15-22). Yet Ruth is cast in the typical male role as the foreigner seeking her fortune in a strange land, while Boaz assumes the traditional female role by providing hospitality and nourishment (CD Special Topic IC.1). While Ruth flirts obsequiously, Boaz praises her loyalty to Naomi and offers a blessing that she might find shelter under Yahweh's "wing" (Hebrew *kanap*).

In a second encounter at the end of the harvest season, subtle flirtation gives way to outright seduction. This time acting on Naomi's instructions, Ruth intentionally seeks out Boaz for a private meeting under the cover of darkness. After uncovering his "feet" (a common biblical euphemism for genitals), she boldly demands that he make good on his earlier blessing. Although the wordplay is usually lost in translation, she asks Boaz to spread over her his own "cloak" (Hebrew *kanap*). Whether or not their romance is literally consummated on the threshing floor, she spends the night and Boaz sends her home early the next morning bearing seed.

In the book's final scene, Boaz follows Ruth's suggestion by establishing himself as her **redeemer** (Hebrew *go'el*)—a kinsman responsible for assuming the role of male protector upon the death of a household head. Such a person might be called upon to restore lost property, pay debts, exact vengeance, or even act as a surrogate husband to provide an heir for the deceased (Lev. 25:25; 27:9-33; Deut. 25:5-11). Boaz cleverly secures his future with Ruth and enhances his own reputation by outfoxing a nearer kinsman. There are many unanswered questions about the legal maneuvering in chapter four (CD Special Topic IC.2). It is especially unclear in verse 5 whether Boaz announces his own intention to marry Ruth or announces that she and the field are a package deal. Either way, a profitable opportunity to gain property suddenly becomes much more complicated and much less profitable for the nearer kinsman. He hastily declines the role of redeemer, allowing Boaz to step in heroically.

While most interpreters appreciate the literary artistry of Ruth, there is less agreement regarding when and why this story was written. The narrator is clearly looking back upon the Judges period from some distance (Judg. 1:1; 4:7). Many recent interpreters place the book of Ruth in the monarchic period because of its concluding Davidic genealogy. They view the book as royal propaganda composed to explain David's Moabite ancestry by depicting Ruth as the ideal foreigner. Such an interpretation is encouraged by Christian Bibles, which place this book before Samuel as a prelude to monarchic history and an introduction to David.

Other interpreters view the story as a postexilic response to the reforms of Ezra and Nehemiah, which prohibited intermarriage and forced Israelite men to expel foreign wives. In contrast to Ezra–Nehemiah, the book of Ruth illustrates that even a woman from Moab could assimilate successfully and beneficially into the covenant community. This interpretation is encouraged by the placement of Ruth among the Writings in the Jewish canon. Regardless of when or why the book was originally composed, it clearly offered postexilic readers an alternative vision of a more inclusive Judaism.

In later Jewish tradition, the book of Ruth became associated with the **Feast of Weeks**, a festival celebrating the harvest and the gift of the law to Israel. As with the Song of Songs, readers may wonder how this book developed a liturgical function. Ruth (unlike the Song) does con-

STUDYING THE OLD TESTAMENT

tain explicit references to God, but the deity rarely acts directly in this story (Ruth 1:6; 4:13). The main characters seem to work out their own problems with minimal divine assistance, although fortunate coincidences could be read as hints of divine providence (Ruth 2:3; 4:1). The Jewish interpretive tradition goes even further by presenting Ruth as the ideal religious convert who pledges her loyalty to the God of Israel (rather than Naomi) and faithfully obeys Torah requirements.

Lamentations

The book of Lamentations originated in the context of Israel's worship, as did the Psalter. But unlike the wide-ranging psalms, which span many centuries, the poems of Lamentations all respond to one particular historical moment—the fall of Jerusalem to Babylon in 587 B.C.E. This central crisis in Israel's history jeopardized her theological traditions and precipitated untold personal suffering among the survivors. This book candidly articulates the grief, anger, and humiliation of a people seemingly rejected and abandoned by their God.

Lamentations consists of five poems corresponding to the book's current chapter divisions. All but the last of these poems are fashioned around the twenty-two-character Hebrew alphabet as acrostics in which each stanza begins with a successive letter—a device usually obscured in translation. Even the final poem, although not an acrostic, nonetheless consists of twenty-two lines. Not only does this structuring device showcase the literary skill of the poet(s), but in Lamentations it may also have been an attempt to express fully Israel's grief from A to Z (or, in Hebrew, from 'aleph to taw).

From a form-critical perspective, these poems contain elements of laments and of funeral songs used by the bereaved to grieve the dead. Whereas the **dirge** lends an air of finality and resignation to the poems, a lament is often a prayer of protest that holds out hope for deliverance. The mixture of these forms reflects a fundamental theological tension within the book—is hope possible in the midst of overwhelming despair? Like many biblical texts, Lamentations attributes the fall of Jerusalem to national sin and divine judgment. Comparable Sumerian laments-over-a-ruined-city date from the late third to the early second millennium. In these parallels, the destruction of a city results from its abandonment by the local god, but eventually the god returns and the city is restored. Such a happy ending is missing in Lamentations.

God is notably absent from the many personae that speak within this book. A narrator describes the desolation of Jerusalem, who is personified as an abandoned and bereaved woman. Daughter Zion speaks in the first person to confess her past sin and describe her present distress. The collective voice of the community mourns the present reality of hunger, rape, and bondage. A nameless male captive acknowledges the deity's role in his present predicament and calls for a return to Yahweh. Only this anonymous speaker hopes that Yahweh will yet help and avenge Israel. Perhaps for that reason interpreters have long favored these verses as the theological key to the whole book (Lam. 3:40-66).

However, this interpretation may supply too easy a resolution to the profound despair articulated in Lamentations. This anonymous hopeful voice is but one speaker within the book, and his words are not allowed to dominate. Lamentations ends not with these few hopeful verses but with the anguished possibility of divine abandonment. Repeated appeals to Yahweh meet with no response. Overall, the book's dominant tone is despondency with little expectation of relief. Despite confessions of sin, the degree of human suffering is portrayed as excessive and intolerable.

Such sentiments doubtless reflect the bleak realities of existence for survivors in the aftermath of the Jerusalem siege. Scattered biblical passages suggest that the tragedy soon found expression in the fasts and rituals of the worshiping community (Jer. 41:5; Zech. 7:1-7; 8:19). The book of Lamentations was likely composed for such occasions, probably by Jews who remained in the ruined city. Unlike Ezekiel or Psalm 137, this text shows no interest in the exilic community. Thus, in the pluralistic chorus of postexilic Judaism, this book represented the voice of

Jews who had suffered in the aftermath of Jerusalem's fall but had never experienced exile.

Both Jewish and Christian tradition has made Jeremiah the author of this text. As early as the third century B.C.E., the Septuagint placed Lamentations alongside the book of Jeremiah and prefaced it with the claim that "Jeremiah sat weeping and composed this lament over Jerusalem and said . . ." Although this prophet's career did coincide with the Babylonian destruction, it is unlikely that he was the author of Lamentations. That tradition likely derives from Jeremiah's own complaints and from the Chronicler's claim that he had composed a lament over Josiah (2 Chr. 35:23).

Christian canons reflect the arrangement of the Septuagint by placing Lamentations near Jeremiah, while the Hebrew canon places it among the liturgical texts of the Megilloth. Jews traditionally recite this book on the **Ninth of Av**, a somber festival that commemorates the many losses suffered by the Jews throughout their history, including the destruction of the temple by Babylon in 587 B.C.E. and again in 70 C.E. by Rome. Christians usually neglect Lamentations, although the cathartic grief of this book has inspired many later writers, composers, and artists (CD Special Topic IC.3).

Esther

The book of Esther is a well-told tale about a narrowly averted genocidal threat against Diaspora Jews of the Persian period. This story takes place at the imperial winter palace in Susa and concentrates on political intrigue among members of the royal court. The character of Ahasuerus provides comic relief as the supposedly omnipotent foreign king who is actually oblivious to intrigue and easily manipulated by advisers. Otherwise, both the plot and the characters are fairly simplistic, with good Jews (Mordecai and Esther) pitted against an evil enemy (Haman).

The storyline of Esther is advanced through a series of reversals culminating in the triumph of the endangered Jews over their would-be persecutors. By the end of the book, their fasting has been replaced by annual feasting and celebration (Esth. 4:16; 9:20-32). Each major character also experiences a complete reversal of fortunes. The Jewish orphan named Esther becomes queen of Persia. Haman, the powerful prime minister, is ironically forced to publicly honor his enemy and then executed on gallows he had prepared for him. The Diaspora Jew Mordecai escapes death, receives royal honors, and becomes the king's new prime minister.

The book is also littered with satire and exaggeration. King Ahasuerus holds a party that lasts 180 days. When defied by Queen Vashti, he petulantly issues an edict buttressing male authority in Persian households. He then selects a more obedient queen by having sexual relations with every eligible young woman in the empire after they are all subjected to a full year of beauty treatments (CD Special Topic IC.4). Because Haman is offended by one Jew, he offers an outrageous sum of money to have all of them killed. He also plans to kill his personal enemy on gallows fifty cubits (roughly 70 feet) high.

Partly because of such details, most scholars do not regard Esther as a historical account. This judgment is supported by the total absence of corroborating data from extra-biblical sources. Surely a royal edict leading to the slaughter of 75,000 Persian subjects (Esth. 9:16) would be mentioned by Persian historians! In fact, extra-biblical sources name Amestris rather than Vashti or Esther as the wife of Ahasuerus (also known as Xerxes I, 486–465 B.C.E.). Moreover, the book of Esther itself is beset by errors and chronological problems. One of the more glaring examples is the assertion that Mordecai was among the captives of Nebuchadnezzar in 597 B.C.E. (Esth. 2:6; some English translations "fix" this problem). This claim would make him and Esther over one hundred years old by the reign of Ahasuerus.

To deny that the book of Esther is a historical account in no way diminishes its significance, especially for Jews living outside of their ancestral homeland during the Second Temple period. Like the stories of Joseph (Gen. 39–41) and Daniel (Dan. 1–6), Esther provides a model of how Diaspora Jews can rise to positions of influence in a foreign court. It also reflects the vulnerability of Diaspora Jews, who lived with the threat of persecution and oppression even under relatively benign Persian rule. Ahasuerus himself is presented as a fairly harmless (if somewhat dim-witted) monarch, but the menace arises from the king's advisors and subjects who are hostile toward the Jews. Recall that Haman, the quintessential enemy, is described as Amalekite rather than Persian (Esth. 3:1; cf. 1 Sam. 15).

Despite its prevailing "us-versus-them" attitude, Esther stops short of encouraging Diaspora Jews to isolate themselves from the larger culture. Both Esther and Mordecai adapt to a Persian environment. Mordecai sits at the king's gate as a member of the royal court and exposes a plot to assassinate Ahasuerus. Esther successfully hides her Jewish identity, marries a foreigner, and apparently ignores Jewish dietary restrictions. Yet the book also insists that Jews must stick together to survive as an ethnic group in a potentially dangerous world. Overall, Esther advocates a middle course for Diaspora Jews between cultural assimilation and sectarian withdrawal.

In its present form, the book explains the origins of the Jewish **Purim** festival, which celebrates Jewish identity and survival in the face of non-Jewish hostility. The name of this festival derives from the "lots" (Hebrew *purim*) that Haman used to determine the day that would have witnessed a Jewish massacre but instead witnessed the slaughter of their enemies (Esth. 3:7). In the carnival-like atmosphere of Purim, the story of Esther is read dramatically amid cheers for Mordecai and jeers for Haman (CD Special Topic IC.5).

Despite the popularity of this festival, however, the book of Esther almost did not make it into the biblical canon. Its status continued to be disputed as late as the third century C.E. Resistance to Esther stemmed in part from its focus on vengeance and bloodshed at the expense of mercy and kindness (Esth. 8:11). To forestall a massacre against the Jews, the book lauds the preemptive massacre of 800 non-Jews in Susa and 75,000 non-Jews throughout the Persian provinces (Esth. 9:1-17). Another problem was the book's total lack of explicit references to God, although a few verses may presuppose divine providence or Jewish election (Esth. 4:14; 6:13). Overall, however, the author of Esther appears to understand Jewish identity in purely ethnic rather than religious terms. Later editors addressed the book's perceived theological deficiency by adding explicit references to God and long prayers attributed to the main characters. These additions were preserved in the Septuagint and are considered deuterocanonical by some modern Christian communities.

Preliminary Exercise IC.1: Jewish Identity in Ruth and Esther
Preliminary Exercise IC.2: Performing the Song and Lamentations
Chart IC.1: The Festal Scrolls
Chart IC.2: How Translators Mask the Song's Eroticism
Chart IC.3: I Adjure You Not to "Awaken" or "Interrupt" Love?
Chart IC.4: Is Yahweh Mentioned in Song 8:6?
Special Topic IC.1: Literary Conventions and the Betrothal Type-Scene
Special Topic IC.2: The Legal Background of Ruth
Special Topic IC.3: Lamentations Lives On in Music, Art, and Literature
Special Topic IC.4: Why Esther Was *Not* a Feminist
Special Topic IC.5: Is Esther a Dangerous Book?

The Megilloth encompasses a gamut of human experiences and emotions from love and loyalty to crisis and grief—a richness further enhanced by the book of Ecclesiastes, which we will examine shortly. Within this heterogeneous collection speak many of the competing voices of Second Temple Judaism from the Diaspora, the return community, and even Judeans who had never experienced exile. That no one voice dominated this lively chorus is demonstrated by the fact that they all eventually found a place in scripture and a role in Israel's worship.

Along our first path through the Writings, we have explored a wide range of texts that reflect the many forms of piety characterizing the Second Temple period. Some of these texts originated in the context of worship, whereas others were secondarily incorporated into the liturgi-

STUDYING THE OLD TESTAMENT

cal calendar. Still others promote a particular form of piety emphasizing the restored temple or strict Torah observance. All of these texts advocate competing visions for postexilic Judaism and provide different answers to the question of Israel's identity. The many perspectives represented here eloquently attest to the pluralism of the Second Temple period.

THE PATH OF WISDOM

Our second tour through the Writings leads us into territory that may seem oddly familiar to modern readers. Contemporary Western culture bombards us with advice on a wide variety of topics. A myriad of books promise to help us better ourselves emotionally, physically, and intellectually. Countless magazine articles tease us with the possibility of more successful relationships in our personal and professional lives. An endless stream of newspaper columnists and talk-show hosts offer to answer our questions and guide our decision making. Even calendars offer daily adages and memorable quotes. It seems that the world is bursting to tell us how to live well and find fulfillment.

Sages in ancient Israel also sought ways to succeed in life and attempted to transmit this knowledge to later generations. This wisdom tradition eventually resulted in a body of literature, some of which survives within Hebrew scripture (Proverbs, Job, and Ecclesiastes) and some of which survives in the Apocrypha (Sirach and the Wisdom of Solomon, CD Special Topic IIA.1). Like the modern advice industry, biblical wisdom also adopts a variety of approaches to its subject matter. It may focus on practical advice for everyday situations or offer philosophical explorations of life's most profound topics, such as the reasons for human suffering and the inevitability of death.

Wisdom books share at least two distinctive features that set them apart from other biblical texts. First, they are surprisingly unconcerned about the fate of Israel. One searches in vain through canonical wisdom books for references to the covenant community, its history, its traditional heroes, or familiar biblical themes (like exodus, law, monarchy, temple, or exile). Exceptions to this rule occur only in the later apocryphal texts (Sir. 44–50; Wis. 11–19). Second, wisdom literature presupposes a basic approach to reality informed by human experience, observation, and reason. This worldview spotlights the individual, who was considered responsible for securing his or her own well-being by making wise choices. While foolish decisions were thought to result in disastrous consequences, wise decisions promised a good life comprised of longevity, health, wealth, honor, and progeny. Such goals were especially important in ancient Israel, which did not develop a concept of an afterlife with rewards and punishments until a very late period.

The wisdom worldview might strike modern readers as naïvely optimistic and strangely non-theological for biblical literature, but in reality its optimism rested upon theological convictions. The sages presumed that wisdom was discernible through human reason, experience, and observation because Yahweh had imposed order upon chaos in the act of creation. In contrast to prophetic oracles, which are presented as direct revelation ("Thus says the Lord"), the sages discerned God's intention for humanity by appealing to more general revelation mediated through the created order. Confidence in the wisdom enterprise rested upon confidence in God as Creator.

Even so, the wisdom movement never totally discounted an element of divine mystery that tempered its optimism. Generally, wise action brought success and folly brought destruction, but human wisdom could not penetrate the mind of Yahweh (Prov. 21:30). Neither did the sages pretend to offer a set of rules that could be interpreted dogmatically. At their best they recognized that the truth of any wise principle depends upon circumstances. In some situations wisdom requires one to "look before you leap," whereas in others "he who hesitates is lost." While

Proverbs subtly hints at this ambiguity (Prov. 26:4-5), Job and Ecclesiastes tackle headlong the limitations of wisdom.

Nonetheless, this worldview offered a viable alternative to inherited traditions that had either failed or proved inadequate for Second Temple Jews. First, wisdom thought eliminated the theologically problematic claim that Yahweh directly controlled historical events. Second, it provided a means of translating Israel's particular claims into a more universal idiom. Rather than emphasizing national election or covenant, the sages proposed a universal Creator who has made wisdom available to all humans. Biblical wisdom freely imitates and borrows from sapiential traditions that had long flourished in Egypt and Mesopotamia, and Israel's quest for knowledge must be understood as part of this larger international movement. Finally, postexilic pluralism is reflected in the inter-canonical dialogue among Proverbs, Job, and Ecclesiastes. For some Jews the codification of older sapiential traditions was a means of reconnecting with Israel's past and reinforcing the status quo. Others used the wisdom enterprise to pose hard questions and deconstruct inherited dogmas.

Proverbs (Prov. 1–3 and 8–12; CD Preliminary Exercises IIA.1 and IIA.2)

Even the casual reader will notice that Proverbs contains many disjointed sayings that tend to blur together when the book is read in one sitting. Any collection of adages is best read slowly and reflectively in small doses. For this reason, an approach like form criticism, which focuses on short units of text, is well-suited for studying Proverbs. Unsurprisingly, the most obvious literary genre in Proverbs is the **proverb** (Hebrew *mashal*)—a pithy saying grounded in experience that encapsulates a truth about life. A closer look, however, reveals that the book contains many literary genres, including admonitions, allegories, aphorisms, better sayings, hymns, and numerical sayings (CD Chart IIA.1).

Israelite sages strategically used a wide variety of forms to communicate their advice effectively and persuasively, packing a maximum of meaning into a few well-chosen words.

But just who were the sages behind Proverbs? Tradition attributes the entire book to Solomon, who reigned over Israel in the tenth century B.C.E. But this king's connection with Proverbs and other wisdom books (Ecclesiastes and the Wisdom of Solomon) is no more historically reliable than David's connection to the Psalter. The claim of Solomonic authorship derives mostly from his legendary reputation as Israel's wisest ruler (1 Kgs. 3:4-28; 10:1-10). The book of Kings credits him with three thousand proverbs dealing with trees, beasts, birds, reptiles, and fish (1 Kgs. 4:29-34). Encyclopedic lists of animals and plants have survived from other ancient Near Eastern cultures, but very little material on these topics appears in the book of Proverbs. If Solomon did produce such wisdom, it has long since disappeared.

In actuality, Solomon is only one of several people named in superscriptions throughout Proverbs as sources for this material (Prov. 1:1; 10:1; 25:1). Also named are "the wise" and two non-Israelites named Agur and Lemuel (Prov. 22:17; 24:23; 30:1; 31:1). These headings do not necessarily contain historically accurate information, but they do indicate that biblical editors viewed Proverbs as an anthology—or, more properly, as an anthology of anthologies—to which many hands contributed. This impression is confirmed by the discovery of an Egyptian wisdom text (Instruction of Amenemope, circa 1200 B.C.E.) that was apparently used as a source for Proverbs 22:17–24:22 (CD Special Topic IIA.2).

A multiplicity of sources is also evident in the content of Proverbs. Some of its sayings seem to presuppose a wealthy, elite audience with access to the king (for example, Prov. 16:12-15; 20:2; 23:1-2; 25:1-8). These proverbs are obviously preexilic and possibly originated in the royal court (Prov. 25:1). In ancient Egypt, wisdom literature was produced by a professional class of sages, who were responsible for advising the king and instructing potential heirs in proper behavior. By analogy, it is possible that professional sages also worked in ancient Israel under royal patronage. Yet many other sayings in Proverbs reflect the concerns of a broader audience and likely originated as folk wisdom. The family would then have provided another context for the production and transmission of wisdom. Mother and father doubtless shared responsibility for educating and socializing their children in the absence of other educational structures (Prov. 1:8; 6:20). Not until the second century B.C.E. is there clear evidence that schools provided a third social setting for the production of wisdom (Sir. 51:1-12).

Proverbs likely received its final shape around the fifth century B.C.E. Little organization is evident in the canonical form of this book aside from the superscriptions that mark off seven once-separate collections (CD Chart IIA.2). The first of these (Prov. 1–9) now functions as an introduction to the book as a whole. Instead of the practical and pithy sayings found elsewhere in Proverbs, these chapters are dominated by longer wisdom poems and instructions that are more overtly theological. Here we find a repeated claim that wisdom begins with the "fear of [Yahweh]" (Prov. 1:7; 9:10; also in Prov. 15:33; Job 28:28; Ps. 111:10; Sir. 1:14). This expression indicates an attitude of awe and reverence for the deity rather than simple fright. Its prominence here and in other wisdom books suggests that this was an important premise of Israelite wisdom.

Another major theme in these chapters—the value and desirability of wisdom—is developed through the literary technique of **personification**. The feminine Hebrew noun *hokmah* ("wisdom") is transformed into an articulate and powerful woman with goddess-like qualities (CD Special Topic IIA.3). **Woman Wisdom** calls disciples to feast at her table and promises blessings to those who seek her. In one remarkable passage she describes herself as the initial act of creation and the agent by which Yahweh brought all else into being (Prov. 8:22-31). This is as close as the biblical tradition comes to assigning a female consort to Yahweh. Wisdom's foil, sometimes called **Woman Folly** or the **Strange**

Woman, is depicted variously as an adulteress, a loose woman, and a prostitute. This personified figure also calls to young men, but she threatens to lure them to their destruction.

Throughout Proverbs, wisdom and folly are depicted as two mutually exclusive roads with very different destinations. Paired sayings often contrast the way of wisdom with the way of folly. The wise (also called the righteous) exhibit appropriate behavior toward elders and superiors and are characterized by a strong work ethic, self-control, moderation, propriety, and generosity. The foolish (also called the wicked) flout authority and indulge in laziness, debauchery, and gossip. In other words, the virtues and vices enumerated by Proverbs tend to reinforce traditional values of the community. The claim that wisdom is grounded in the created order established by Yahweh gave divine sanction to these social expectations.

Proverbs generally affirms a **retribution theology** that links wise/righteous actions to reward and foolish/wicked actions to punishment (CD Chart IIA.3). Indeed, observation would indicate that wise and foolish behavior usually lead to predictable consequences. Rash words often presage later regrets. Generosity is typically appreciated. An industrious and diligent person is more likely to succeed than a lazy drunkard. Good table manners make for a more pleasant dining experience. **Conventional wisdom**, like that found in Proverbs, describes what usually happens under normal circumstances and voices the shared assumptions and expectations that enable community life.

Doubtless wisdom literature like Proverbs was a useful tool for teaching community values and acceptable social behavior to young people. Doubtless it also served to justify privileges enjoyed by wealthy and powerful members of society. Where wisdom is believed to result in wealth, it is but a small step beyond Proverbs to see wealth as evidence of wisdom. Conversely, the repeated observation that laziness leads to ruin can be twisted into blaming the poor for their poverty. This overly simplistic interpretation of Proverbs threatened to reduce the wisdom enterprise to a self-serving system of moralistic clichés.

Yet several destabilizing proverbs suggest that the principle of retribution theology was not absolute. Some sayings admit that material benefits do not always accrue to the wise/righteous and virtue is recommended as its own reward (Prov. 15:16; 16:8, 19; 17:1). Other proverbs acknowledge that the deity is elusive and the future inscrutable to human wisdom (Prov. 16:2, 9; 19:21; 20:24; 21:2, 30-31). In the book of Proverbs, these occasional warnings are easily overshadowed by the sheer volume of other sayings that affirm conventional wisdom. Even so, the sages at their best were capable of self-critical reflection, as seen in the counter-voices of Job and Ecclesiastes.

Preliminary Exercise IIA.1: A Closer Look at Proverbs
Preliminary Exercise IIA.2: Proverbs and *The Analects of Confucius*
Chart IIA.1: Common Genres in Wisdom Literature
Chart IIA.2: Individual Collections in Proverbs
Chart IIA.3: Wisdom's Adaptation of Retribution Theology
Special Topic IIA.1: Deuterocanonical Wisdom Literature
Special Topic IIA.2: Proverbs in an Ancient Near Eastern Context
Special Topic IIA.3: Woman Wisdom and Other Women in Proverbs

Job (Job 1–7; 29–31; 38–42; CD Preliminary Exercises IIB.1 and IIB.2)

Proverbs might be regarded as the embodiment of Israel's conventional wisdom because it describes how things usually work under normal circumstances. But Israel's sages recognized that life was not always conventional, consequences were not always predictable, and people did not always get what they deserved. For biblical Israel, nothing could have illustrated that fact more plainly than the reality of exile followed by centuries of political domination. This devastating crisis and its lingering aftermath exposed the inadequacy of Deuteronomic theology and all other forms of retribution theology that supposedly guaranteed that "you reap what you sow."

Ironically, the same wisdom movement that produced Proverbs also provided tools for critiquing conventional wisdom. Some of Israel's sages attempted to come to terms with questions raised by the reality of undue suffering. Insofar as Job illustrates the failure of retribution theology, this book resounds loudly in an exilic and postexilic context. Yet the fundamental issues that it addresses transcend any one historical time and place. Long before Job was written, several ancient Near Eastern wisdom texts had already probed comparable questions, often employing similar literary genres (CD Special Topic IIB.1). Throughout the ages the themes explored by Job have continued to inspire thoughtful reflection (CD Special Topic IIB.2). Here we find biblical literature at its best and most provocative.

However, many readers have difficulty fully appreciating this book because they approach it with preconceived ideas. Popular imagination has made Job into a clichéd symbol of the patient sufferer, who stoically endures unbearable pain and loss without ever cursing or questioning God. Yet an honest appraisal reveals a more complex character, whose pious submission gives way to defiance in later chapters. In fact, there almost seem to be two different Jobs in this book—the raging Job in the central poetic dialogue (Job 3:1–42:6) and the patient Job in the narrative tale that frames it (Job 1–2; 42:7-17).

The dissonance between these two sections of the book goes beyond contrasting characterizations of Job and different literary modes (poetry vs. prose). Whereas the dialogue upends retribution theology, the book's framing tale provides a traditional happy ending that seems to reinstate it. Such conflicting perspectives might indicate a separate origin for the two parts of this book. The prophet Ezekiel refers to Job as a folk hero renowned for his righteousness (Ezek. 14:14, 20). This may suggest the pious story framing Job was once a separate folktale to which the central chapters were later added. Whatever its origin, the canonical book of Job has jarring tensions that resist easy resolution and entice readers to continue thinking.

Job's readers first encounter what seems to be a fairy tale about a one-dimensional character who lived "once upon a time" in a far-off land. In keeping with the universalism of wisdom literature, there is nothing particularly Israelite about this story or its main character. Job is merely described as a blameless and upright man who feared God. Presumably as a result of his righteousness, he has been blessed with wealth, honor, and progeny, all of which are described in idyllic terms. His life provides a living testimony that conventional wisdom and its system of retribution theology work.

But then the scene shifts from earth to heaven, where readers are made privy to information hidden from Job—his idyllic life is about to be shattered through no fault of his own but as the result of a conversation between God and a member of the divine council called "the Adversary" (Hebrew *ha-satan*). This figure is not the later Judeo-Christian personification of evil known as Satan, even though most English Bibles persist with this misleading translation (CD Special Topic IIB.3). The presence of a definite article on the noun tells us that it is intended to be a title rather than a name. The Adversary is simply a heavenly functionary who serves as a prosecuting attorney answerable to Yahweh. This character does nothing without divine authorization and disappears after the second chapter. In contrast to modern Judeo-Christian thought, the book of Job never comes close to explaining away undeserved suffering by blaming Satan.

Although the Adversary is not a major character in Job, he does raise one of the book's key issues—the feasibility of disinterested righteousness. When Yahweh brags about Job's religious devotion, *ha-satan* questions whether it is genuine. Was Job righteous only because he was rewarded for such behavior? Yahweh agrees to test Job by allowing him (and his household) to suffer. Calamity strikes without warning, claiming his wealth and the lives of his children, but Job blesses Yahweh and submits to adversity. After another conversation with the Adversary, Yahweh allows an attack directly upon Job's own body. But again he refuses to accuse God of injustice.

The book changes dramatically in chapter 3 as poetry replaces prose and the long-suffering Job finally speaks out in frustration. He wishes that he had never been born or had died at birth rather than live to see such misfortune. These anguished cries set off a debate between Job and his so-called friends **Eliphaz**, **Bildad**, and **Zophar**, who have come to "comfort" him. Despite the powerful rhetoric, most readers run out of steam before completing all three rounds of this debate (CD Chart IIB.1). Overall, the voices of Job's friends represent orthodox religion and retribution theology. Not only do they presume that wickedness leads to suffering, they also reverse that logic by interpreting Job's misfortune as evidence of sin. In effect, they sacrifice Job in order to preserve their belief in a fair God who guarantees that people get what they deserve.

Job, however, refuses to uphold traditional doctrines at the cost of denying his own experience, and the narrative prologue has left readers with no choice other than to agree with his plea of innocence (CD Special Topic IIB.4). Nonetheless, Job clearly shares with his friends the assumption that suffering is (or should be) rooted in guilt. He is merely indignant that this principle of retribution no longer seems to work in his case. As the dialogue progresses Job becomes angrier and angrier as he increasingly ignores his friends and addresses his complaints directly to God. In his final soliloquy, Job dares God to produce evidence of his guilt and tries to provoke a face-to-face confrontation with the deity (Job 29–31).

Readers may expect an immediate theophany following Job's words, but first a new character named **Elihu** speaks (Job 32–37). Although he pretentiously claims to correct both Job and his friends, in reality Elihu's rant brings little that is new to the debate. Only then does God finally appear, granting Job an awesome theophany but no answers. The deity neither accuses Job of sin nor tells him why he is suffering. Apparently, the issues of innocent suffering and theodicy that have so preoccupied the book's human characters do not concern the deity. Instead Job is asked a series of rhetorical questions that affirm God's power over the universe—something that no one in the book has ever questioned.

Readers can only speculate as to why God responds in this seemingly inappropriate way. Perhaps the intent is to awe Job into submission by emphasizing the enormous gap between creature and Creator. Perhaps the deity intends to shift the focus of attention from humanity to the whole of creation or to force Job to admit that he knows very little about the intricate mysteries of the universe.

When Job finds himself unable or unwilling to respond (Job 40:3-5), the deity goes on to describe two frightening monsters—Behemoth and Leviathan. Both of these creatures are drawn from ancient Near Eastern mythology, where they symbolize the forces of chaos that existed before creation and occasionally threaten to reassert themselves. Yet Yahweh exerts complete mastery over these monsters, basically reducing them to pets. Again we are left to speculate over the intent of these images. Do they simply reinforce the impression of God's power? Or do these images mock the efforts exerted by Job and his friends to ensnare and control Yahweh?

Job eventually does manage a short and enigmatic response, and these few verses comprise one of the most closely scrutinized passages in the Bible (Job 42:1-6). Job first acknowledges Yahweh's power, which he had never actually questioned. He then admits the limitations of his own wisdom, which had after all been based on hearsay. But now that God has appeared to Job, second-hand information ("I had heard of you by the hearing of the ear") has given way to firsthand experience ("now my eye sees you"). Conventional wisdom has been displaced by something else, although the substance of Job's new insight is not explicitly revealed to the reader. Verse 6 is clearly pivotal but is especially difficult to interpret and perhaps intentionally ambiguous (CD Chart IIB.2). We could imagine Job's repentance is tongue-in-cheek. In that case, he does not really relinquish his argument although compelled to bow before a superior force. However, the verse is more often read as a pious affirmation of faith from a man who no longer expects God to provide answers or rewards.

The closing narrative is a bit of a letdown after the radical thoughts provoked by the dialogue. Events come full circle in a return to normalcy when Job's fortunes are restored twofold (although we might legitimately question whether his children can simply be replaced). Should we conclude that retribution theology, which was rejected in the dialogue, has now been reinstated? As the book of Job now stands, does the framing narrative undermine the poetic dialogue? Despite the book's "happy ending," it is difficult for thoughtful readers to fall comfortably back into the mindset of conventional wisdom. We cannot help but notice that God rebukes the friends, who advocated retribution theology, and commends Job, who dared to question inherited doctrines. Despite the apparent return to normalcy, Job is left with a new appreciation for God's power and freedom and no guarantees for the future.

Preliminary Exercise IIB.1: A Closer Look at Job
Preliminary Exercise IIB.2: The Ambiguous Ending of Job
Chart IIB.1: The Structure of Job
Chart IIB.2: Translating Job 42:6
Special Topic IIB.1: Job in an Ancient Near Eastern Context
Special Topic IIB.2: Job Lives On in Literature and Verse
Special Topic IIB.3: The Origin of Satan
Special Topic IIB.4: I Know That My Redeemer Lives (Job 19:25-26)

Ecclesiastes (Ecc. 1–4; 6; 9; 12; CD Preliminary Exercises IIC.1 and IIC.2)

Like the author of Job, the sage responsible for Ecclesiastes stood at the fringes of the wisdom movement as a skeptical counter-voice against the optimistically conventional wisdom of Proverbs. Whereas Job explores the problem of innocent suffering and the possibility of genuine piety, Ecclesiastes questions the purpose of human existence and whether anything can ultimately give life meaning. These challenges to traditional theology grew naturally out of wisdom's emphasis on human experience and observation. New experiences and candid observations demanded endless renegotiation of inherited doctrines.

Ecclesiastes, like Proverbs, is traditionally attributed to Solomon, Israel's "patron saint" of wisdom, although he almost certainly did not write this book. The author does temporarily adopt the persona of Solomon to support the pretense of having sampled everything life has to offer (Ecc. 1:12–2:26). Only Israel's wisest and wealthiest king would be free to pursue such an experiment unencumbered. Yet the author soon discards that persona and in later chapters talks about monarchy as an outsider (Ecc. 4:13-16; 5:8-9; 8:2-6; 10:4). Even if the pretense of Solomonic authorship was more convincingly enacted, the late form of Hebrew used in Ecclesiastes renders a monarchic date impossible. The presence of Aramaic forms and Persian loan words indicate a postexilic date of composition, likely in the late fourth or early third century B.C.E.

If Solomon did not write Ecclesiastes, then who did? The book's author is most often called **Qoheleth** (Ecc. 1:1-2, 12; 7:27; 12:8-10), a Hebrew participle form meaning the "Assembler" and the Hebrew title of the book (translated by the Septuagint as *Ekklēsiastēs*). Because this participle sometimes appears with a definite article, it is probably a title rather than a personal name, but just what Qoheleth assembled is unclear. The book's final verses describe him as a wisdom teacher who gathered pupils for instruction (Ecc. 12:9-10). This view is reflected in most modern English translations, which render Qoheleth as "Teacher" whereas older translations often used "Preacher."

With the exception of the opening and closing verses (Ecc. 1:1; 12:9-14), most of the book appears to derive from the hand of Qoheleth himself in the form of a first-person monologue or reflection. Attentive readers will notice several recurring themes in the book, some of which invite comparison with other texts from the ancient world (CD Special Topic IIC.1). Readers should be aware that any attempt to condense the message of Ecclesiastes inevitably fails to measure up to the brilliance of the original work, but we can nonetheless list several important features of the book.

First, discerning readers will notice an abundance of repeated words and phrases that set the tone of Ecclesiastes. Qoheleth poetically describes many human pursuits as "chasing after wind," or exercises in futility. Toil and weariness are the lot of humanity and the world is hopelessly crooked. Most important, Qoheleth judges everything "under the sun" to be **vanity** (Hebrew *hebel*). This key term—which literally means "breath" or "vapor"—is variously translated as emptiness, meaningless, useless, futility, and absurdity. The abundance of translations hints at the richness of this evocative image, which appears most forcibly in a mantra at the beginning and end of the book: "Vanity of vanities! All is vanity" (Ecc. 1:2; 12:8).

Second, Qoheleth, like Job, rejects retribution theology, which was the central premise of conventional wisdom. In other words, Ecclesiastes denies that the wisdom enterprise could deliver what it all too often promised. There is no guarantee that the wise/righteous will be rewarded and the foolish/wicked punished. Rather, the bestowal of blessings appears to be random if not downright unfair (Ecc. 7:15-17; 8:14). Even in the cases where people do get what they deserve, this situation is only temporary. A good person who works hard and prospers will nonetheless die just like a fool (Ecc. 1:14-17; 6:1-6). This universal fate swallowed up all merit-based distinctions. Lacking any concept of a meaningful afterlife, Qoheleth assumed that death canceled everything (Ecc. 3:19-21; 9:10). Having irrevocably severed the tie between deed and consequence, he concludes that nothing humans can do has any ultimate significance.

Third, unlike Job, Qoheleth was not confronted and overpowered by God in a whirlwind theophany. In fact, the deity is rather distant in Ecclesiastes (Ecc. 5:1-2). Yahweh, the personal name of Israel's deity, never appears in this book. Conventional wisdom held that knowledge of God was mediated through the created order. Whereas Proverbs celebrates the predictable regularity of creation, Qoheleth finds the endless circularity of nature a reason for despair (Ecc. 1:3-11). Although he questions neither God's existence nor sovereignty, Qoheleth warns that the deity is inaccessible to human beings. Our limited human vantage point makes it impossible to comprehend God's plans or determine the appropriate action for any occasion (Ecc. 3:1-11; 8:16-17). Like Job, Ecclesiastes reinforces limitations of human wisdom and the incomprehensible mystery of God.

Fourth, in light of his other observations, Qoheleth counsels enjoyment of what life has to offer while it lasts. This is not an endorsement of hedonism but a call to find satisfaction in life's simple pleasures (Ecc. 2:24-26; 3:12-13, 22; 5:17-19; 8:15; 9:7-10; 11:7-10). That advice is addressed particularly to young people, who would all too soon experience the relentless onslaught of old age—a subject that seems to have morbidly fascinated Qoheleth (Ecc. 11:7–12:7). This *carpe diem* philosophy is usually interpreted as a sign of hopeless resignation, but it could also be heard more positively as an appeal to live serenely in the present moment rather than vainly attempting to ensure the future.

Finally, careful readers of Ecclesiastes will discover a few teachings that stand in tension with the main theses expressed in this book. For example, Qoheleth occasionally does affirm that God will eventually judge the wicked and reward the righteous (Ecc. 3:17; 11:9). We could view such verses as additions by a later editor who wanted to soften or correct Qoheleth's radical teaching. Editorial activity is most obvious in the two conclusions appended to the end of the book. Verses 9-10 clearly derive from an admirer, while verses 11-14 appear to qualify Qoheleth's indictment of traditional theology. Yet it is difficult to dismiss every traditional passage in Ecclesiastes as a corrective by a later editor. At times Qoheleth quotes conventional sayings in order to refute or revise them (Ecc. 3:1-11; 8:12-14). The tensions in the book may also be a deliberate attempt to mirror life's inherent contradictions.

It is rather remarkable that this unorthodox book of wisdom made its way into the biblical canon. Along with that of the Song of Songs, the canonical status of Ecclesiastes continued to be hotly debated into the second century C.E. Its canonization was likely eased by the book's association with Solomon and its adoption as the standard liturgical reading at the annual Feast of Tabernacles (a commemoration of Israel's wilderness wandering). The book's survival and eventual acceptance show that Qoheleth's words rang true to some Jews struggling to live at the mercy of foreign rulers in a world where God might seem remote and human effort ineffectual. Because the words of this book have continued to ring true to later readers, it has exerted a lasting influence throughout the ages (CD Special Topic IIC.2).

Preliminary Exercise IIC.1: A Closer Look at Ecclesiastes
Preliminary Exercise IIC.2: Bumper Sticker Wisdom
Special Topic IIC.1: Ecclesiastes in an Ancient Near Eastern Context
Special Topic IIC.2: Ecclesiastes Lives On in Music and Literature

The path of wisdom has lacked many of the familiar landmarks that we encountered on previous stages of our journey through Hebrew scripture. The absence of Mosaic-exodus traditions and Davidic-Zion theology in particular makes the wisdom literature stand out as an alien body within the biblical canon. In these books we have found not particular concerns of Israel but universal concerns of humanity. Clearly, these sages were not afraid to ask difficult questions about life and faith. Neither were they afraid to rethink inherited doctrines in light of human experience and reason. The inner canonical dialogue among Proverbs, Job, and Ecclesiastes gives us some indication of the diversity and theological depth of postexilic Judaism.

THE PATH OF APOCALYPTIC

On our final path through the Writings we will examine the book of Daniel, which contains the only fully developed **apocalypse** in the Hebrew Bible. Unfortunately, few genres of literature have been as widely misunderstood as this one. Throughout the ages, countless misguided interpreters have claimed to discover elaborate blueprints of the end-times in apocalyptic writings (CD Special Topic IIIA.1). Apocalyptic language has become so commonplace in the modern world that it is regularly applied to political threats like a nuclear holocaust and ecological dangers like global warming. End-time scenarios have been further popularized in recent years by authors and filmmakers (CD Special Topic IIIA.2). Apocalyptic concepts continue to be a subject of fascination for modern audiences as the specter of *The Day After* (the title of a 1983 film about a nuclear apocalypse) has receded only to be replaced by *The Day After Tomorrow* (the title of a 2004 film about an ecological apocalypse).

Because apocalyptic themes seem so familiar, we are often tempted to impose our modern preconceptions on this ancient literary genre. But Daniel is best understood alongside similar texts that first emerged during the Hellenistic period and continued to appear well into the Common Era (ca. 300 B.C.E.–200 C.E.). Many of these Jewish and early Christian apocalypses have survived in addition to Daniel and the New Testament book of Revelation. We can identify several distinguishing features in this body of literature, although not every feature necessarily appears in every apocalypse. Familiarity with common traits of the apocalyptic genre will aid our understanding of Daniel.

The term *apocalypse* derives from a Greek word meaning to "uncover" or "reveal" (Greek *apokaluptein*). In its most basic form, an apocalypse is a narrative in which a heavenly messenger reveals otherwise inaccessible information to a seer, usually through enigmatic dreams and visions that require interpretation. The messenger, who serves as both guide and interpreter, may be an angel or a human who was transported to heaven before death such as Enoch (Gen. 5:24) or Elijah (2 Kgs. 2:11). The human recipient of the revelation often appears as a famous hero from the past (Adam, Abraham, Moses, and so on). Although an apocalypse is usually presented as that hero's first-person report, the real author is clearly a much later person writing a **pseudonymous** account.

Although the precise content of the revelation varies, there are two main types of apocalypses. In the first kind the seer is taken on an otherworldly journey that includes a guided tour of the supernatural realm. The second kind features a review of history that appears predictive when viewed pseudonymously through the eyes of an ancient seer. This literary illusion is called *ex eventu* prophecy, or prophecy "after the fact." Only at the end of a historical review might the author hazard a genuine and usually vague prediction of events to occur in the near future. Both kinds of apocalypse indulge in fantastic imagery that overwhelms readers and invites them to share in the wonderment of the seer.

In addition to basic similarities in form and content, apocalypses also share a distinctive theological perspective that might be conveniently labeled **apocalypticism**. Some of these ideas may occasionally appear in other types of literature, but they tend to be especially concentrated here. The foundational premise of this worldview is the existence of a supernatural realm that determines what transpires on earth. In contrast to the Bible's historical and prophetic traditions, apocalyptic literature does not imagine that this influence flows in the other direction. In an apocalypse, divine plans are not affected by human actions nor are God's purposes accomplished through human agents.

Apocalypticism is also marked by a profound dissatisfaction with the current world order and a preoccupation with **eschatology** (derived from *eschaton*, the Greek word for "end"). Although circumstances on earth are currently unsatisfactory, an eschatological judgment is anticipated that will bring a decisive end to the present world order as a prelude to renewal. Within this broad framework, apocalyptic literature exhibits a wide variety of eschatological expectations, ranging from the judgment of all humanity after a cosmic destruction to individual judgment after death. In contrast to the minimalist view of the afterlife found elsewhere in the Hebrew Bible, apocalyptic literature embraces the Hellenistic idea of personal immortality with posthumous rewards and punishments.

An apocalyptic worldview contrasts the present world order with the coming age that was expected to follow eschatological judgment. Whereas the current age is marked by injustice and the oppression of God's people, the new age will set things right. This is but one example of the **dualism** that often leads apocalyptic thought to adopt a binary (either-or) way of viewing the world that allows no ambiguities. A similar distinction is drawn between this world and the supernatural realm. Sometimes apocalypses even posit a cosmic dualism within the supernatural realm between forces of good and forces of evil. Although never really challenging the supremacy of God, lesser angelic and demonic beings are pitted against one another. Correspondingly, humanity is also divided into two groups: (1) the elect who will ultimately be rewarded for their faithfulness to God and (2) the rest who will ultimately be punished for their persecution of the elect.

Readers might legitimately wonder how this new worldview suddenly emerged in Israel during the Hellenistic period. Yet many aspects of apocalypticism were not entirely new. Important points of connection exist with earlier prophetic traditions that had anticipated a coming Day of Yahweh. Several late prophetic texts might be viewed as "**proto-apocalyptic**" due to their extensive use of symbolic visions or their descriptions of an ideal future age (for example, Ezekiel; Isa. 24–27; Zech. 9–14). It is possible that these passages reflect a transitional stage between prophecy and apocalyptic. Other points of connection suggest influence from Babylonian, Persian, or Hellenistic traditions. Vestiges of ancient myths are also evident in apocalyptic literature. Like any theological perspective, Jewish apocalypticism probably did not spring entirely from any one of these sources (CD Special Topic IIIA.3). Although its growth was likely fostered by many different strands, ultimately apocalypticism must be recognized as more than the sum of its antecedents.

Readers might also wonder who produced these highly imaginative apocalypses and for what purpose. It is evident that most apocalyptic texts emerged from perceived crisis situations and must be understood in that context. Although the nature of the crisis might vary from real persecution to simple culture shock, apocalypticists shared the conviction that all was not as it should be. Rightly or wrongly, they felt alienated or deprived within the prevailing social order. An apocalypse is then the literary manifestation of deep-seated dissatisfaction. Having lost confidence that circumstances could improve through natural means, disillusioned apocalypticists shifted their hopes from this age to the next. Perhaps supernatural forces would accomplish the salvation that human agency could not.

Apocalyptic texts should, therefore, be rightly understood as a literary form of protest against a world order that is experienced as unjust. It insists that the God of Israel is in control of history despite all evidence to the contrary. It also provides a means of affirming the ultimate triumph of God's justice in the face of perceived injustice. Finally, apocalyptic literature makes life in the midst of crisis more bearable by allowing its audience to view their own hardships as part of a larger struggle between the forces of good and evil and encouraging them to persevere in the knowledge that their side would be victorious.

Daniel (Dan. 1–7; 10–12; CD Preliminary Exercises IIIA.1 and IIIA.2)

The book of Daniel is perhaps the most familiar yet misunderstood book in Hebrew scripture. Its title immediately conjures images of would-be martyrs walking unscathed through a fiery furnace or sitting unharmed in a lions' den. Here we also find the origin of common English expressions such as "feet of clay" and "the writing on the wall." Other expressions like "son of man," which some New Testament writers borrow as a designation for Jesus, remind us that Daniel formed part of the apocalyptic seedbed of early Christianity (CD Special Topic IIIA.4). Unfortunately, this book also has served as a favorite source for charlatans who take verses out of context to construct detailed end-time predictions, often correlating biblical images with people and events in the contemporary world. Such usage ignores the historical context of Daniel and runs contrary to the nature of apocalyptic literature.

In fact, only part of this book may be properly classified as apocalyptic literature. Daniel divides neatly in half based upon its content. Part one of this book is a collection of heroic tales that feature Jews in the court of foreign kings during the Babylonian exile (Dan. 1–6). Part two is a series of apocalypses that offer an interpretation of ancient Near Eastern history from the sixth to the second centuries B.C.E. (Dan. 7–12). These two sections of the book are knit together in at least two significant ways. First, the book is composed in two languages, Hebrew and Aramaic. The extended Aramaic section in the middle of Daniel spans most of the tales in part one and the first apocalypse in part two (Dan. 2:4b–7:28). Second, the book is unified by the figure of Daniel himself, who acts as protagonist in most of the earlier chapters and as seer in the latter chapters.

The name Daniel may derive from a legendary character named Dan'il, who appears in Canaanite literature and whom the exilic prophet Ezekiel describes as a bygone exemplar of wisdom and virtue (Ezek. 14:14, 20; 28:3). If so, the author of Daniel transforms this character into a wise and pious Jewish youth. Whether or not Daniel should be identified with Dan'il, the stories found here likely represent just a few of many tales that circulated about him. Three additional stories are preserved in the Septuagint and regarded as deuterocanonical by Catholic and Orthodox churches (CD Special Topic IIIA.5).

Daniel 1–6 contains two kinds of stories—those about resisting assimilation and those about interpreting divine messages. In the first kind of story, Daniel (and to a lesser extent Shadrach, Meshach, and Abednego) serves as a model for Diaspora Jews by maintaining his Jewish identity in the face of pressures to conform to the dominant culture. Like the apocryphal characters Judith and Tobit, Daniel and his compatriots faithfully observe the laws and traditions of their ancestors.

They refuse to compromise Jewish dietary laws or pray to anyone other than Yahweh despite threats of royal displeasure and martyrdom (Dan. 1; 3; 6). At the same time Daniel, like Joseph, manages to rise to a position of influence in a foreign court, aided by his God-given skill in dream interpretation. These stories reassure readers that God protects the faithful and rewards them with success. Daniel and company flourish on their kosher diet and are miraculously shielded from harm in the fiery furnace and the lions' den.

In the second kind of story found in Daniel 1–6, God enables Daniel to interpret divine messages for foreign rulers that arrive in the shape of dreams and mysterious writing. These stories underline God's control of the historical process, especially the fates of seemingly invincible rulers and kingdoms. In one dream, a statue made of four different materials represents the succession of four earthly kingdoms, specifically Babylon and three successive powers, each weaker than the previous. Just as this statue is smashed by a stone, these kingdoms will one day fall before the kingdom of God. Another dream presages temporary madness for the arrogant King Nebuchadnezzar.

God's judgment against arrogant rulers and oppressive kingdoms is especially apparent in the familiar tale of Belshazzar's banquet (Dan. 5). This story, set on the eve of Babylon's fall, depicts Belshazzar presiding at a raucous feast and defiling stolen vessels from the Jerusalem temple. God's judgment is rendered by a mysterious hand that inscribes upon the wall the words "Mene, mene, tekel and parsin." These words can be read either as weights (mina, shekel, and two half-minas) or as verbs (number, weigh, and divide). Once again only Daniel can decipher the message—God has numbered Belshazzar's days, weighed his worth, and now will divide his kingdom between the Medes and the Persians.

Although the tales in part one of Daniel are set during Babylonian exile, a number of historical errors suggest that they were written many years later. To cite just a few examples, Jerusalem fell during the reign of Jehoiachin, not in the days of his father Jehoiakim, as claimed in Daniel

STUDYING THE OLD TESTAMENT

(Dan. 1:1-2). Nabonidus, rather than Belshazzar, was the son and successor of Nebuchadnezzar (cf. Dan. 5). It was during the reign of Nabonidus that Babylon fell to Cyrus the Persian, not the otherwise unknown figure of Darius the Mede (Dan. 5:31). Darius was, however, the name of the Persian king who eventually succeeded Cyrus. Such errors indicate that these stories were written at a time long after the exile by an author with only a sketchy knowledge of Babylonian and Persian monarchs.

At some point these stories were gathered together by the author of Daniel and made to introduce a series of apocalyptic visions (Dan. 7–12). As always with apocalyptic literature, we cannot fully appreciate part two of Daniel without some knowledge of the historical setting from which it emerged. Apocalypses are generally dated through careful analysis of their content against what we know about Israel's history. Daniel 7–12 gives special prominence to an unnamed ruler who profanes the Jerusalem temple by setting up an "abomination that makes desolate" and persecutes "the people who are loyal to their God" (Dan. 11:31-32). The description of this figure calls to mind the Seleucid ruler Antiochus IV Epiphanes (175–164 B.C.E.). In fact, Daniel's four visions provide an accurate review of major events in ancient Near Eastern history down to 167 B.C.E. We may assume that this historical summary is actually prophecy after the fact placed pseudonymously on the lips of a young seer in Babylonian captivity. Only when dealing with the latter years of Antiochus's reign do these visions become inaccurate (Dan. 11:39-45). For this reason, part two of Daniel is typically dated to around 167 B.C.E., making this the latest book in the Hebrew Bible.

Readers should recall from the historical outline provided in chapter 1 that the **Seleucid Dynasty** was one of the many offshoots of Alexander the Great's conquest of the eastern Mediterranean world. Alexander had radically transformed the ancient Near East by introducing Greek, or Hellenic, culture. **Hellenization** was embraced by many Jews and resisted by others, most especially by a group of observant Jews called the **Hasidim** (meaning "the righteous ones"). The pressure to adopt Greek customs increased when Judea fell under Seleucid control in the early second century, especially under the rule of Antiochus IV. In an attempt to strengthen his control over his vast empire, Antiochus decided to eradicate all local religious and cultural practices. It became a capital offense for Jews to circumcise their sons, observe the Sabbath, or own a copy of the Torah. Antiochus forced many Jews to eat pork and take part in Greek rituals. He even erected a statue of Zeus in the Jerusalem temple—a desecrating act that would certainly be considered a desolating abomination!

These outrages gave rise to a resistance movement led by Mattathias and his son Judas, also known as "the Maccabee" (meaning "the hammer"). Using guerilla tactics, Judas Maccabeus won a series of victories over the larger and more powerful Seleucid army. The **Maccabean Revolt** ended four years later in 164 B.C.E. when Jewish forces gained control of Jerusalem and purified the temple—an event commemorated yearly by Jews in the festival of **Hanukkah** (CD Special Topic IIIA.6). Although the composition of Daniel preceded this victory, the book likely encouraged the Maccabean resistance.

Antiochus's program of enforced Hellenization was almost certainly the crisis that gave birth to the apocalypses preserved in Daniel, and the book must be read in this context. In chapters 7–12, we find many of the elements generally expected in apocalyptic literature. The third-person narrative of earlier chapters is abruptly replaced by first-person reports of Daniel's visions filled with images of fantastic beasts and tantalizing glimpses of the supernatural realm. The significance of these visions eludes Daniel until they are explained to him by various heavenly interpreters, including the angel Gabriel. Through a series of interlocking apocalypses, these chapters chart the rise and fall of ancient Near Eastern powers from the sixth through the second centuries B.C.E.

In his first vision Daniel watches four wondrous beasts emerge from the primordial waters of chaos (Dan. 7). These beasts are identified with four successive empires: the Babylonians, the Medes, the Persians, and the Greeks. Here and elsewhere the "little horn" likely represents Antiochus IV himself. Judgment is rendered upon the beasts by God (here called the "Ancient of Days") and executed by a mysterious heavenly figure called "one like a son of man"—perhaps the angel Michael, who executes God's judgments in chapter 10.

The second vision represents the victory of Alexander the Great (the goat) over the Medes and Persians (the ram). The third vision updates Jeremiah's prophecy that Israel would be in exile for seventy years (Jer. 25:11-12; 29:10). By extending this period to seventy weeks of years (490 years), Daniel explains Israel's continued subjugation to foreign rulers and projects her restoration further into the future. The final and longest vision describes the struggle between the Ptolemies and the Seleucids for control of Judea, especially emphasizing the suffering of the faithful under Antiochus IV. Taken as a whole these visions demonstrate that the succession of human empires is under God's absolute control and promise that the kingdom of God will prevail over its adversaries in the not-too-distant eschatological future.

The book ends with a message of hope for those who die prior to God's judgment (perhaps as martyrs for the faith). In the Hebrew Bible's first and only unambiguous reference to **resurrection**, Daniel is assured that the dead will be raised to everlasting reward or punishment as befitting apocalyptic dualism (Dan. 12:1-4). He is also instructed to keep these visions sealed until the appropriate time to perpetuate the literary fiction that these events had been predicted long ago.

The reign of Antiochus ended, but it was not superseded by the kingdom of God. Yet the book of Daniel was preserved and eventually canonized anyway. In part, that was because Daniel's visions were already being reinterpreted in reference to the Roman Empire. The theological value of this book does not rest in its ability to predict the future. Rather its value lies in its insistent conviction that a just God will not allow the evil kingdoms of this world to have the last word.

The Journey Continues

Because diversity is the hallmark of the Writings, it is difficult to draw general conclusions about this collection. What is most striking about this section of the canon is the wide variety of theological perspectives that it allows to stand in tension. The Chronicler's temple-centered Judaism is juxtaposed with Ezra–Nehemiah's Torah piety. The inclusiveness of Ruth strains against the exclusiveness of Esther. The conventional wisdom of Proverbs stands alongside Job and Ecclesiastes, and the this-worldly wisdom found in these three books competes with the eschatologically focused apocalypticism of Daniel. What results is a rich intra-canonical dialogue that fosters a robust pluralism rather than imposing a single worldview.

In a sense, the three paths that we have explored in this chapter—worship, wisdom, and apocalyptic—are somewhat arbitrary. The books within the Writings can and have been grouped in many different configurations. But the paths that we have traced here do represent some of the major interpretive trajectories within Second Temple Judaism as Israel's ancestral faith was reconfigured to meet postexilic realities. The authors of these books did not shy away from asking difficult questions or rethinking inherited doctrines in light of new experiences. This process has continued through the ages as each new generation of Jews and Christians appropriates for itself the faith of its ancestors.

THE JOURNEY CONTINUES

Reflecting on our exploration of Hebrew scripture, readers may be justifiably impressed by the great variety of literary genres and rich diversity of religious thought found in its pages. In our reading we have encountered epic narratives and short stories, hymns and erotic poetry, proverbs and essays, oracles and visions. Competing theological perspectives speak in the midst of these literary forms. The conditional understanding of covenant expressed by Mosaic traditions is balanced by the irrevocable promises vouchsafed to Abraham and David. The assumption that Yahweh operates within the normal course of human history is challenged by the apocalyptic worldview of Daniel. The assurance of divine justice that dominates prophetic literature is met by counterarguments in the Psalms, Job, and Ecclesiastes.

These theological crosscurrents are a reminder that the Hebrew Bible is the product of many contributors writing under different social, political, economic, and historical circumstances. We better appreciate biblical literature when we allow ourselves to hear these voices speaking distinctly rather than searching for a uniform biblical theology. Rather than imposing inflexible doctrines, different biblical texts offer a wide range of theological perspectives. This diversity is, in fact, one of the Hebrew Bible's greatest strengths and the key to its enduring value in the postbiblical world.

Although our journey through scripture ends with the book of Daniel, the story of the Jewish people and their faith does not end with the Maccabean Revolt. In fact, the centuries following the overthrow of Antiochus IV Epiphanes were among the most significant and creative eras of Jewish history. This period witnessed the proliferation of several distinct parties within Judaism, two of which developed into religious movements that flourish to this day—namely, Rabbinic Judaism and Christianity. These centuries also witnessed a flowering of postbiblical literature as Jewish communities continued to adapt their inherited traditions to meet changing circumstances.

Although the Maccabean Revolt secured a brief period of Jewish independence, the **Hasmonean Dynasty** formed by the Maccabees squandered most of its time and resources in squabbling over succession. They also managed to alienate more traditional elements of the Jewish population by claiming for themselves the prerogatives of both king and high priest. A series of assassinations and foreign alliances eventually culminated in civil war and the forfeiture of Jewish independence to Rome in 63 B.C.E. Rome would directly or indirectly rule Palestine for the next several centuries, exacting heavy tribute and brutally crushing Jewish rebellions in the late 60s and early 130s C.E. The first of these two rebellions resulted in the destruction of the Second Temple in 70 C.E., an event that would determine the future course of Judaism.

In the midst of these historical developments arose several competing groups that advocated distinctive interpretations of the Jewish faith. We have already discussed some aspects of the increasing pluralism that characterized the Second Temple period. Samaritans stood at odds with Jerusalem Jews. Judeans who had not experienced the exile competed with the return community, who considered themselves the true Israel. Tensions also existed between Palestinian and Diaspora Jews. Another way of describing the many emergent forms of Judaism during this period derives from the writings of a first-century C.E. Jewish historian named Flavius Josephus. Josephus lists four competing parties, each with its own theological and political agenda: Sadducees, Essenes, Pharisees, and an unnamed "fourth philosophy."

STUDYING THE OLD TESTAMENT

The **Sadducees** were one of the more influential Jewish movements prior to 70 C.E., largely because their numbers were drawn from the priestly establishment and aristocracy. As the privileged members of Jewish society, they were not above collaborating with the Romans to protect their own economic and political interests. They also tended to assume a conservative stance in religious matters, recognizing the authority of the Torah alone and insisting on a strictly literal interpretation. However, the destruction of Jerusalem's lucrative temple cult in 70 C.E. robbed the Sadducees of their power base and led to their disappearance as a force in Judaism.

At the opposite end of the political spectrum stood Josephus's unnamed "fourth philosophy," which he describes as extremely nationalistic and revolutionary. For convenience's sake, we can label this loosely defined group the **Zealots**, the name of a particular nationalistic party that appeared in the mid-first century C.E. The Zealots advocated acts of resistance toward Rome, ranging from withholding taxes to assassinations and open rebellion. Inspired by apocalyptic expectations of deliverance, they willingly suffered torture or martyrdom for their cause. Messianic claims circulated around many leaders of this party, including Judas the Galilean and Simon bar Kochba. The Zealots were active forces in both ill-fated Jewish revolts against Rome. A handful of revolutionaries actually managed to hold the mountaintop fortress of Masada for years following the First Revolt (66–73 C.E.) before ultimately committing mass suicide rather than surrender. But the Second Revolt (132–135 C.E.) ended with enough bloodshed and devastation to quell nationalistic aspirations once and for all.

The **Essenes** were also defined by their apocalyptic expectations. Believing that the messianic era and Day of Judgment were close at hand, the Essenes withdrew from Judean society, which they viewed as hopelessly corrupt. They rejected the authority of the temple priesthood and formed ascetic communities dedicated to study and ritual purity. Initiates were required to undergo extensive training and surrender private property to the community.

The Qumran community associated with the Dead Sea Scrolls was most likely part of the Essene movement. Such an impression is created by *The Community Rule*, one of the nonbiblical manuscripts found among the scrolls, which appears to have served as a constitution for the Jews at Qumran. It provides rather stringent procedures for membership, a strict disciplinary code, and references to the group's founder, who is called the Teacher of Righteousness. In the manner of apocalyptic dualism, the Qumran writings describe their own community as the children of light whereas all other people (including other Jews) are described as children of darkness. *The War Scroll* describes an imminent battle in which the children of light would fight alongside angelic forces to crush the children of darkness. The Essenes may have felt that this battle was at hand with the First Revolt against Rome. In any case, the Qumran community seems to have been destroyed by Roman armies in this conflict, leaving behind only the library of scrolls hidden in nearby caves.

The **Pharisees** were the party that eventually became dominant and developed into the Rabbinic Judaism that is practiced today. Unlike more conservative Jewish movements, the Pharisees adapted traditional Jewish beliefs and customs to accommodate the changed conditions of Second Temple Judaism. They embraced popular Hellenistic ideas like the immortality of the soul, the resurrection of the dead, and posthumous judgment. They also recognized alongside the written Torah an oral interpretive tradition called the **Oral Torah**, which they claimed had been handed down from Moses at Sinai. These oral traditions applied priestly purity regulations to all Jews, creating a decentralized form of Jewish piety that could be practiced in daily life apart from the temple. Pharisaic piety found a natural home in Jewish synagogues both in Palestine and in the wider Diaspora.

Beginning in 200 C.E. the rabbinic successors of the Pharisees collected and codified the Oral Torah into a work called the **Mishnah**. But as discussions of the Torah and Mishnah continued, more interpretive traditions emerged. In the late fifth and early sixth centuries, rabbinic scholars working in Palestine and Babylon produced two separate elaborations of the Mishnah that became known as the **Talmud**. The Babylonian Talmud is generally considered more authoritative and holds near-canonical status in modern Judaism alongside other rabbinic literature.

A fifth form of Judaism during this period was the emerging Christian movement, whose adherents identified the crucified Jesus of Nazareth as the promised Davidic messiah. Jesus himself and all of his earliest followers were Jews steeped in the traditions of their ancestors. For this reason, Christianity and the New Testament cannot be understood apart from the Hebrew Bible. By the end of the first century, non-Jewish converts to the movement began to outnumber Jewish Christians, which contributed in large part to its eventual emergence as a separate faith.

The many manifestations of Judaism that competed with one another in the Maccabean and Roman periods gave rise to a large and varied body of literature composed in Hebrew, Aramaic, and Greek. The Dead Sea Scrolls, rabbinic literature, the New Testament, and the texts that Christian communities would later call the Deuterocanon or Apocrypha maintained strong ties to Hebrew scripture. This burgeoning literary activity attests to the continuing vitality of biblical traditions for later communities of faith.

INDEX

Oral Torah, 298

parallelism, 176, 253
Pentateuch. See Torah
Persian Empire, 2, 6, 90, 93, 218–21, 241
Pharisees, 296, 298–99
Philistines, 2, 5, 34, 39, 135–36, 139, 141,
    144–46
poetry, 167, 176, 252–53, 263
priesthood, 64, 69, 84, 89–90, 93, 103,
    116, 134–35, 154, 179, 189, 207,
    229–31, 245, 297
Priestly Code, 72, 83–86
prophecy,
    ancient Near Eastern, 191–92
    definition of, 96–97
    social origins of, 188–94
Proverbs, 20, 240–41, 269, 271–75, 280,
    282, 284, 294
Psalms, 20, 65, 240–41, 251–56

Roman Empire, 265, 296–98
Ruth, 22, 240, 260–63, 294

Sabbath, 26, 45–46, 75–76, 88, 200, 226,
    250, 292
Sadducees, 296–97
Samaritans, 241, 243, 247, 249–50, 296
Samuel, First and Second, 95–97, 119,
    131–54, 244–46
satan, 30, 229, 277
Second Temple
    construction of, 220–21, 226–30
    destruction of, 296
    idealization of, 216–17
    role in postexilic Judaism of,
        230–31, 236, 248–50, 254–55,
        292, 296–98
Seleucid Dynasty, 7, 291–93
Septuagint, viii–ix, 8–11, 265, 268, 289
Servant Songs, 224–25
Sinai/Mosaic covenant
    Davidic covenant in tension with
        the, 96, 119, 131, 140–41,
        148–49, 165, 209

prophetic literature and, 160, 178,
    185, 189–90, 209
Torah and the, 42, 63, 64, 71–86
social location, 18–19, 40
Solomon's Temple
    Chronicler's History and, 246–47
    construction of, 5, 150–57
    desecration and reforms of, 128–31,
        163–64, 197
    destruction of, 6, 44–45, 51, 66, 82,
        124, 137, 199–200, 243, 263–65
    prophetic attitudes toward, 183,
        194, 207–10, 213–16
    sacrificial cult, 83–84
Song of Songs, 10, 240, 242, 257–60,
    262–63
succession narrative, 151–54
synagogue, 243, 248–49
Syro-Ephraimite War, 172, 183–85

Talmud, 299
tabernacle, 82–84, 92
Ten Commandments, 72–76, 80, 85
theodicy, 49, 204–5, 215, 231, 278
theophany
    ancestral traditions and, 50, 55–57
    Deuteronomistic traditions and,
        101–2, 135, 157, 161
    prophetic call as, 68–69, 183, 213
    Sinai/Mosaic traditions and, 68–69,
        72, 76, 79, 101
    wisdom tradition and, 278, 282
Torah
    canonical placement of, viii, 10,
        23–25
    literary origins of, 35–46
translation, 11–15

Vulgate, 11–12

wilderness traditions, 64, 86–93
wisdom tradition, 269–84
    ancient Near Eastern, 271–72, 276
    definition of, 269–71
    Solomon's association with, 272,
        281, 284

304

INDEX

theology of, 270–71, 273–75, 278–80, 282–83

Writings, viii, 239–242

Zealots, 297

Zechariah, 168–69, 194, 222, 228–30

Zephaniah, 168–69, 201–3

Zion theology

Latter Prophets and, 174, 185–87, 189–90, 208–9, 213–16, 226–27

Psalms and, 254, 256

See also Davidic covenant